MW00683139

KENNETH
GEORGE
McKENZIE

1892–1964

THE FOUNDING OF
CANADIAN NEUROSURGERY

KENNETH GEORGE McKENZIE

1892–1964

THE FOUNDING OF CANADIAN NEUROSURGERY

T.P. MORLEY

Fitzhenry & Whiteside

Kenneth George McKenzie
Copyright © 2004 Thomas P. Morley

Fitzhenry & Whiteside Limited
195 Allstate Parkway
Markham, Ontario L3R 4T8

In the United States:
121 Harvard Avenue, Suite 2
Allston, Massachusetts 02134

Fitzhenry & Whiteside acknowledges with thanks the Canada Council for the Arts, the Government of Canada through its Book Publishing Industry Development Program, and the Ontario Arts Council for their support of our publishing program.

National Library of Canada Cataloguing in Publication

Morley, Thomas P.
Kenneth George McKenzie and the founding of neurosurgery in Canada /
Thomas P. Morley.

Includes index.
ISBN 1-55041-779-7

1. McKenzie, Kenneth George, 1892–1964.   2. Neurosurgeons—Canada—Biography.
I. Title.

RD592.9.M34M67 2003   617.4'8'092   C2003-900591-7

U.S. Publisher Cataloging-in-Publication Data
(Library of Congress Standards)

Morley, Thomas P.
Kenneth George McKenzie : and the founding of neurosurgery in Canada /
Thomas P. Morley. — 1st ed.
[232] p. : ill. ; cm.
Includes index.
Summary: The thirty-year career of Kenneth George McKenzie dedicated to the art and technique of neurosurgery. McKenzie led the way as an innovator and inventor to perfect the surgeon's art.
ISBN 1-55041-779-7
1. Neurosurgeons — Canada — Biography.   2. McKenzie, Kenneth George.
I. Title.
617/.4/ 8/092 B   21   RD592.9. M1561.M842   2003

Cover design: Intuitive Design International Ltd.
Interior design and typesetting: Daniel Crack, Kinetics Design
Printed and bound in Canada

TABLE OF CONTENTS

PREFACE AND ACKNOWLEDGEMENTS

Towards the end of his life Kenneth McKenzie admitted with disarming candour that he had for the first time, just discovered the glory of Shakespeare and regretted it had taken him so long. He had also recently experienced the peculiar magic of print: "Could I *really* have written that?" he laughed admiringly as he read one of his old articles. When hurricane Hazel hit Toronto in 1954, the Don River rose to the basement ceiling of the McKenzie home. Unlike a neighbour who also stored his personal documents in the basement, McKenzie did not salvage the soggy material by drying it out, but decided to abandon it all to the garbage collector. I have no idea what was lost — perhaps the missing letters to his parents from the trenches, or university and hospital correspondence that might have shed more light on his aspirations and struggles in the early years of the specialty.

Many of McKenzie's reports, published and unpublished, were at the forefront of neurosurgical development at the time. In a study involving highly technical matters with its own vocabulary, an obvious difficulty needs to be overcome. I have rejected an attempt in the surgical sections to completely satisfy either professional or lay readers but have resorted to compromise in favour of the latter. I hope the result is within reach of non-medical readers, yet holding the interest of the others.

I have drawn heavily on family recollections and scrap books and on the Oral History Interviews conducted for the University of Toronto, Faculty of Medicine, by the Hannah Institute for the History of Medicine/Associated Medical Services, Inc. (Interviewer, Valerie Schatzker; transcription of 48 interviews, Sheila Snelgrove; comprehensive index, Martina Hardwick. Ms. Schatzker conducted interviews between 1982 and 1992.) Associated Medical Services also kindly contributed to the cost of typing the manuscript. Of McKenzie's colleagues and former residents I am especially indebted to the late Frank Turnbull, the late E. Harry Botterell, the late Charles G. Drake, William M. Lougheed, the late Rupert Warren, the late Norman Delarue, the late William S. Keith, the late Eric A. Linell and Janet Wallace, R.N., all of whom gave me extensive interviews and some, over the years, revealing letters.

Mrs. Irene McKenzie, Dr. McKenzie's widow, died shortly before interviews for this biography were first undertaken. Members of the family who have been unstinting in their assistance and production of photographs are the children of the second generation, the late Jean Graham, Dorothy McKenzie, Margo Angus-Kelly, Frederick A. McKenzie; and, of the third generation, Joan Schwanz and Susan Angus-Kelly. In search of material for McKenzie in the First World War, I consulted a number of curators and archivists who, at considerable inconvenience to themselves, put their resources at my disposal: L/Col. R. Eyeions, Curator, Royal Army Medical Corps Historical Museum in Aldershot; Mr. David Jones, Curator of the museum of the Essex Regiment; Major Peter Chisholm, Curator of the Museum and Archives of the South Staffordshire Regiment; and Mr. Arthur Manville, of the Royal Canadian Military Institute, Toronto.

To Boguslawa Trojan and Monica Dingle of the Toronto Academy Library for many searches and photocopying. To Margaret van Every, Archivist, TGH; James Herder, Editor of the St. Andrew's College's *The Andrean*; John Fowler, President of the Toronto Academy of Medicine for the preservation of the typescript of McKenzie's paper (1932) on vestibular nerve section for Ménière's syndrome; Stuart Vandewater for guidance to Queen's University's Botterell archives; William O. Geisler for sharing his first-hand knowledge of the part Botterell and Jousse played in the spinal injuries story; to Henry Barnett, Harold Warwick and John A. McLachlin for information surrounding the time of McKenzie's contact with the University of Western Ontario. Michael Thibault, Librarian, Royal College of Physicians and Surgeons of Canada; James T. Connor, TGH historian; Margot MacKay, medical artist, U of T; Ellen Illman, Librarian, Monkton (Ontario) Library, now moved to the Stratford–Perth (Ontario) Library and Archives; Kathy Wideman, Stratford–Perth Archives; William Halliday, Department of Pathology, TGH, for finding the specimen and for arranging the photography of McKenzie's first spinal cord tumour; N.B. Rewcastle, Department of Pathology, University of Calgary; Felicity Pope, Canadian Museum of Health and Medicine when it was situated at the TGH but now, alas, dispersed; Ani Orchanian, Archivist TGH; Grace Scott, widow of the late John W. Scott; Mary Wildridge and Anne Baker for grammatical and syntactical improvements; to Dorothy van Will for the typing of the whole MS and its countless revisions; and to Penny Hozy and Richard Dionne of Fitzhenry & Whiteside for painstaking improvements to sequence and layout of the original "final" MS. Finally, I am grateful to my wife for putting up with many inconveniences while the work took precedence over domestic affairs, and for her criticism, sometimes favourable, sometimes sharp, but with which I almost always eventually agreed.

T.P. MORLEY
Uxbridge, Ontario
2003

INTRODUCTION

This is an account of the life of Kenneth George McKenzie as seen by a very junior colleague in the first place, now a retired successor to McKenzie and Harry Botterell at the University of Toronto and the Toronto General Hospital. When people ask me what I am up to in my retirement and I say I am writing the story of Canada's first neurosurgeon, more often than not the inquirer comments that surely the Wilder Penfield story is so well known that there's nothing important to add! When Harry Botterell died in 1997 leaving a trail of glory behind him, I decided to incorporate all three figureheads into McKenzie's biography. Each man made his own mark in Canadian neurosurgery but of the three, McKenzie's contribution is the least well known. My story is not a judgment of a competition for enduring fame; it is an attempt to bring McKenzie's personality and life's work to a wider audience than his immediate surviving colleagues and intimates.

T.P. MORLEY
Uxbridge, Ontario
2003

Main Street, Monkton, Ontario, 1987

ONE

BEGINNINGS

DR. ALEXANDER FELSTEAD MCKENZIE (1865–1954)
OF MONKTON, ONTARIO

Monkton, Ontario, a hamlet with a population of a few hundred, lies at the intersection of Highways 33 and 55. The countryside is as flat as a prairie, the bed of a vast, freshwater inland lake, created before the ice dam receded from the St. Lawrence valley, leaving it flat and fertile. Unlike the western prairie, the whole area was forested until the European invasion turned it into farmland. Each allotment of 200 acres, once cleared of trees, was enough for a settler to live on: 160 acres mixed farming and 40 acres, the "back forty," left as hardwood bush for firewood and wildlife shelter.

During the two hundred years of their existence, the farms have grown in acreage but have fallen in numbers.[1,2,3] Many "back forties" have shrunk or vanished altogether, making way for huge fields that feed the great hungry, expensive machines that have displaced ox, horse and human muscle. Agribusiness has moved in. The farmer may be the hired manager of what were once his father's fields.

In spite of change the countryside is a landscape of quiet prosperity. Great barns, each proudly bearing at its gable-end the family name, watch over, at a little distance, the trim house and garden, while the rest of the farm buildings cluster round its base. Even these fine old barns are seldom replaced unless by long, low, prefabricated steel and aluminum sheds, while the hay crop rests rolled up in white plastic at the edge of the field looking, from a distance, like huge sewer pipes waiting to be buried. Only on the few remaining Mennonite farms do you see wheat sheaves, stacked in their little pyramids awaiting collection by horse and cart, survivors of an earlier age.

I arrived in Monkton on a brilliant summer day in 1987 in search of first-hand information about the McKenzie family. On the advice of a passing inhabitant I entered the one-chair barbershop. It was hard to penetrate the gloom after the bright sunlight outside. The window was small and thick tobacco smoke burned the eyes. Two pink points glowing on the far side of the shop led to the seated smokers, silent on the entry of a stranger. The barber, sprawled in the one chair used for his business, and the newcomer introduced themselves to each other and pleasantries interrupted whatever discussions had been taking place before the intrusion.

The barber offered the stranger one of the waiting chairs against the wall next to the smokers. No, he never knew a McKenzie, but the name was familiar, he added tactfully. His two seated friends, Murray Brown, aged 92, and Ross Shine, a year or two younger, remembered Kenneth McKenzie.[4] Murray went to primary school with Ken, but couldn't remember much else. Ross, however, had vivid recollections of Ken and the old doctor, Ken's father, A.F. McKenzie. Like everyone else in Monkton, Murray and Ross had been patients of Dr. McKenzie. There was no choice; he was the only one. You didn't go to him, he sent for you. When you had a sore throat and it wouldn't go away he gave you a shot, and if you cut yourself playing outside he gave you another. Ken, they said, was just an ordinary kid, always outside. "He became some sort of a head surgeon, didn't he? I didn't see him after that," Murray said. "I know he joined up and went to France, but that was after he left Monkton."

Kenneth McKenzie's father, Dr. Alexander Felstead McKenzie, was born on the 6th of May, 1865, in Goderich, Ontario, the fourth son of George and Mary McKenzie. He received his medical education at the Toronto School of Medicine, a proprietary school affiliated with Victoria University. The affiliation enabled him to obtain the Bachelor of Medicine (M.B.) degree from the University of Toronto in 1884, but the licensing authority, the College of Physicians and Surgeons of Ontario,

Part of the direct McKenzie line, George (88), A.F. (55), K.G. (27), and Jean (2)

Alexander Felstead McKenzie,
K.G.'s father

held up the issuance of a licence for almost two years until after he turned twenty-one. For seven months during these years, he was taken on as assistant to Dr. T. Smellie who was contracted to provide medical services to workmen building the Canadian Pacific Railway line east from Port Arthur (Thunder Bay). A.F. McKenzie's first practice was in Belgrave, Huron County, not far from Goderich. There he met Margaret Pake of Wingham, Ontario.

Margaret (A.F. called her Maggie) was descended from James Pake, a United Empire Loyalist who, in 1788, came

Margaret Pake
married A.F. McKenzie in 1864

with his brother Samuel to Upper Canada from Tappan, New Jersey. James was given a grant of land of 200 acres and his two oldest sons 100 acres each. The third son, Samuel, married Julia Parliament from Tappan on April 9, 1798 when he was thirty and she fifteen. They had twelve children, of which Amos was born on June 22, 1820. Amos married Susan Hunter on February 20, 1849 who became widowed in 1876 with 8 children. The youngest, Margaret Pake, married Dr. A.F. McKenzie in 1889.

A.F.'s first practice after receiving his licence in 1885 was in Belmore, Ontario. He moved to Belgrave a month later having earned only $2.25 at Belmore. For the next four years his annual cash income averaged $1,033.00, enough to support a bachelor but not a married couple. After spending two months attending the New York Polyclinic for postgraduate study, on August 14, 1889, A.F. married Margaret,[5] who was working as a schoolteacher. Shortly afterwards they moved to Toronto where their only child, Kenneth George, was born in 1892. Dr. McKenzie, Sr. practised in Toronto for six years before moving to Monkton.

Some years later they moved again to Toronto where, for a short time during World War I, Dr. McKenzie, Sr. was assistant medical superintendent to the Toronto General Hospital. During succeeding years he practised in Oakville, Toronto and Alliston until, in 1925, the McKenzies returned to Monkton, this time to stay.

As was usual in the country, the doctor practised from his home during the Monkton years. In the small, rural community he knew everyone and directed their medical care from the cradle to the grave. Many patients, and some doctors, including A.F., preferred delivery of babies at their homes rather than in hospital. It didn't take many unexpected deaths before a hospital's reputation, however undeserved, was of a place from which the return journey was in a coffin. There was no

A.F. McKenzie, K.G.'s father, in his office dispensary at Monkton

ambulance to take the rural sick to a distant hospital and back even after the arrival of the first automobiles. A sick patient felt secure in her home attended by her own physician. On the other hand, the trust patients had in their doctor was commonly fortified by the absence of another in the district to choose from. In the dispensary in the doctor's house, he personally prepared medicines (often spiked with asafoetida or a bitter to enhance effectiveness through the repulsive taste), ointments, powders, pills, plasters and poultices. The doctor would roll pills, fold papers in the correct manner for powders and, of course, precisely measure out the components from his basic stock to fill his prescriptions.

In 1925, when the McKenzies finally settled in Monkton, the telephone was still a rarity. By then, across the whole of the United States there were only fifteen telephones for every hundred people. When the doctor was needed urgently, someone in the household had to go and fetch him. Knowing his patients, the doctor would have a fair idea which call had to be answered immediately and which could wait until the next day. False alarms were uncommon; patients were reluctant to send urgently for the doctor unless their distress was great. Respect between patients and doctor was a two-way street.

The Doctor's house, Monkton, Ontario

A.F. McKenzie was a man of few spoken words. His wife, by contrast, was outgoing and communicative and, socially speaking at least, was the more dominant of the two. It was she who disciplined the young Kenneth and any of his friends when they needed it. When she caught Kenneth and a friend smoking tea leaves in clay pipes in the shelter of a haystack, she summarily pulled their pants down and spanked their bare bottoms. She was a good, kind mother but her belief in the innate naughtiness of boys was unshakeable. When the Doctor gave Ken a rifle, she made sure a round was jammed in the barrel, rendering it, she thought, unusable even by boys. Maggie soon discovered they had underestimated her son's interest in mechanical things; Kenneth had persuaded the village smith to restore the gun to working order. His enterprise inevitably earned him punishment and the gun's confiscation.

The union of the doctor and his wife was a happy one. They complemented each other in temperament and had no reason or desire to tread the other's ground. A.F. spent his working days in his office, examining patients or preparing their medications in the little pharmacy adjacent to the examining room, and in writing and keeping the accounts of the practice and the house. In the days before the automobile they got about by horse and buggy and A.F. took great pride in his modest stable. Mrs. McKenzie ruled the home and decided which social functions she and her husband should attend, for they were somewhat aloof from their neighbours. Having been a teacher in her younger days, Margaret's active brain was fed by any worthwhile books she could lay her hands on; she quickly exhausted the supply the Monkton library had to offer. When he grew up and left Monkton, Ken regularly sent her gifts from Britnell's bookshop in Toronto to satisfy her intellectual hunger.

Margaret McKenzie, K.G.'s mother
— CITY OF TORONTO ARCHIVES G AND M. –135959

As a boy Kenneth spent his time with his school friends outdoors or in their houses rather than in his own, for, as his own children later discovered, the McKenzie house held little attraction — no toy box stuffed with undreamed of wonders, no outdated or outworn clothes for make-believe and laughter. Home was for grownups, not for unbridled, noisy children; Victorian–Edwardian domestic decorum was the ruling code.

A young Kenneth with one of his father's horses

The doctor's taciturnity hid his amiable and generous nature. The care he gave his patients for so many decades was expression enough of his friendship towards them. The village rejoiced in his generosity when he severed five acres, of the thirty-five he owned, as a gift to Monkton for a public park — provided no horse racing would ever be allowed there. He reserved the remaining thirty acres for his much admired standard-bred horses: McGrador, Lady Grey, Lady Brown and Jack X[4]. Dr. McKenzie was the first in Monkton to own an automobile (1915), but the fate of his beloved horses is not known.

A.F. had a vigorous mind and a happy compulsion to record events. When he was not attending to his practice he kept a diary full of family genealogical data, events, accounts, social information on patients, especially marriages and deaths, and professional correspondence with colleagues. His isolation from medical company did not stand in the way of his submitting articles to medical journals, most of which were accepted. The first, "Fibro-cystic tumour of the uterus," a case report with "exhibition of specimen," to the Huron [Ontario] Medical Association, appeared in the *Dominion Medical Monthly* of September 1898, four years after his graduation. The last, "Notes on one hundred obstetrical cases in rural practice," was published in the *Canadian Medical Association Journal* of August 1934. Here he made a strong case for obstetrical deliveries in the home rather than in hospital. In 1932 the institutional maternal death rate was 9.3 per 1,000, while the non-institutional rate was 2.3. He allowed that the high hospital death rate was in part due to admission of serious obstetrical cases, but his report of 100 cases of home delivery without the death of a single mother or infant supported his thesis. McKenzie admitted the argument over institutional versus home delivery was not settled, but from his experience he had good reason to believe the trend away from home care to the hospital was undesirable.

The force of his argument was weakening by the time it was published by the arrival of Sulfonilamide and other members of the sulphonamide family. These manufactured drugs were spectacularly successful against infection by the streptococcus bacterium, the prevalent scourge of puerperal infection in hospitals. The inevitability of bacterial adaptation and resistance to sulphonamides and antibiotics was yet hardly a threat; but McKenzie lived long enough after his publication to be vindicated by reports of the hazard of hospital infections, this time due not to contamination but to resistant bacteria following widespread and unnecessary use of sulphonamides and antibiotics.

Between the first and the last of his publications, A.F. wrote articles on medical nomenclature (1899), the clinical significance of "tracheal breathing" (1906) and, in the same vein, he reported "Two respiratory symptoms of serious import" (1909). There followed "Medical Heresy" (1913), a report of three cases of acrodynia (1923) and an article on aortic thrombosis (1931). (*See* Appendix B *for complete references.*)

The subject of "tracheal breathing," as he called a particular clinical sign, occupied his thoughts for decades, from the time of his first article on the subject in 1898, until 1937 when he finally let the matter drop. He observed that when breathing comes in gasps accompanied by a downward movement of the larynx and even the jaw, death is not far off. McKenzie was curious to know the mechanism of the laryngeal movement, not simply the *how*, but also the *why*. He had already learned from experience the significance of the sign. At a time when, in the absence of technological aids, a doctor had to rely on his wits and experience, a sign of impending death was invaluable to the management of the patient and, as important, the patient's family. He inquired of his colleagues seeking an explanation of this common sign. He puzzled over it for forty years, on and off, reading the medical literature and raising the matter with friends. He was not convinced by the answers he received, and he would not be subdued.

Jabez Elliott (1873–1942) was a prominent physician in Toronto, an expert in the treatment of tuberculosis and well known in medical circles in Canada and the United States. In 1932 A.F. McKenzie, still chafing after 25 years over the mystery of "tracheal breathing," wrote another paper on the subject which he was advised to send to Dr. Elliott with the request that he forward it to the editor of the *Canadian Medical Association Journal*, Dr. A.G. Nicholls. Elliott's response was authoritative, diplomatic and professorial:

Aug. 24, 32.
Dear Dr. McKenzie,

I shall be very glad to send on your MSS to the Editor, but would ask you to consider some term other than tracheal breathing. The terms vesicular breathing, bronchial breathing indicate what we hear through the stethoscope as does tracheal breathing — vide the books on auscultation. The phenomenon you describe as tracheal breathing has been described as "riding of the larynx" and as such known to indicate serious respiratory disturbance [while] others ... speak of "up and down movements of the thyroid cartilage" or of the larynx or cricoid.

The works of the Prof. of Anatomy at Western Univ., Dr. Macklin indicate that in normal health there is tracheal and bronchial movement but these are not called tracheal or bronchial breathing. Look up his writings.

Sincerely yours
J.H. Elliott

McKenzie's long and immediate reply was courteous. He was "much obliged for your friendly comments and criticism." He then launched into a three-page argument to support his disagreement with Elliott. There was nothing in his tone to suggest he was stung by Elliott's letter but he found there was plenty of substance in it to argue over. It was also a cue to revive another but related subject which had prompted an earlier paper by McKenzie, on medical nomenclature:

> ... Again so far as I know the term "tracheal breathing" is not in actual use by chest men. I may be mistaken about this but I do not remember even seeing it in print except in my own articles referred to in my paper. Of course if the term is in actual use by throat and chest men that rules it out for my purpose but if not I think I have about as good a claim on it as anybody else as I have been using it for over twenty-five years!

McKenzie apologizes for taking up Elliott's time but asks him for references to the actual use of the term "tracheal breathing" by throat or chest men, the use of the term "riding of the larynx," and to Macklin's article. He makes a note at the end of the file copy of his letter to Elliott — which he had copied by hand — "Received no reply to above from Dr. Elliott."

A.F. held definite views on the politics of medical practice and the organization of medical societies. He was a strong advocate of continuing medical education, influenced by his own isolation from contact and conversation with colleagues. Another preoccupation included a prescription for a doctor's library[6] on the lines of Osler's advice in "Aequanimitas." He also reflected on a long life[7] in a light-hearted speech with serious undertones, and gave a thoughtful paper (not published) entitled "The Local Medical Association" (1915) in which he discussed medico-legal, organizational and political matters the profession had to face.

McKenzie Sr. felt strongly enough about the importance of continuing medical education, particularly for practitioners working in isolation as he was, that he appeared on his own behalf with a brief on the subject before Mr. Justice Hodgkins, chairman of a royal commission on medical practice in 1949.[8] Understandably, McKenzie felt slighted by the commissioner's ignoring the issue he had raised, but it was some consolation, on the strength of his submission, to find himself chairman of the Ontario Medical Association Committee on Education.

If, when he was a young schoolboy, Kenneth did not readily appreciate his father's qualities, as he grew to manhood he inherited them. Neither man disclosed his emotions and feelings though both openly and critically examined the value of their own medical decisions in articles they wrote in medical journals. Like his father, Kenneth was outwardly unruffled under stress. At the hospital, especially in the operating room, his self-control was legendary, and at home, while the children were around, it took the form of quiet, kindly and unyielding discipline. Whether his father discussed with Kenneth his aptitude for a medical career is unknown, but the home environment surely influenced

A.F. McKenzie

FOUR GENERATIONS
OF DOCTORS

K.G. McKenzie

Frederick
McKenzie

Joan Pivnick
*(granddaughter
of K.G.)*

not only the direction, but also the intensity of his son's pursuit of medicine.

A.F. McKenzie kept a diary sporadically from 1903 to 1943. It begins on August 11, 1903 with the death of "Grandfather Wm. Bailey at 97 years 5 months" and ends 179 pages later with the dates and places of birth of himself, his wife Margaret, his son Kenneth and Kenneth's wife, Irene. The birth dates and full names of Kenneth's four children complete the record: Jean Marie (1918), Dorothy Irene (1919), Margaret [Margo] Biette (1921) and Frederick Alexander (1927). By 1943, when he was 81 years old, the script is shaky but the entries are as informative and emphatic as they had ever been.

The diary records the mundane daily round of his life interspersed with episodes of minor illness (the "grippe" frequently attacks Maggie with abdominal pain and fever, but neither A.F. nor Kenneth are spared) and visits to neighbours and relatives. The purchase of a horse is less often mentioned than a sale. A.F.'s interests outside his practice lay in the farm and his harness horses until the automobile supplanted them. Thirty-eight acres of "farm property" were leased for $2,700 in 1913, and he calculated his "financial standing" that year at $9,000, which included $500 for "rigs, harness and utensils about house, Mina and Lady Brown," the two horses.

When A.F. and Maggie took a trip in the automobile, gas and oil consumption, distance and time, depreciation and estimated cost per mile (4.66 cents) were meticulously reported. Household, professional and farm accounts have their place in the record. He tabulates his practice earnings from the time of graduation in 1884, when he worked on the CPR, to 1910, the date he made the entry. The lean years were in Toronto from 1890 to 1895, when his annual income from the practice averaged $1,030, which represented only 72% of payments charged. The percentage of collections rose to 87% when he moved to rural Monkton, where, from 1896 to 1901, his annual income steadily increased from $1,050 to a maximum in 1907 of $3,131. A periodic personal "Financial Standing" shows the couple enjoyed a modest affluence dependent in part on A.F.'s real estate dealings and income from rentals for property he owned in and around Monkton.

Apart from the recording of events, the journal also served as a commonplace book in which A.F. reproduced passages, poems or aphorisms of a religious or philosophical bent, which pointed to his own beliefs and doubts. From Carlyle's "Sartor Resartus," for example:

Love not pleasure; love God. This is the "Everlasting Yea," wherein all contradiction is solved: wherein whoso walks and works, it is well with him ... (p. 172)

But whence? — O Heaven, whither? Sense knows not; Faith knows not; only that it is through Mystery to Mystery, from God and to God ... (p. 239)

And, from Browning's "Bishop Blougram's Apology"[9]:

I act for, talk for, live for this world now,
As this world calls for action, life and talk –
No prejudice to what next world may prove,
Whose new laws and requirements my best pledge
To observe them, is that I observe these now,
Doing hereafter what I do meanwhile.
Let us concede (gratuitously though)
Next life releases the soul of body, yields
Pure spiritual enjoyments: well, my friend,
Why lose this life in the meantime, since its use
May be to make the next life more intense?

A.F.'s admiration for Blougram's apostasy reflected his own doubts about the sacrosanctity of man-made, church-inspired doctrine rather than reliance on personal beliefs or scriptural interpretation. The portrayal of the bishop's questioning the church's doctrine and polity was in keeping with A.F.'s presbyterian inclination.

An extract from "Life in Other Worlds," by R.A. Proctor, begins with an inquiry into the place of man in his world, "constantly learning to subordinate his individual interests to those of society at large, or rather to identify his interests with those of the larger organism of which he is a part ...." The passage picked out by A.F. ends with a cosmological reflection of universal order created out of apparent chaos: "The arrangement which seems so wasteful of space and time and matter and force, may in reality involve the most perfect possible use and employment of every portion of space, every instant of time, every particle of matter, every form of force."

Whether A.F. confined his musings and private thoughts to himself or discussed them with his son is not revealed. Kenneth was probably even more reserved than his father. His own children had little or no recollection of his baring his soul and Kenneth's views on such profound topics are unknown. But beneath Kenneth's reserve, it may be safely assumed, he absorbed, through his own and his father's shield of silence, wisdom and deep filial affection. The current wave of "tell-all-and-feel-better" challenged the privacy of the Scottish temperament; profound questions and personal troubles were on the whole best contemplated and resolved without outside help. To A.F., the written word could be more comfortable than the spoken in his communications to his son. This inscription on the flyleaf of a book he gave him may be the nearest he got to passing on to Ken a fragment of unsolicited wisdom:

The boatman reaches shore partly by pulling and partly by letting go.
The archer strikes his target partly by pulling and partly by letting go.

Old Persian proverb

On one occasion, on Sunday, September 26, 1909, the eve of Kenneth's departure to the University of Toronto medical school, A.F.'s diary lifts a corner of the veil to reveal the author's love for his son:

Kenneth leaves for the University tomorrow. This afternoon the weather was cool and threatening rain but we took a nice long walk over the farm and through Bettger's bush. Kenneth showed me the largest tree in the bush, a magnificent maple that girths about 16 1/2 feet = to a diameter of 5 1/4 feet. He has been more of a companion to us this summer than ever before and his mother and I shall miss him very much.

It was not in his nature for A.F. to tell Kenneth to his face he was proud of him and loved him. But the rest of the entries, of Kenneth's comings and goings, of Irene and the children, the details of Kenneth's WWI postings, of A.F.'s gift to him of Lady Brown (a three-year-old) and, on another occasion, of $1,500,

Kenneth McKenzie

indirectly tell the real story. A.F.'s attention and affection grew as Kenneth eased into manhood.

We know from Kenneth's daughter Dorothy that Maggie, though not as restrained nor austere as A.F., did not seem to have the knack of making her grandchildren's visits joyful and exciting. But whatever the grandchildren might have thought about the Monkton establishment, Kenneth and his parents made up a quietly happy family.

McKenzie (right) with his parents at their 60th wedding anniversary in 1949

THE ALAMEDA TIMES-STAR
SASKATCHEWAN ~ OCTOBER 4, 1951

Dr. Alexander F. McKenzie, of Monkton, Ontario, is the oldest practicing physician in the British Empire. On the occasion of his 65th year of practice last year Dr. A.F. McKenzie was singularly honored by his colleagues, by the King and Queen, and by the Lieutenant Governor [sic] of Canada.

The Sovereign's recognition took the form of a letter from Buckingham Palace signed by a Palace official, and the Ontario Medical Association elected him to a well-deserved life membership. Alexander Felstead McKenzie died in his ninetieth year on the 2nd of February, 1954, and was buried in the Maitland cemetery at Goderich, the town of his birth.

Of all the character traits Kenneth inherited from his father none was more firmly embedded than quiet doggedness, a refusal to surrender the bone. Every puzzle has a solution, every idea a development. A.F's struggle to understand the physiology and pathology of "tracheal breathing" engaged his mind for about as long as his son Kenneth George strove for neurosurgical perfection in the ward and operating room.

ENDNOTES — CHAPTER 1

1. Noble, H.F. "Recent Trends in Occupied Farm Land in Southern Ontario." Voluntary paper prepared for the annual meeting of the Agricultural Institute of Canada, Canadian Agricultural Economics Society Section, 19 June 1963. Published by the Ontario Department of Agriculture, from the Farm Economics Branch.
2. Evans S. *The Back Forty: Farm life in the Ottawa Valley.* Burnstown, Ontario: General Store Publishing House Inc., 1990: 13. ISBN 0-919431-37-2.
3. Canada Year Book 1992. Ottawa: Statistics Canada, 1991. ISBN 0-660-14056-X.
4. Interview at Monkton in 1989 with Murray Brown (aged 92) and Ross Shine, primary school contemporaries of Kenneth.
5. Margaret's maiden name, as recorded by A.F. in his diary, was Pake. Her mother's maiden name was Hunter. In a detailed report of the celebration of the McKenzies' diamond wedding in *The Monkton Times* of 18 August 1949, Margaret's maiden name appears as Pakenham.

6. McKenzie, A.F. "A working library." *The Canadian Doctor* (March, 1940): 24–29.
7. See Appendix C, ref. 3.
8. *Globe and Mail* (13 August 1949).
9. Bishop Blougram of the poem was modelled on Cardinal Nicholas Patrick Stephen Wiseman (1802–1865). Near the end of his life he was forced by the Curia to abandon many of his liberalizing views which included support for the Association for the Promotion of the Unity of Christendom.

St. Andrew's College first cricket XI.
McKenzie is on far right of middle row.

— COURTESY ST. ANDREW'S COLLEGE

TWO

EDUCATION
AND WORLD WAR I

Education

It was natural, if not inevitable, that his parents chose to give Ken an education to fit him for professional life. They assumed he would follow his father into medicine by way of the medical school at Toronto of which A.F. was an alumnus. For this to come about he would need scholastic discipline to pass high school grades leading to the university entrance examination. The McKenzies lived modestly and could afford the fees of a private school.

There was from early times in Canada brisk interdenominational competition for the capture of souls, not only among the Aboriginal communities in remote areas but also in the schools of cities and countryside. The desire for ecumenical cooperation in education as in matters ecclesiastical was not generally apparent. In the public school system in Ontario, however, there was no recognition of the various sects within the protestant communion. Indeed, religious, scriptural teaching was prohibited to anticipate partisan disputes and crippling interdenominational strife. Pedagogic acknowledgement of the existence of a Christian God in the public protestant schools boiled down to the daily recital of the Lord's Prayer and the singing of the (British) National Anthem. If a child was to receive religious instruction it had to be at home or in private school. The McKenzies' adherence to the Scottish Presbyterian tradition over other denominations governed their decision to send Kenneth, in 1905, to St. Andrew's College in Toronto. Although the school had only been founded a few years earlier, it had already won a high reputation.[1]

Private schools in the province were patterned on the British so-called "public" schools, which, by the middle of the nineteenth century, were so successful that the influential and wealthy middle class had control of their governance. Thus the original concept of a school for everyone, where the emphasis was on Christianity, scholarship, social responsibility and probity, was subverted by the few who could afford to realize the dream and take command of the system. In boys' schools of the genre, in Canada as in Britain, the academic emphasis in Kenneth's day was on Latin, Greek, English, French, History and Mathematics, and a basic knowledge of the Scriptures. A good memory was a greater asset than an inquiring mind; argument, research and intellectual growth could be left to the days at university or, for the most gifted, the very last months of schooling. Encounters with the opposite sex — in girls' as in boys' private schools — were, with enthusiastic parental approval, distractions avoided by absolute segregation. Early rising, a rigorous workout before schoolwork began, compulsory team sports and stern discipline, imposed for the most part by senior boys, contributed to a much admired Spartan policy.

Ken joined St. Andrew's in its new premises in the prestigious Rosedale district of Toronto. The school had prospered from the very beginning. The rigorous scholastic education that went hand-in-hand with an emphasis on manners and decorum, was exactly what its supporters demanded. Pride of school and pride of country were matched by a simultaneous pride in a strong British connection, emotional, political and economic. The cadet corps was and is an important and enduring part of the school's life. Military duty, hard work and patriotism were not regarded as embarrassments by boys trained to lead in the community and, soon enough, in war.

As a competitor in the life of the school, Kenneth's success at St. Andrew's was in athletics, and this he carried over into University. He played in the 2nd rugby team and in the first cricket team, but he shone in wrestling and, to a lesser extent, in boxing. St. Andrew's came into national prominence when "Dutch" Bollard, "the youngest schoolboy ever to achieve so great a success [came] 2nd in the Canadian wrestling championship, winning the silver medal of the Canadian Amateur

Athletic Union."[2] Ken put in a good performance at cricket but was drawn toward wrestling, the sport in which Bollard had brought such distinction to the school. Wrestling suited his independent temperament and slight physique and remained his favourite athletic sport. In his second year at university he was the intercollegiate wrestling champion in his weight class; they nicknamed him "Rubber" McKenzie because of his agility in the ring.

On the other hand, Kenneth was not particularly distinguished in class. His athletic activities are recorded in St. Andrew's College *Review* of midsummer 1908, but not his academic achievements, other than his class standings which were less than brilliant. In 1909 he successfully passed the provincial junior matriculation examinations and the same year entered the University of Toronto. We might deduce from Kenneth's marks in these examinations that his favourite subjects were those on which he scored highest: geometry 85/100; algebra 69/100; physics 65/100; Latin composition 64/100; Latin authors 57/100. In English composition and literature, ancient history and Greek authors and composition, he narrowly avoided failure. But he blossomed at medical school, and, by contrast, ended his university career with the silver medal.

In spite of a mediocre performance at St. Andrew's, he must have retained a respect and affection for the school; when he was approaching retirement age, he was active in the Old Boys' Association and sat on the Board of Governors, eventually as Chairman.

When K.G. McKenzie was a medical student at the University of Toronto, the curriculum and the profile of the student body were very different from today, eighty years later.[3] Most students passed directly into medicine from high school and were therefore younger than in later decades when higher academic standards were required. In 1910, 49% of the fathers of medical students were from the professional or business classes. By 1922 the figure had risen to 59%. One reason for the overwhelming entry of the wealthy was simply that they were able to bear the fees and living expenses the long medical course demanded. On the other hand, summer employment in hotels, in the forests and mines, construction and transportation, opened the doors of the medical school to young men who were prepared to work and pay for their education. But higher standards in urban than in rural schools was a more potent cause of intake imbalance across the social spectrum. City schools were able to pay for specialist teachers that rural boards could not afford, and urban private schools were correctly perceived as pro-

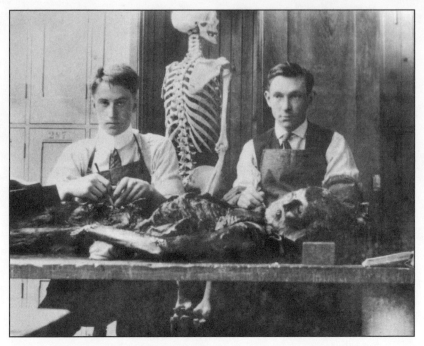

McKenzie (left) at medical school, U of T

viding a more rigorous academic program with sights set on university entrance.

The medical school curriculum in the early decades of the twentieth century at Toronto, as elsewhere, was divided into preclinical (basic science) and clinical years. Chemistry, physics and biology were preliminary subjects to be passed before the main preclinical course was undertaken. Each period covered two to three years. Frequent examination, particularly in the preclinical years, closely monitored the student's performance. Up to 30% of the first year intake failed to pass and had to repeat the year if they chose to continue as medical students. The failure rate in subsequent years was greatly reduced.

The subjects that occupied the longest hours of study were anatomy and physiology, followed by pathology and bacteriology, pharmacology and materia medica, the last including weights and measures (drachms, ounces, minims, etc., a confusion of systems and conversions abhorred by the student before the metric system became universal). Detailed anatomy of the human body was of prime importance since the practitioner on graduation was entitled to carry out surgical operations, limited in scope only by his own conscience. (The first step to control surgical standards in Canada was taken in 1929 with the creation of the Royal College of Physicians and Surgeons of Canada.) The clinical years were spent in the teaching hospital, with attendance at formal lectures by the appointed staff supplemented with bedside instruction on patients, emergency medicine and surgery, and obstetrics. The clinical years left little time for extramural pastimes.

A.F.'s diary follows Kenneth's career through University with tantalizingly short entries:

"*Monday, March 6th 1911. Heard that Kenneth won the Varsity Championship for wrestling 125 lb. Class. Won the 115 lb. Class last year.*" Perhaps there were no letters from Kenneth telling his parents of his success; A.F. had fortunately "heard" about it.

"*May 27th 1911. Kenneth passed his second year in medicine without any stars. Gave him Lady Brown — 3 yrs. old.*" His success in winning the silver medal in his final year is not mentioned when the time arrives.

"*Monday, Sep. 18th. Kenneth returned from Wingham where he has been for a little over three weeks training Allerly. When he first went he drove him a half mile in 1.50. The day he came home he drove him a full mile in 3.02 1/2.*"

"*Tues. Feb. 27th [1912]. Went to Toronto last Saturday to see Kenneth wrestle in the intercollegiate games in the 125 lb. Class. Much to my delight he won from the McGill man in the afternoon securing a fall. In the evening he defeated the Kingston [Queen's] man getting the decision on points. The Kingston man was older and had previously won in the same class. Enjoyed the little holiday.*" A.F. pasted a clipping of the match from the Toronto Star:

"*The feature bout of the wrestling was the struggle in the welterweight final between Garvock of Queen's and McKenzie of Varsity ... It was a tight decision which went to McKenzie. A funny incident occurred during this bout. Garvock, in reaching for a fast head hold, swatted McKenzie on the face, and the Varsity lad came back with a resounding smack which made the crowd yell with delight ...*"

"Rubber" McKenzie was a nickname fairly earned.

World War I

Kenneth graduated from medical school in the early summer of 1914 redeeming his mediocre scholastic standing by winning the silver medal in his last year. War was declared on August 4th. The next day he signed on for the Canadian Army Medical Corps (the "Royal" insignia had not yet been bestowed on the corps). Early in 1915 the British War Office asked the Canadian Army Medical Corps (CAMC) for 100 Canadian doctors under 40 to volunteer for service with the RAMC. Before the end of the year 260 Canadian doctors had been commissioned in the RAMC to serve with British forces and, by the end of the war, 416 medical volunteers from Canada had made the transfer, since they could not all be absorbed into the Canadian forces.[4] McKenzie sailed for England in May 1915, and on landing he was seconded to the British Royal Army Medical Corps.

Other names of early volunteers in the CAMC list included R.L. Shields, G.C. Anglin, J.N. Humphrey and H. Crassweller, all K.G.'s contemporaries at medical school in Toronto. Altogether there were 36 doctors listed as lieutenants in the CAMC and all were seconded to the RAMC.

Lt. K.G. McKenzie CAMC in May, 1915, on the eve of his sailing to England

The exact chronology of K.G.'s First World War experiences is uncertain. The University of Toronto Roll of Service is written from information provided in retrospect by K.G.'s father where the dates do not always agree with the official record. Since the Canadian Army Medical Corps (CAMC) was not fully organized at the beginning of the war when K.G. enlisted, there is also some doubt about the accuracy of the official record. The occasional brief mention of letters from Kenneth in his father's diary sometimes sheds light on their contents.

From these records we know that K.G. landed in France in August 1915. He was attached to the 25th General Hospital for two months before his posting in October to the 10th Battalion of the Essex Regiment. At the hospital he enjoyed the practical experience of laboratory work. "We received," his father records in his diary, "a couple of letters from Kenneth from France, in one of which he gave me some good advice as to what to read and how to do my laboratory work." But the peace and comfort of the hospital was not to last long. In November, as winter was setting in, he was transferred to the 10th Essex holding the line between Arras in the north and Amiens in the *départment* of Somme. The nearest town was Albert, which, including the cathedral, had been "sadly knocked about by the German fire."[5] The battalion had relieved the 8th Suffolk a short time before K.G. arrived in the trenches.

By the time of the armistice in 1918, the 10th Essex had won more battle honours than any other battalion in the regiment. The cost was heavy. Five thousand officers and men passed through the battalion, of whom 1,100 were killed or died of their wounds.

When Ken joined the battalion in November 1915 activity was sporadic and the front static. Trench repair was the order of the day. Snipers and sappers (tunnelling and setting mines) were active on both sides and voices, when raised, could be heard coming from the enemy trenches. The battalion was taken out of the line after two months and marched to the western suburb of Corbie to enjoy the Christmas season. The proposed capture of an enemy salient had been cancelled, a happy postponement and rest from vile weather and mud-filled trenches. Corbie, with its shelter, hot food, Christmas pudding and generous seasonal libations to the accompaniment of the regimental band, was a blessed interlude. On December 28th the battalion marched to Albert and the next morning took over a sector of the line north of Bécourt. The trenches in places were still two to three feet deep with mud.

On the night of January 31st, 1916, the popular battalion com-
mander, Lt.-Col. J.F. Radcliffe, was killed by a shell as he sat in a dugout
"talking to 2nd Lieut. Bryerley and the Regimental Medical Officer"
who, however, is not named; but since McKenzie was the only MD on
the strength when Radcliffe was killed, there is no reason to believe it
was anyone else. A group photograph of the battalion's officers taken
in December 1915 shows McKenzie at one end of the back row. It is
not surprising his name is not recorded in the war diary of the battalion. He was a raw, newly graduated doctor, a non-combatant, the
sole Canadian among seasoned British messmates — an unenviable
situation for the reticent young Canadian. War diaries periodically
listed casualties. Officers were mentioned by name; other ranks were
anonymous statistics. The centuries-old British caste structure perpetu-
ated the discrimination between officers and "other ranks." McKenzie
was an officer, certainly, but probably the latest to join the battalion and,
unlike the others, had no battle experience. In any operational unit
neither a doctor nor a padré was taken into the heart of the fold until
he proved himself under fire. The front was static during the winter of
1915–1916. The slaughter of the Somme was yet to descend on the
opposing armies. By then, Ken was on his way to Mesopotamia.

On February 16th, 1916, in the war diary of the 10th Essex, there is a
record of "an unusual casualty inasmuch as during stand-to the sentry
over the ammunition reserve died of a tumour on the brain." Who but
the M.O. could have ventured the diagnosis of brain tumour? And
what possible medical justification was there to make it? The sentry's
sudden death could only have been caused by a cerebral haemorrhage,
a reasonable if tentative diagnosis in the circumstance. Or was the M.O.
already interested in neurological disorders and on the lookout for
examples? If so, this was the only indication, however slight, that K.G.
showed any interest in neurology before chance took him to the Peter
Bent Brigham Hospital at Harvard and a neurosurgical residency under
the renowned Dr. Harvey Cushing a few years later.

In March McKenzie was transferred to the 2nd battalion of the
South Staffordshire Regiment which was holding the front immediately to the right of the 13th Essex between Albert and Arras. At the
time of his posting, the G.O.C. IV Corps, General Sir H.H. Wilson,
K.C.B., inspected the battalion; its strength on parade was 15 officers
and 492 other ranks. The battalion was withdrawn from the front for a
rest and to attend a demonstration of flamethrowers (by this time both
sides were using them by the hundreds) and all NCOs were instructed

Irene Biette of Tillsonburg
married K.G. in 1916

by a Sgt. Major in the use of the bayonet in combat. Back in the line, fire from mortars and rifle grenades was "very accurate." A gas alarm from the 13th Essex mercifully didn't come to anything for the South Staffs. So the days wore on: shelling, sniping, patrols and occasional zeppelin sightings; German aircraft were out in considerable numbers to direct their artillery.[6]

McKenzie left France on six weeks' home leave shortly before the carnage of the battle of the Somme, which began on July 1, 1916. He would return to another theatre of war, this time to Mesopotamia, arriving soon after the surrender of the allied force to the Turks at Kut-al-Amara and the death march of the defeated British and Indian garrison that followed.

While on leave he had just enough time to return to Canada and marry Irene Biette of Tillsonburg. (Monkton and Tillsonburg are not too far apart for the son of a doctor and the daughter of a banker to have met on social occasions, but the particulars of their first meeting are unrecorded.) The "military wedding of much interest was solemnized at high noon on June 5 at the residence of Mr. and Mrs. Frederick Biette," and was conducted by the Reverend J.H. McBain. A buffet luncheon was served and "the dining room was decorated with yellow roses and the table was centred with roses surrounded with tulle and tiny Union Jacks." The couple spent a brief honeymoon in Muskoka, returning by train to Monkton and an enthusiastic welcome, as reported in the *Monkton Times*:

The reception and demonstration was organized by the Monkton Men's Patriotic League, and several hundred men, women and children were present when the train pulled in. When the gallant Captain and his bride alighted from the train great cheers went up from the assemblage and the atmosphere was almost fanned into a cyclone by the flags of the school children. A dozen automobiles were draped in Union Jacks and the flags of the allies ... The procession finally pulled up at the old home where the school children were in waiting and led by Mr. Edgar Wilson sang, "The Maple Leaf Forever," "We'll Never Let The Old Flag Fall," "Men of the North" and "God Save the King." ... Mr. Fred Armstrong, on behalf of the League, read an address of welcome to the Capt. and Mrs. McKenzie, while Reeve Wm. Scott presented him with a gold piece. The Capt. was then given three cheers and a tiger after which the assemblage dispersed, permitting him to spend with his family the few brief days that are left him before his return to the front "Somewhere in France."[7]

Capt. K.G. McKenzie, RAMC, and Irene Biette on their wedding day at the Biettes' Bidwell Street home in Tillsonburg, Ontario, June 15, 1916

"Throughout the years I knew him [McKenzie]," Bill Keith, McKenzie's first resident neurosurgeon (1930–1931), wrote,[8] "I don't recall that he ever referred to his service in World War I. I thought we should try to fill in the gap in our knowledge of the life of this great surgeon. With this in mind I arranged to visit Mrs. McKenzie in her home. My wife and I spent a very happy hour there on February 2nd, 1976." Irene related to the Keiths how, as K.G.'s voyage back to Canada drew to an end, his ship picked up the River Pilot at Farther Point near Rimouski, about 120 miles from Quebec City. As the Pilot climbed on board, Ken dropped into the tender and made it to shore. His resourceful move allowed him to reach his Ontario home a day and a half earlier than if he had stayed on board.

When the time came to leave Monkton, the town put on a triumphal motor cavalcade in the couple's honour. Irene sat on the fire reel next to the Chief on the way from Ken's home to the station where they caught a train back to Chatham to rejoin her parents. Bill Keith continues:

> In the course of this trip they had to change trains at a junction. For some reason or other they missed the junction. When Ken discovered this he pulled the emergency cord and stopped the train. Irene remembers the angry conductor coming through the car saying, "Who pulled the cord?" She replied, "That man up there," pointing down the car. Ken had disappeared somewhere. She got off the train and the two of them walked back to the junction. For many years the phrase "that man up there" was used in the McKenzie home to explain all sorts of unusual situations ...

The McKenzies spent the rest of Ken's leave in Chatham until the time came for him to return to the war. Bill Keith:

> The eastbound train arrived in Chatham about 10 p.m. It was not very far from the Biette home to the railroad station. When the train whistled, Ken paid a last fond farewell and the sound of his running footsteps in military boots disappeared down the driveway. The train reached the station and then Irene heard the heavy military boots returning with an almost breathless message, "I've forgotten my glasses." He was given a pair of glasses, his footsteps disappeared again but the train remained silent and then the footsteps returned with Ken gasping, "These are not my glasses." Finally he got his own glasses and the footsteps died away again. Shortly thereafter the train started up and this really was the departure. I am sure the conductor felt justified in delaying the train that long in order to return a soldier to the war.

When Bill Keith visited her on this occasion, Irene didn't know of or chose not to relate Ken's experiences in the war. Perhaps Bill did not press her further for details; perhaps she never knew because, in keeping with his natural reticence, Ken might not even have told his wife.

It wasn't to the Western Front he was sent on his return, but to the 40th General Hospital in Mesopotamia. A British and Indian force had been sent to thwart a German and Turkish push southwards through Mesopotamia to Basra and the head of the Persian Gulf. The overland route from eastern Europe to India lay through Mesopotamia, and the oil refinery and pipeline terminals were situated at Abadan on the Shatt al Arab, the final common discharge of the Tigris and Euphrates into the Gulf. It was Germany's strategy not only to establish the overland route to India but also, and more importantly, to deny Middle East oil to the Allies.

By the time McKenzie reached Mesopotamia, the successful Turkish siege of Al Kut (the farthest point up the Tigris the British-Indian expedition reached in its attempt to take Baghdad) was over and the defeated garrison marched north to captivity in Anatolia. Of the 2,500 British prisoners-of-war at Kut, 1,750 died on the march; 2,500 Indian soldiers out of 9,300 captured similarly fell by the wayside. Starvation, scurvy, beri-beri, thirst, heat, abandonment and violence towards stragglers was their fate. Not until late in February, 1917, was Kut recaptured.[9]

At the 40th General there were more diseases than battle wounds to attend to. As at Gallipoli and in other theatres, amoebic and bacillary dysentery, hepatitis and malaria were prevalent and disabling. Kenneth would have continued happily in the hospital's laboratory, but the job was taken from him, "unjustly," he bitterly claimed in a letter to his father,[10] when he was posted to the Officers' Convalescent Depot. He was interested in the laboratory diagnosis of disease by means of clinical chemistry and bacteriology, an approach to the management of illness akin to his later striving to improve operative techniques and instrumentation in neurosurgery. He understood himself well enough to know that neither general practice nor medical neurology would completely satisfy him, just as ward work in the 40th General held less appeal than the solving of puzzles in the laboratory.

Monotony was intense; there were no amusements, nor any change from the dull daily task. The men who had come from England and had previously had no great experience of a summer in the tropics became depressed. The sick rate rose with alarming rapidity and the patients showed little or no recuperative power. During June, 1916, there were seldom fewer than 1,000 cases in the field ambulances each day; during July this figure rose to 1,500, while later the number in hospital exceeded 2,000. The chief causes of admission were dysentery, diarrhoea, jaundice, enteric fevers, sand-fly fever, malaria, effects of heat, septic sores and minor surgical conditions. They were over-crowded and there was a deficiency of tents.[11]

After six months at the 40th General, he was posted as medical officer to the Officers' Convalescent Depot, Mesopotamia, until he sailed for England on April 28, 1917.

The slow journey from Basra to Dover, which included an overland interlude across the length of France from the Mediterranean to the English Channel stopping first at Bombay, was relieved by a ten-day posting to a hospital outside Alexandria. No medical duties were required; the hospital was a convenient billet for the handful of M.O.s until a ship arrived to take them to Marseilles. There were seven medical officers on board the troopship from Basra: six graduates from the Toronto class of 1916 and one, McKenzie, from 1915. They spent a weekend in Cairo, climbed the Cheops pyramid and, like all good tourists, civil and military, were photographed perched on camels beside the sphinx.[12] Apart from one submarine alert, handled by the escorting Japanese destroyers with depth charges, the passage in a

K.G. and medical friends on leave at the pyramids, 1917. All from class of 1916 except McKenzie (1915). *Back row, from the left*: C.J.M. Willoughby, K.G. McKenzie, Harry B. Hetherington, Lamont Hill, James A. Dickson. *Front*: Bethune Maitland, Percy Sargeant.

— PHOTO FROM WILLOUGHBY, C.J. McN. FROM LEECHES TO LASERS: A CENTURY OF MEDICAL EXPERIENCES OF A CANADIAN DOCTOR 1911 TO 1991. PUBLISHED BY THE AUTHOR.

crowded troopship across the Mediterranean was without incident: calm seas, sunshine and the bliss of a step nearer home. They were lucky; within days of their sailing from Alexandria, another troopship, the *Transylvania*, was torpedoed with the loss of 413 soldiers; 2,500 were saved by the escorting Japanese destroyer, *Matsu*.[9]

Back in Toronto, McKenzie spent eighteen months at the CAMC Hospital, Davisville, until his transfer to Christie Street Hospital where the sick and wounded from overseas were gathered. His demobilization was delayed until April, five months after the armistice, probably to help in the medical examination ("boarding") of troops before discharge, a dreary routine of documentation M.O.s hoped to avoid.

Soldiers returning from battle seldom keep completely silent about their experiences; they usually have something to say at least about the exploits of comrades if not of themselves. It is often held that veterans who have experienced action stay silent to bury the memory of the horrors of close engagement. But their silence is rarely absolute. Stories come out now and then as the years pass. Yet it appears that Ken never talked about his innermost thoughts while he was on the Western Front, even to his family. There was nothing in trench warfare to glorify, and it was tedious to try to describe winter in the trenches under mortar and sniper fire to an audience who, without the experience, could never feel it. And it was not his style to indulge in even the hint of a boast at hardships endured. He had learned by now that pain and tough experiences were no easier to bear for the telling, a lesson that would stand him in good stead when administrative struggles in the Toronto General Hospital (TGH) were lost and when surgical operations failed to fulfill his expectations.

ENDNOTES — CHAPTER 2

1. For a history of St. Andrew's College see: Scoular, W. *Not an Ordinary Place. A St. Andrew's Centenary*. Published by St. Andrew's College, Aurora, Ontario (1998): 526+viii. ISBN 0-9684598-0-3.
2. St. Andrew's College *Review* (Midsummer 1908): 37.
3. For a full discussion of socio-economic factors governing entry to Ontario universities see: Gidney, R.D. and W.P.J. Millar. "Medical Students at the University of Toronto, 1920–40: A Profile." *Canad. Bull. Med. Hist.* 13 (1996): 29–52.

4. Duguid A.F. *Official History of the Canadian forces in the Great War*. Vol. 1:164 n.d. Ottawa: Minister of National Defence.

5. Burrows, John W., FSA. *The Essex Regiment* (1935): 146. The story covering the time McKenzie was with the Essex Regiment is taken from Burrows who in turn depended heavily on the Commanding Officer's war diary, a responsibility of every C.O. particularly in combat areas, but which was not infrequently delegated to an adjutant or other officer.

6. Information in this paragraph is taken from the War Diary of the South Staffordshire Regiment: Regimental H.Q., Whittington Barracks, Lichfield, Staffordshire, courtesy of Major Maurice Beedle.

7. *The Monkton Times* (15 June 1916).

8. WSK. A memorandum for private circulation received from him in May 1976.

9. Gilbert, Martin. *First World War*. Toronto: Stoddart Publishing Co. Limited. 1994. ISBN 0-7737-2848-1.

10. Entry in A.F. McKenzie's diary 6 March 1917: "Had a letter from Kenneth yesterday in which he speaks of his disappointment at not being able to keep his laboratory work. Thinks he was unjustly displaced."

11. Medical Services. *Surgery of the War*. HMSO (1922). Chap. X: Reorganization in Mesopotamia (247).

12. Willoughby, C.J.M. *From Leeches to Lasers. A Century of Medical Experiences of a Canadian Doctor*. Published by the author (1991): 121. ISBN 0-9695527-0-X. Copies may be obtained from Royal Inland Hospital, 311 Columbia St., Kamloops, B.C.

Harvey Cushing with postgraduate assistants in 1922: K.G. McKenzie (left), Cushing, and James Paterson Ross (elected President of the Royal College of Surgeons of England 1957–1960)

THREE

THE FOUNDING OF
CANADIAN NEUROSURGERY

This story is about Kenneth McKenzie's part in the founding of Canadian neurosurgery. As Wilder Penfield declared in the title to his autobiography, no man stands alone in such an enterprise.[1]

A triptych to the memory of the founders of modern Canadian neurosurgery would bear on each of its panels an image of McKenzie, Penfield and E. Harry Botterell. Edward Archibald (1872–1945) would be posed in a supporting but still prominent position in the tableau. As a leader in the McGill medical school Archibald's neurosurgical contributions were substantial.[2,3] He lived and worked earlier than McKenzie as a general surgeon with a particular interest in chest and pancreatic surgery and, to a lesser extent, in the surgery of trauma to the head. His most important contribution to the neurosurgical literature (385 pages) appeared in *American Practice of Surgery*[4] in 1908. But his attention was not focused on neurosurgery to the exclusion of other interests.[5] In a preliminary discussion with Penfield before his appointment to McGill was confirmed, Archibald said he wanted Penfield to take over his brain surgery practice to leave time for him to carry on with chest surgery, where his main interest lay. Archibald's reputation won him the chair of surgery at McGill in 1928; and in 1935 he was elected president of the American Surgical Association. Perhaps it was as well for North American surgery that he forsook further neurosurgical interest in favour of the larger field of leadership in education. One of his rôles was as a key player in establishing the American Board of Surgery.

Wilder Graves Penfield

Wilder Graves Penfield[6] (1891–1976)

Wilder Penfield was born in Spokane, Washington, where he lived until he was eight years old. From his earliest days he received from his mother the prescription for success. Following her doctor husband's departure from the family, Jean Jefferson Penfield took command. She held strong views on the course his life should take and Wilder, unprotesting, matched his ambition with hers. The closeness between them lasted all their lives, recorded and preserved in their exchange of letters. In his autobiography[1] Penfield writes:

> Mother had the gift of making her son feel that she relied on his strength, believed in him and trusted him. In order to win this three-year scholarship [*a Rhodes Scholarship at Oxford*], all I had to do, during the next eight years, was to make myself into an "all-round" scholar and leader of other boys. The fact that my mind was really that of a plodder, and that my gangling body was slow and awkward, would be, it seemed, no obstacle whatever.

Mother and son set their sights at long range even before Penfield went into medicine. His future unfolded along lines jointly ordained by them. It was a life of unrelieved but exhilarating toil, with no escape from the drudgery that is a part of scholarship. He enjoyed the slogging for the harvest it promised.

Throughout his later boyhood, up to the Princeton years, Penfield's eyes had been set on a Rhodes Scholarship. He strengthened his puny muscles, hardened himself to physical pain, studied the meaning of leadership and raised the level of his scholastic standing. These, he calculated, were the essentials to success at the Rhodes Scholarship stakes. The Rhodes Trust stipulated that the applicant should be an outstanding all-rounder, so he taught school, played and coached the Princeton varsity football team, wrestled and boxed.

Rhodes House, the administrative and social centre of the scholarship program, did not guarantee its scholars membership in an Oxford college. Penfield won the Rhodes Scholarship he was after, but to enjoy the facilities of the House and enter into the life of the university, membership in a college was necessary. Acceptance by a college depended on success at "responsions," a simple screening test of elementary knowledge demanded of all candidates to the University, including an examination in Latin. Penfield was accepted by Merton College, the oldest in the University (a claim contested by Balliol and, more flippantly, by University College), but he first had to satisfy the college he had a working knowledge of classical Greek. Having failed his first attempt at responsions, now he also had to cram the rudiments of Greek into his head before he could become a bona fide member of the ancient foundation. He worked at it while doing a course in human anatomy at Harvard and, before that, while a schoolteacher. It was a gruelling time, but he passed both exams, responsions and college entrance, at the next attempt. He learned a few days later that Greek had already been removed from the requirements for admission to Merton and the university.

At Oxford he came under the influence of the great experimental neurophysiologist, Sir Charles Sherrington, and was befriended by Sir William Osler, Regius Professor of Medicine. There could have been no better start in life for a medical student with academic aspirations. On returning to the United States, he was taken back by Johns Hopkins for his final year and, in 1918, he graduated in medicine. The Peter Bent Brigham Hospital in Boston appointed Penfield a general surgical intern for twelve months about the time Harvey Cushing returned from the First World War to take up his position as Chief Surgeon at the hospital. Penfield took advantage of Cushing's presence in the hospital to learn from him by observation and by attendance at teaching sessions. He was not, however, part of his resident staff.

Penfield's return to Oxford and Sherrington's laboratory for a year was followed by a Beit Memorial Fellowship, applied for on his behalf by Sherrington. The Fellowship was his ticket to the National Hospital for Nervous and Mental Diseases (more conveniently known as Queen Square) in London, where reigned the greatest clinical neurologists of the country. It was Queen Square's heyday. Neurology was supreme.

Neurological diagnosis depended on a searching history and signs from physical examination, with anatomical and pathological correlation; a knowledge of the natural course of nervous disease, and therefore the ability to make a prognosis completed the attributes of the mature neurologist. A neurologist had to trust to his own unaided skill and experience to make a diagnosis. There were almost no biochemical tests of value. X-rays were primitive and were useful only to demonstrate fractures and other abnormalities of the skull. High hopes were lavished on the diagnostic possibilities of the electroencephalogram as soon as it was introduced by Berger in 1929. But it was not much help to the surgeon in the localization of operable lesions in the brain. Its most important place was to be in the diagnosis and surgical treatment of epilepsy, the area of specialization in which Penfield and his colleagues at the Montreal Neurological Institute (MNI) would become the pre-eminent authorities.

Surgery of the brain and spinal cord, hardly out of its infancy, was controlled — sometimes with good reason — by the medical neurologist. Every patient admitted to the hospital was placed under the care of a neurologist who decided if and when transfer to a neurosurgeon would be desirable. Such condescension was an affront the fiery Queen Square surgeon, Sir Victor Horsley, was never able to efface. Horsley, the first identifiable neurosurgeon in the modern sense, died not long before Penfield studied at Queen Square. He succumbed on July 16, 1916, to heat exhaustion in the Middle East while inspecting army medical establishments, because he refused to wear tropical uniform, a War Office injunction he regarded as undignified for an officer.[7]

Edward Archibald, chief of surgery at the Royal Victoria Hospital in Montreal, sought out Penfield in 1928[8] to upgrade surgery of the nervous system at McGill. Penfield, aware of the strength of his position in the academic marketplace, prized out of the chief surgeon without much difficulty greater contractual concessions than Archibald at first intended: nothing less, in fact, than the promise of what became the Montreal Neurological Institute, an academically autonomous, physically separate, multidisciplinary treatment, research and teaching institution within the confines of McGill's medical school. It was a far cry from Archibald's original plan to refurbish his department with an up-to-date but limited extension of nervous system surgery on a par with other developing subspecialties. Under the leadership of Penfield, with Archibald's blessing, the first plans were drawn up in 1929. A generous grant from the Rockefeller Foundation enabled construction of the Institute to begin, and in 1934 its doors opened.

Impatient to bring his plans to reality, Penfield brought with him from Baltimore and New York attending staff as well as the more junior research and house staff and key nursing staff. He did not spend time looking for Canadian talent in the neurosciences to support him. The pickings in any case were meagre since the few suitable candidates in the country were fully occupied building their own departments of anatomy, physiology, pathology, psychiatry and radiology. At the time, between the wars, Montreal, Toronto and Winnipeg were the only Canadian hunting grounds.

The MNI was opened by Sir Edward Beatty, the Chancellor of McGill University, on September 27, 1934. William V. Cone and Arthur R. Elvidge were Penfield's attending surgical staff colleagues; Joseph P. Evans, William T. Grant, David L. Reeves and Arne Torkildsen, all to become eminent neurosurgeons, were Research Fellows or House Staff.[9]

E. Harry Botterell

Edmund Harry Botterell, O.C.[10] (1906–1998)

Harry Botterell was born in Vancouver, but the family moved to Winnipeg six months after his birth. At ten he was sent as a boarder to Ridley College, St. Catharines, Ontario, before entering McGill University, Montreal. During the first year of his Arts/Med Course his father died (1924). The interests of the family dictated his return home to Winnipeg where he completed his medical education with the M.D. degree from the University of Manitoba (1930). His early appointments were: Surgical intern/resident Winnipeg General Hospital; Resident Physician, Montreal General Hospital (1931–1932); demonstrator in anatomy,

University of Toronto (1932–1933); surgical resident at Toronto General Hospital to Dr. W.E. Gallie (1933–1934); clinical clerk and locum tenens house physician, National Hospital for Nervous Diseases, Queen Square, London (1934–1935); research assistant in John Fulton's experimental neurophysiology laboratory, Yale University (1935–1936).

He was appointed lecturer in neurophysiology, University of Toronto, lecturer in neurosurgery and assistant to Dr. K.G. McKenzie, Toronto General Hospital, from 1936 to 1940. During the Second World War he was a neurosurgical specialist, Royal Canadian Army Medical Corps with the rank of Lieutenant-Colonel, posted to no.1 Canadian Neurological and Plastic Surgical Military Hospital, Basingstoke, England (1940–1945). He was appointed to the neurosurgical attending staff, Toronto General Hospital, in 1945, under Kenneth McKenzie for the last seven years of his reign.

Harry was a big man, strong in body and resolve. Returning to Winnipeg to be near his family after his father's death, he continued his medical studies, as well as overseeing his family and influencing important family decisions. He had hardly crossed the threshold to adulthood when he took over this, the first of his many heavy respon-sibilities. In the process he steadily became a master of administration. Reform was his passion.

•••

The founders' personalities and achievements could not have been more diverse, each with his peculiar obsession to excel: McKenzie to perfect the surgeon's art, Penfield to bring contemporary science to neurological research, and Botterell to seed Canadian medical schools across the country with a crop from his own cultivar, "the best damn neurosurgical centre in North America," as he privately vowed he would make the neurosurgical division at TGH.[11]

There were a few others in Canada who, after the First World War, being general surgeons of repute, opened the skull to remove brain tumours and blood clots and who, less commonly, exposed the spinal cord to relieve pressure from tumours or fractured vertebrae, but they could not hold a candle to those whom Harvey Cushing had trained. Cushing, like Horsley and Macewen before him, showed what was possible in the surgery of the nervous system with newer operating techniques and pioneering determination. Some surgeons looked askance at the extension of the surgical specialty into brain and spinal cord, at least until success in the new branch was widely demonstrated. Instead, they would avoid an operation that could be beneficial were they at ease in its execution. A cautious surgeon is commendable in the professional and public mind compared to the innovator whose work can so readily be dismissed as "experimental." The solid reputation in Toronto of the established surgeons did not encourage change.

The great-hearted W. Edward Gallie (1882–1959), Professor of Surgery at Toronto and later Dean,[12] wrote, several years after his retirement, to a raw, recent arrival in the university division of neurosurgery:

Medical Arts Building
Bloor and St. George Sts.
Toronto 5
April 21, 1955.

Dear Morley,

... I have just read your address on "The Growth of Neurosurgery,"
with the greatest interest ... because it deals with a part of the history of
neurosurgery with which I have had some sort of contact. For instance,
I knew Horsley, Macewen, Cushing, and Dandy. Oddly, I found all four
to be similar in at least two regards. They were all brilliant contributors
to our knowledge, and undoubtedly great figures in medical history, but
they were all disagreeable, pompous, and tremendously impressed with
their importance.

Dandy, who was about my own age, made me sick, as he did most of
the members of the Interurban Surgical Club to which we belonged, and
yet, as you say, he made perhaps the most important contribution to
cerebral diagnosis ever made.

I recall going to Baltimore with the Club, somewhere around 1917 or
1918, and seeing several of the first patients in whom he had injected air
into the ventricles. His presentation left me wondering how a man could
get so puffed up. But, there, rest his soul, for he really was something,
and you must bless him every day in the study of neurological patients.

With kindest regards,
Sincerely,
W.E. Gallie

Yet Kenneth McKenzie, who trained under Cushing in 1922, maintained a respectful and even affectionate relationship with his mentor, as shown in the letter Cushing wrote him from Yale on December 28, 1936:

Dear Ken:

Thanks for your Christmas note which was much appreciated. I am always glad to hear from you and to learn what is going on. Van [Nostrand[13]] sent me a Christmas card with a map showing how to find his farm, and I shall hope someday to have a look at it and see him at the plow. It is nice that you and he should be so near together so that you can keep in touch with one another's work. I am naturally very proud of you both.

I am glad to learn that your operating-room problems have been straightened out and that things are going well. Your Ménière syndrome business must be very gratifying. I still hear from some of my old ganglion cases done twenty years ago.

Yes, I suppose Cairns[14] is bound for Oxford, though he keeps mum about it for the appointment has not been exactly made public.

With greetings to Irene and the Children, and best wishes for the New Year, I am

Always affectionately yours,
Harvey Cushing

Through McKenzie, the skepticism towards neurosurgery in Toronto changed to cautious approval, but not immediately. In the early years of his appointment to TGH his surgical colleagues were eventually relieved to have the burden of care lifted from their shoulders for conditions they imperfectly understood. Admiration followed for the results of operations they themselves dared not attempt. McKenzie established a neurosurgical reputation no one in the medical school at Toronto could match.

When McKenzie graduated in medicine before the Great War, Toronto was a busy, parochial community. It failed to equal Montreal's aura of comfortable sophistication, a blending of old world poise with new world vigour, so it settled down to making money and looking to a future of mercantile success to rival its neighbour. Anglophones in Westmount, in control of Montreal industrially and politically, looked out disdainfully from the heights of Mount Royal on the city to the west. Hogtown, they called it, blithely corrupting the name Hogg's Hollow, now a wealthy district on the banks of the Don River, to emphasize the disparagement. The old joke of the foreigner who confessed the only thing he knew for certain about Toronto was that McGill was there, was gleefully circulated in Montreal's clubland and drawing rooms. Although the social chasm between the English and French communities was deep, the French tradition endowed the city with a richness appreciated by American visitors and even guardedly admitted by anglophones. To Americans of culture, Montreal was the only Canadian city that could hold a candle to the great metropolises of the Atlantic seaboard. The British were less lavish in praise of their Montreal cousins. Samuel Butler's satirical dig at Montreal's perceived philistinism in "Psalm of Montreal"[15] had heads nodding in approval.

Preferrest thou the gospel of Montreal to the gospel of Hellas,
The gospel of thy connexion with Mr. Spurgeon's haberdasher to
the gospel of the Discobolus?

The medical school at the University of Toronto began to emerge from Montreal's shadow during and especially after the Great War. The loss overseas of so many alumni from each school impelled those who returned, and those who had remained, to renewal and reform. In Montreal, Edward Archibald and, in Toronto, Duncan Graham in medicine, Clarence Starr and W.E. Gallie in surgery, were prime movers.

It is not clear why McKenzie, the silver medallist of his year and the son of a prominent Toronto medical graduate in general practice, was passed over for an appointment to the resident staff. Partly it was, unwittingly, of his own doing. Immediately after graduating in 1914, he volunteered for overseas war service, which left him vulnerable when he returned after the armistice. The Hospital guaranteed tenure to all returned junior hospital medical staff who were appointed before the war, but McKenzie could not qualify since he never stayed behind long enough in the first place even to apply.

The medical school at Toronto did not particularly want McKenzie, whose ambition to become a surgeon stemmed from his undergraduate days when he watched Dr. Herbert Bruce skillfully remove an appendix. The fledgling specialty of neurological surgery was established in only a few centres in the United States and seemed an unpromising field for a surgical career, especially at TGH. The Department of Surgery was satisfied with its performance and was not anxious to surrender the care of head injury to a newcomer. The orthodox care of the head injury at that time was "expectant" — the jargon for doing nothing but waiting for full consciousness to return. Meanwhile, any scalp or facial wounds could be attended to. It was a protocol believed to be well within a general surgeon's capability, but the competence to diagnose intracranial complications such as blood clots, and the training to deal with them surgically, was not. The change came with the appointment of C.L. Starr to the chair. His appointment followed that of Duncan Graham (1882–1974) who had recently been made the first full-time salaried University Professor of Medicine in North America.

Graham graduated in medicine from Toronto some nine years before war broke out in 1914. With a number of other Toronto graduates, including McKenzie, he enlisted in the Canadian Army Medical Corps and volunteered for overseas service. His posting took him to Salonika in the Crimea where he made his name. Although he had published as co-author a number of articles in the bacteriological literature before the war, it was Graham's paper in the *Lancet* on dysentery among the British Salonika Force that caught the attention of the authorities at home. His administrative ability, backed by his scientific reputation, made him the successful candidate for the professorship of medicine in the University.[16]

The president of the University of Toronto, Sir Robert Falconer, and Sir Joseph Flavelle, Chairman of the hospital's Board of Trustees, agreed the hospital had to be converted from its historic role as a community hospital to a modern university teaching hospital. The appointment of Graham as Professor of Medicine in the University and Chief of Medical Staff in the hospital was the necessary first step. To build a department of surgery equal to any on the continent, reforms in administration along the lines Duncan Graham had already laid out for the Department of Medicine were necessary.

C.L. Starr (1868–1920),[17] Graham's opposite number as head of the Department of Surgery in the hospital and university, held similar views on the way a teaching hospital should be run. Starr was appointed to the Hospital for Sick Children as chief of orthopaedic surgery in 1895. W.E. Gallie joined him as his senior assistant. Starr, Gallie and Graham became the leading lights in the two major clinical departments, medicine and surgery. Both Graham and Starr were protected from total dependence on private practice, Starr by a grant from the Rockefeller Foundation (1921) and Graham by an endowment (1918) to the university of a chair in medicine named after the donors, Sir John and Lady Eaton.

The privilege of looking after patients in the "public" wards was granted only to "attending" physicians recommended by the head of the department. They agreed to teach and take care of their patients in the public wards without payment. Patients, in return, would allow medical students to assist the staff doctor in their care as part of their training. A minority of beds would be set aside for patients who chose to pay for professional attention by appointed staff doctors. As a rule, medical students did not visit these "private" patients, an exclusion later experience has shown to be unnecessary and undesirable.

In this way hospital patients, it was assumed, would be served by the best practitioners and the medical school by the best teachers, all without any cost to either hospital or university, since the fee-bearing beds were provided by the hospital in a separate building, the Private Patients Pavilion, the preserve of the appointed staff from which they could earn their living. This arrangement was severely strained in the 1930s. The hospital depended on a substantial income from private beds. When, during the Depression, admissions fell, the Board relented a little by encouraging selected physicians who were not on the strength of the hospital-university staff to admit patients to private beds previously denied them. At the same time, the administrative and professional link between hospital and university was strengthened to the benefit of each, though mutual rivalry between the two institutions lingered until a joint advisory liaison committee was formed to smooth over such contentious issues as staff appointments and budget.

Graham, by the simple device of securing a letter of resignation from every doctor on the staff of the department of medicine before he agreed to his own appointment, which was confirmed in 1919, began his career at the hospital in complete control. Those who failed to deliver also failed to be re-appointed. Some who did comply with Graham's draconian demand still found themselves left out in the cold, but the university and hospital stood firm in support of Graham, while the disaffected prepared for battle. The affronted practitioners took their outrage to the Ontario Medical Association, which gave them its support, and the quarrel eventually landed in the lap of the Provincial Legislature. The storm blew itself out in 1923 with the ending of the parliamentary session and the defeat of Drury's adminis-tration by the Conservatives under Ferguson. Starr, with Graham, had kept his head down while the battle raged and did not enter into the debate, at least not publicly.

On his return to civilian life in 1919, with no opening in the junior surgical resident ranks, McKenzie established himself in general practice, but without much enthusiasm. He received neither patronage nor encouragement from colleagues in university or hospital to embark on a surgical career, much less one in neurosurgery.

Portrait of Harvey Cushing presented by him to Clarence Starr at the time of McKenzie's appointment as resident to Cushing

In 1922, the Faculty of Medicine in the University of Toronto recommended to the Trustees that a "Charles Mickle Fellowship be given for 1922–1923 to Harvey Cushing, M.D., Moseley Professor of Surgery at the Peter Bent Brigham Hospital, Harvard University."[18] Under the terms of the gift, Doctor William Mickle, the Toronto gold medallist in medicine of 1866 (*see* Appendix G) gave $50,000 to the University so that an annual scholarship could be given to the member of the medical profession who had done the most "during the preceding ten years to advance sound knowledge of a practical kind in medical art or science." Cushing, on receipt of the Fellowship, suggested the scholarship of $1,000 he received be put towards the support of a young man from Toronto interested in spending a year as Cushing's resident at the Brigham.

As soon as the opportunity came, through Harvey Cushing's generosity, to finance a man to be Cushing's resident for a year, Starr saw his chance at last to satisfy McKenzie's desire to become a surgeon. It was only then that neurosurgery became the focus of McKenzie's ambition. Up to that point he would have accepted any junior appointment just to get his foot into the surgical door.

When Starr offered McKenzie the chance to respond to Cushing's request for a trainee, McKenzie accepted without hesitation and packed his bags for Boston, leaving his wife and three small daughters at home for a year, as dictated by Cushing. War had already separated Kenneth and Irene for the first three years of their marriage, but they agreed the opportunity could not be missed, particularly as it carried with it an assurance from C.L. Starr there would be a junior position on the surgical staff at TGH on his return from Boston.

McKenzie obtained the appointment in 1922 following his predecessors as Cushing's fourth resident.[19] By that time Cushing was well established in neurosurgery at the Brigham. He had demonstrated that it was possible to remove brain tumours with the reasonable expectation of survival and restoration of function. Condemnation of operations on the brain and spinal cord had given way to cautious approval in a few major centres. Archibald in Montreal had published his extensive experience in brain trauma and Thorburn (1861–1923), in Manchester, in his 1889 monograph, "A Contribution to the Surgery of the spinal Cord,"[20] had proved his authority on spinal injuries and, more significantly, on the accurate assessment of level of injury by physical neurological examination. Of Thorburn's eighty-two articles, forty-six were on neurosurgery or neurology, but he forsook the neurosurgical field, "realising that practitioners were ceasing to send him general surgical cases and that he was heading for economic disaster."[21, 22]

In his 1940 memorial to Cushing[23] McKenzie writes on the man as he saw him while spending a year as his resident. The introductory training in neurosurgery with Cushing packed at least two years' experience into the one. Long hours, insufficient sleep and confinement to the hospital except for, perhaps, half a day a month, was the usual routine at the time — and continued to be so for most neurosurgical residents in other schools up to the Second World War. Cushing's demands on his resident were not more severe than on himself. In particular, the most detailed recording of history, neurological signs and every operation undertaken on the service was an absolute necessity. Cushing himself made good drawings of the operative field to complement his own written record, but McKenzie, it seems, did not have Cushing's artistic talents. Even so, his crude drawings added understanding to his dictated notes.

McKenzie seems to have been encouraged by the secret of Cushing's success as he saw it. In contrast to the "brilliance" Halsted attributed to Cushing when he was his resident in general surgery at Johns Hopkins, to McKenzie his "genius lay in the fact that with average mentality and good health he set his course for the top and never became sidetracked or slackened the pace." McKenzie believed that what Halsted interpreted as brilliance was a feature of a man "who worked unusually hard and more efficiently than the average." McKenzie, never claiming brilliance in himself, would have been convinced that success could come simply from sustained hard work and that he too was up to it.

In 1954, listening to K.G. talking about his experience with Cushing and his impression of his teacher, I dictated a memo directly afterwards. It was not a verbatim record. I reproduce here extracts as I wrote them, without editorial revision:

... Perhaps a great contribution made was the impression that he [Cushing] indelibly wrote on his pupils' minds that even the smallest thing in clinical surgery really matters. The irony is that no one working with such a man can make any great contribution. He is overshadowed and smothered ... He [Cushing] was determined to become a famous man ... He never inspired devotion except from one man (Horrax). He was completely unapproachable and gave the impression that this sternness and lack of any emotion was calculated to build legend around himself ... He felt his life would have been completely wasted if the memory of it had died with him ... He was always talking about his mortality figures, and he became so obsessed with the idea of having a lower mortality than anyone else of whatever branch of surgery he might be dealing with that his clinical judgment was sometimes distorted.

Walter Dandy was in great contrast to this and he used to say that mortality figures did not interest him, and what he meant by that was simply that if one was always competing to keep one's mortality down in a branch of surgery that is developing, then development would cease, and this attitude in no way conflicted with the highest consideration of medical ethics. For instance, in a malignant brain tumour Dandy would make an attempt at radical excision where Cushing in the same tumour would only take out a very small piece. This would often result in Cushing's patient dying just as soon as Dandy's from the tumour itself rather than the operative removal ... Dandy was much more concerned to produce useful citizens than low mortality figures.

Cushing worked at very high pressure and never relaxed. Whatever he did, he did seriously. If he played tennis he hated to lose, but he only took exercise because he thought it was good for him, not because he enjoyed it. K.G. could not have stayed with him for long. He felt that the force of Cushing's personality would have extinguished his own. Cushing was always very fair to his juniors even if he drove them hard, and he would always stand up for them in any dispute between them and colleagues ... and patients.

McKenzie's assessment of Cushing in 1954 had changed little from the time he published the article in the American Journal of Psychiatry a year after Cushing's death in 1939.

Joint Command

In the world of hospital and university, McKenzie at first faced constraints that could be relieved only by the goodwill of his contemporaries or patronage from his seniors, favours not readily dispensed. His arrival on the scene was, after all, largely due to his own initiative and persistence. McKenzie, it will be recalled, missed a junior internship in surgery at TGH because he volunteered for military service immediately after graduation while others put in at least six months as interns. Only those who had been so employed before enlistment were promised renewal of engagement when they returned as veterans. The hospital and university kept to the somewhat officious rule in spite of McKenzie's repeated applications as a veteran. He had no sponsor until C.L. Starr saw an opportunity in Cushing's offer to transfer the $1,000 prize money awarded him by the Mickle Foundation. And sending the ambitious young man to Boston for a year would be a means at least to get McKenzie off his back. On his return from Cushing, McKenzie's ambition could no longer be denied. A student of the leading American neurosurgeon surely had to be taken seriously. But even with Cushing's sponsorship in his record, McKenzie's first years were a struggle.

In 1923 he accepted the position of general surgical resident to C.B. Shuttleworth, a probationary year before his appointment to the attending staff as neurosurgeon could be ratified. He received his board and lodging and a small salary, but thereafter he was on his own. At first he had to look after general surgical cases or go hungry. But following success with a few patients with trigeminal neuralgia and traumatic intracranial haematoma, and a willingness to tackle cerebral tumours which others had neither the knowledge nor skill to undertake, he was able to follow his heart's desire by surviving on a practice limited to neurological disorders.

A less determined man than McKenzie would have given up in despair of ever being able to support himself in the early 1920s from the proceeds of a practice limited to surgery of the nervous system. Seven or eight years passed following his return to Toronto before he could survive without a sweetening of general surgical cases — abdominal emergencies, thyroidectomies and bodily injuries other than to the head. Work in these areas, though, was not easy to come by. An established surgeon would sometimes ask for his assistance at an operation on a private patient, more as a kindness than a necessity, especially when senior surgical residents from other services did not appreciate being displaced in the operating room from the position of first assistant to the chief.

His primary obligation to the public, the General and the University, was to fill a gaping hole. Neurosurgical patients up to that time had been poorly handled; comparison with leading Ivy League American centres discredited Toronto. The TGH had been unable to fulfill the aspirations of its trustees to create "a hospital perfectly complete" so long as surgery of the nervous system was neglected. McKenzie's second, but no less imperative responsibility was to fly the Canadian flag by attending American neurosurgical meetings and participating in their clinical programs with papers which were later published.

The medical school at Toronto was already well known in the United States. It had scored well in the Flexner Report to the Carnegie Foundation (1910), joining McGill to become one of only two schools in Canada to win the report's approval. In 1921 the Toronto Medical School became world renowned as soon as the work of Banting, Best, Collip and McLeod in the conquest of diabetes became known.

To the young McKenzie, with no neurosurgical colleagues to compare notes with, Toronto was at first a barren land. But he kept up his contacts in the United States and extended them through the patronage of Cushing. They became his close friends throughout his life,[24] particularly Glen Spurling, Eustace Semmes and Ed Fincher.[25] With them he talked neurosurgery and golfed and fished at the periodic meetings of the societies to which Cushing had directly or indirectly sponsored him.

As with McKenzie, a year as surgical resident with Cushing at Peter Bent Brigham turned Glen Spurling's desire from a career in general surgery to neurosurgery. He established the neurosurgical service at the Louisville General Hospital in 1926 and remained at its head until retirement in 1960. He was one of the founders of the Harvey Cushing Society (1931) and, as one of its delegates, with representation from the Society of Neurological Surgeons (the "Senior Society"), formed the Board of Neurological Surgery and later became its chairman. In the army during the Second World War, as Assistant Chief of General Surgery, he was responsible for all U.S. military neurosurgical services in Europe.

Eustace Semmes, Professor of Surgery (Neurosurgery), University of Tennessee in Memphis, received the Distinguished Service Award of the

Society of Neurological Surgeons (1976). He joined Spurling and Fincher on the scientific program at the second meeting (1933) of the Harvey Cushing Society with his paper, "Pathological Physiology of Cord Injuries." It was at this meeting K.G. McKenzie, with six others, was "invited to join the Society."

Ed Fincher had been a student of Cushing at the Peter Bent Brigham and of Alfred Adson and Winchell Craig at the Mayo Clinic. He was elected President of the Society of Neurological Surgeons (1955–1956); he practised in Atlanta.

In this company McKenzie was hailed as one of their own and through them was voted into the highest echelons of American neurosurgery. K.G. regularly attended the meetings of the Society of Neurological Surgeons, the only neurosurgical society at the time. Cushing, with the close cooperation of Ernest Sachs, formed the society in 1920. Penfield (1942) and McKenzie (1948) were in due course each elected president.

McKenzie's appointment as resident to Cushing heralded the close

Meeting of Society of Neurological Surgeons, New York Neurological Institute, December 1929. *Standing, from left*: Byron Stookey, Wilder Penfield, Loyal Davis, Samuel Clark Harvey, Kenneth G. McKenzie, Max Peet, Charles Bagley, Harry Hyland Kerr, Carl Rand, Ernest Sachs, Jay Keegan, William Jason Mixter, Charles E. Dowman, Francis Grant, Winchell Craig. *Sitting*: Charles Elsberg, Charles H. Frazier, Howard Naffziger, Harvey Cushing, Alfred S. Taylor relationship between Canadian and American neurosurgeons. The huge increase of neurosurgeons in both countries after World War II diminished the Canadian need for communication across the border at the senior level. But many Canadian neurosurgeons still believe it essential to their continuing education to be elected to at least one of the several American Societies.

The Society of Neurological Surgeons chose to deny itself excessive

---

CANADIAN NEUROLOGICAL ASSOCIATION

FIRST ANNUAL MEETING

MONTREAL, MAY 20 - 21, 1949

PROGRAM

FRIDAY, MAY 20TH

9 A.M.   REGISTRATION - MONTREAL NEUROLOGICAL INSTITUTE.

9.30-12.45 MORNING SESSION. AMPHITHEATRE M.N.I.

9.30-10.30 SYMPOSIUM ON LESIONS ABOUT FORAMEN MAGNUM

NEUROLOGICAL ASPECTS - J.P. ROBB
RADIOLOGICAL DIAGNOSIS - D.L. MCRAE
ARNOLD-CHIARI MALFORMATION - K.G.MCKENZIE AND J.W. CLUFF
AN UNUSUAL FORAMEN MAGNUM SYNDROME - F.H. O'BRIEN

10.30   NON-SIGNIFICANT VENTRICULAR SHIFT IN PNEUMOGRAMS.
                                          - D.C. EAGLESHAM

10.50   CEREBRAL HEMORRHAGE OR BRAIN TUMOUR.
                                          - C. BERTRAND AND D. LAFIA

11.10   ACOUSTIC NEUROMA. THE USUAL SYNDROME AND ITS VARIATION,
        BASED ON STUDY OF 97 VERIFIED CASES.
                                          - K.G. MCKENZIE

11.40   THREE UNUSUAL BRAIN TUMOURS - A PATHOLOGICAL STUDY.
                                          - E.A. LINELL

12.00   PREPARATION AND USE IN SURGERY OF AN ARTIFICIAL SPINAL FLUID
                                          - K.A.C.ELLIOTT AND
                                            R.LEWIS

1.15 P.M. LUNCH FOR MEMBERS, ROYAL VICTORIA HOSPITAL, DOCTORS' DINING ROOM

2.30-5.00 P.M. AFTERNOON SESSION. UNIVERSITE DE MONTRÉAL, 2900 M .ROYAL BLVD.
                (TRANSPORT WILL BE FURNISHED FOR THOSE WHO WISH IT)

2.30   ENCEPHALOMYELITIS   - R.G. ARMOUR

3.00   A STUDY OF CERTAIN ALTERATIONS IN SPEECH DURING STIMULATION OF
        SPECIFIC CORTICAL REGIONS. - L. ROBERTS

3.20   STUDIES ON THE BIOCHEMICAL MECHANISM OF EPILEPSY
                                          - D.MCEACHERN & K.A.C. ELLIOTT

3.50   PSYCHOSOMATIC PROBLEMS RELATED TO THE GENERAL-ADAPTATION-SYNDROME.
                                          - H. SELYE,
                                            PROFESSOR-DIRECTOR,
                                            INSTITUTE OF EXPERIMENTAL MEDICINE
                                            AND SURGERY, U. DE M.

Program of first annual meeting, Canadian Neurological Association, 1949 growth in order to preserve the original intimacy amongst its members. As more neurosurgeons arrived on the scene, trained by the very same members who were sometimes reluctant to admit them to the Society, the next generation decided to form its own society. Foreseeing the great increase of neurosurgeons in the country and the threat to the intimacy and quality of the "Senior Society," Cushing gave his blessing to the first newcomer. The new society was named The Harvey Cushing Society at its formation in 1931. The Canadians, McKenzie (1936), Frank Turnbull (1949) and Charles G. Drake (1977, after it changed its name to the American Association of Neurological Surgeons), were each elected President.

The medical school in Toronto took another spurt forward when William Edward Gallie became Professor of Surgery in the University and head of surgery at Toronto General Hospital after Starr's death in December of 1928. He had already advocated an organized system for the training of surgeons. Now he was in a position to do something about it. In a letter to Sir Heneage Ogilvie,[26] Gallie wrote:

> [Fifty] years ago, when I was first appointed to the staff of the General Hospital, the surgical staff was composed of a group of independent surgeons, nearly all Fellows of the Royal College of Surgeons of England, each doing whatever he pleased and without the slightest interest in training surgeons. The chief interest, indeed, of these surgeons, was to use their hospital appointments to increase their private practices. As far as I know no surgeon had been trained in Canada up to that time.
>
> Then came the change. Clarence Starr was made Professor of Surgery and Surgeon-in-Chief of the General Hospital. At the same time I succeeded him as Surgeon-in-Chief of the Children's Hospital, and the two of us worked together to try to establish here in Toronto a real school for surgeons. Then after a few years Professor Starr died, and I was transferred to the General, and made Professor of Surgery. That was 1929.

Gallie was admired by students and colleagues of all ages; his administrative gifts were particularly effective from the genial but decisive manner of their delivery. His other distinctions included: Hunterian Professor, Royal College of Surgeons of England (1924); President, American Orthopedic Association (1932); Moynihan Lecturer and Gold Medallist of the Royal College of Surgeons of England (1947), the 20th Gold Medal winner in the 150 years since its inception; Dean of Medicine, University of Toronto (1936–1946); successor to C.L. Starr as Surgeon-in-Chief, Hospital for Sick Children, Toronto (1921); following Starr as Professor and Surgeon-in-Chief at the Toronto General Hospital (1929); President, American College of Surgeons (1941–1946) during W.W. II, holding the fort until the war was over; President, American Surgical Association (1948).

After C.L. Starr died in 1928, Gallie was appointed, simultaneously, Dean of Medicine, Professor of Surgery and Surgeon-in-Chief at the Toronto General Hospital.

Gallie was most supportive of McKenzie. As soon as his new position could be officially ratified by the hospital and university together, he successfully urged the hospital board of trustees to build an operating room dedicated to neurosurgery alone (1929), finally acknowledging McKenzie's persistent plea.

Although McKenzie had been *de facto* head of a struggling subspecialty of neurosurgery, official recognition of a separate division within surgery was not granted until Gallie's promotion to the chair of the surgical department. Thereafter, with his position clarified as head of the division, McKenzie was assured of a fair hearing over the development of neurosurgery in the hospital. His reasoned and persistent request for an operating room of his own had finally been granted. It was built at basement level with outside access to the hospital gardens. There was a small area for a secretary and a space just big enough for surgeons to change (there were no lockers), where a cracked corner hand basin held together with Elastoplast served as a urinal. These trivial inconveniences were overlooked by McKenzie in the joy of the larger benefaction. He no longer had to wait until the end of the day for an operating room to become free. It was all his own. After World War II a second room was added so that the hours spent in preliminary air encephalograms and other pre-operative investigations no longer held up shorter operations.

K.G.'s clinical burden during this time was, in some measure, of his own making. From his early experience with the difficulty of building a purely neurosurgical practice and from his observation of some U.S. clinics where, he believed, overstaffing was responsible for less than optimal individual performance, he resisted new appointments to his service. Instead, he relied heavily upon general surgical residents of other specialties who, under the Gallie surgical training scheme in the university, were attached to him for six months. The arrangement satisfied both his reluctance to train too many neurosurgeons and, on the other hand, it supplied general surgeons to the province who were competent to look after that most common of all neurosurgical conditions, the acute head injury. Some, including Dean Joseph MacFarlane and Professor Robert M. Janes, saw McKenzie's policy as selfishness,[27] but wisely steered clear of interfering in a decision of the divisional head.

McKenzie knew what it meant to bring up a family on a small income. By 1931, when Frank Turnbull (1904–2000) was appointed K.G.'s first neurosurgical resident for full a year, McKenzie was almost able to shed his non-neurosurgical patients, leaving him with only twenty-five cases of brain tumour in the year. And he managed to pay Turnbull $25 per month for his assistance in the operating room, even with fewer private patients than "public," non-paying patients. He eventually attained to a reasonable prosperity from his private patients (there was no other professional source of income) but he was never rich. His will in 1964 was probated at $94,728, which included his house, car and investments. After state medicine had come to Canada in the late 1950s, he thought the officially scheduled fee of $350 for total care of a patient with a brain tumour was "pretty good," although it was modest compared to most European and United States neurosurgical scales.

Over the whole of McKenzie's active career he resisted the temptation to build up the division of neurosurgery by prematurely appointing new colleagues, a tendency he believed he could see developing in some continental centres. His decision to limit the number of neurosurgeons being trained wasn't based on financial greed or selfishness. He thought the practice of neurosurgery, at least in Toronto, would not support another staff neurosurgeon so long as the university was unwilling to subsidize even a junior appointee, a policy the university did not reverse until the 1950s.

After the Second World War, when his protégé Charles Drake was setting up the first neurosurgical unit at the University of Western Ontario in London, Ontario, he warned Drake not to take on attending staff too early or he would find there was not enough practice in the community for two to share, an admonition Drake was thankful to have received.[28]

Charles Drake had been closer to McKenzie than any other resident assigned to him. Temperamentally they were similar and this was reflected in their teaching. K.G. wrote one long, detailed handout to medical students of about twenty pages on how to take a neurologically focused history and carry out a detailed clinical examination of the nervous system. But having written the instruction pamphlet, he handed it over to the resident to teach medical students the basic lessons. His favourite teaching method was discussion with assistants over coffee after an operation on any or all aspects of the patient, disease and operation just concluded. He treated his residents without intentional intimidation, as if they were his equal.

Drake tells the following anecdote about his mentor:

> One night a man arrived at the Emergency department with an extradural haematoma, according to [Drake's] diagnosis.
>
> Dr. McKenzie was at a formal dinner down at the Royal York Hotel. Anyway, I called him there. The message came back, "Are you sure?" He came up and I was just trembling [that] when he operated there would be nothing there. But there was a big extradural. I remember him complimenting me on it. He came up in his dinner jacket. And he sent me a copy of the operative note that he dictated, and I kept it for a long time.
>
> Then I came to my last day there. It was the fall of 1944. We had made rounds and we were coming down the elevator in the Pavilion and we got off ... and he said, "Drake, have you enjoyed the service?" And I said, "Yes, Sir." And he mentioned something about his having enjoyed having me around for this extra bit of time, and that I had helped out ... And then his next words I remember clearly. He said, "Well, look. After the war, if you're still interested, come back and see me." We shook hands and that was it.

When Drake was discharged from the army, K.G. and Gallie decided he should return to the university surgical training program in neurosurgery. McKenzie, sensitive as always to his own deficiency in basic neurophysiology and neurology, comparing his attainments unfavourably to Penfield's more "scientific" background, sent Drake for two years' anatomy and neurophysiology at the University of Western Ontario under Murray Barr, F.R. Miller and George W. Stavraky. Then, as with Botterell earlier, he was sent to John Fulton's laboratory at Yale where he studied functional localization in the anterior cerebellum of the spider monkey.

To wind up Drake's postgraduate tour McKenzie sent him to a number of European neurological centres. He met Professor Norman Dott in Edinburgh only to find him in bed with a broken hip. Dott referred him to a general surgical colleague in the north of Scotland who lent his car to Charlie and his wife, Ruth, to take them to an innkeeper acquaintance who, in turn, put Charlie on to some of the best salmon water in Scotland. Back in Edinburgh he watched John Gillingham,[29] Dott's Chief Assistant, place a lesion in the ansa reticularis for Parkinson's disease according to the method of Gérard Guiot[30] in Paris. The Drakes would soon be visiting Guiot at his clinic and enjoying the hospitality of this quiet, gentle and refined man.

Drake then went on to Stockholm, where McKenzie wanted him to find out how Herbert Olivecrona spared the facial nerve while removing an acoustic neuroma. Olivecrona[31] was away but his assistant, Palle Taarnhøj, filled Drake in on Olivecrona's technique.

Before he returned to Britain, Drake visited the neurosurgical clinic of Professor H. Verbiest at Utrecht. In England he spent some time with Sir Geoffrey Jefferson's unit in Manchester, Sir Hugh Cairns in Oxford, and the neurologists and neurosurgeon (Wylie McKissock) at Queen Square. He watched McKissock operate and remarked, upon the speed at which he removed an acoustic neuroma. Drake judged McKenzie equal in speed but superior in technique.

Thus was McKenzie's prescription for Drake's introduction to neurosurgery completed. He had given him an incomparably better basic and advanced training than his own.[32,33] And he had introduced and addicted him to fly fishing for trout and salmon, and pheasant and duck hunting, as befitted a surrogate father to his surrogate son who had lost his own father ten days before his birth.

As a teacher, McKenzie was respected and admired by both his peers and his resident assistants. Bill Lougheed,[34] who developed the use of hypothermia in intracranial surgery,[35,36] remembered McKenzie "not so much [as a planner] but as someone who was a great teacher and who was a great surgeon, and who had that ability to come in [to the OR] and just stand there, or even assist you. He didn't do it all himself nor leave you to do it." Lougheed recalls:

I was helping him with an acoustic one time and it was one that [Dr. X] had done. The patient came back and K.G. was taking it out. I was assisting by just gently retracting on the acoustic. In the end the fifth nerve was divided and I guess I must have divided it by my periosteal elevator (acting as a retractor) on the top of the tumour. His only comment was, at the end of the procedure, "I guess you didn't see the fifth nerve, Bill." So clearly I had divided it. That was all that was said. It was his reputation [at stake], not mine. A great example.

McKenzie, who had no scientific research training beyond what he had picked up in medical school, was determined to perfect the neurosurgical art to his maximum ability, and to pass it on to the few residents who, he hoped, would settle down in Canada in centres large enough to support them with private practice. His gift to medical training remained in clinical neurosurgery and in this he excelled beyond the two other founders, Penfield and Botterell, who arrived on the neurosurgical stage after him with their own special gifts.

ENDNOTES — CHAPTER 3

1. Penfield, Wilder. *No Man Alone: A Neurosurgeon's Life*. Boston/Toronto: Little, Brown & Co., 1977.
2. Penfield, W. "History of Canadian Surgery: Edward Archibald (1872–1945)." *Canad. J. Surg.* 1 (1958):167–174.
3. Feindel, W. "Neurosurgery at the Montreal Neurological Institute and McGill University Hospitals." *Neurosurgery* 39 (1996): 830–839.
4. Archibald E. "Surgical affections and wounds of the head." In *American Practice of Surgery*. Vol 5. Bryant and Back, Eds. New York: Wood, 1908.
5. Penfield, Wilder. *No Man Alone* (1977: 123)
6. Eccles, J. and W. Feindel. "Wilder Graves Penfield 1891–1976." In *Biographical Memoirs of Fellows of the Royal Society* 24 (1978): 473–513.
7. Sir Victor Horsley (1857–1916) met his end in Mesopotamia at about the same time as McKenzie arrived at the 40th General Hospital Mesopotamia, Imperial Expeditionary Force, on July 6, 1916. McKenzie mentioned "seeing Sir Victor [in Mesopotamia] once during the First World War" in his paper he read in 1958 at the opening of the new neurosurgical unit at the TGH (Ch. 3 endnote 7). That was before McKenzie had any leaning towards a neurological or neurosurgical career. (See also Paget, S. *Sir Victor Horsley: A study of his life and work*. London: Constable, 1919).
8. Robb, P. *The Development of Neurology at McGill*. Montreal University (1989): 125, xii. Privately published by the author. Available from the Montreal Neurological Institute.
9. Montreal Neurological Institute. *Neurological Biographies and Addresses* (1936): Preface. London: Oxford University Press.
10. For memorial notices from nine of his contemporary colleagues, see "E. Harry Botterell. A series of papers commemorating his life and contributions." *Canad. J. Neurol. Sci.* 26 (1999): 230–246.
11. John W. Scott to TPM. Verbal recollection (September 1989).
12. *William Edward Gallie: Surgeon Seeker, Teacher, Friend*. Copyright The Gallie Club (1978). 62 pp. Printed by the University of Toronto Press.

ISBN 0-9690930-0-4. Introduction by R.I. Harris (12 pp) gives a picture of the successes and personal attributes of Gallie. Copies may be obtained from the Department of Surgery, Room 310, Banting Institute, University of Toronto, Toronto, ON, M5G 1L5.

13. F.H. van Nostrand (1896–1975). University of Toronto neuropsychiatrist.
14. Sir Hugh Cairns (1896–1952). Born in Australia; Rhodes Scholar (1919). Awarded a Rockefeller Travelling Scholarship as resident to Harvey Cushing at the Peter Bent Brigham Hospital for one year (1926). The first Nuffield Professor of Surgery at Oxford (1937). (For a full account of the Life of Cairns, see: Jefferson, Sir Geoffrey. "Memories of Hugh Cairns." *J. Neurol., neurosurg., psychiat.* 22 [1959]: 155–166).
15. Samuel Butler (1835–1902). "Psalm of Montreal" was written in Montreal in 1875 and published in *The Spectator* in 1878. In a number of later anthologies the words of the refrain after each stanza have been rendered: "O God! O Montreal!" The correct version, "O God! Oh Montreal!" is an intended exclamatory rebuke.
16. Kerr, R.B. and D. Waugh. *Duncan Graham: Medical Reformer and Educator.* Toronto and Oxford: Hannah Institute and Dundurn Press, 1989.
17. Janes, R.M. "Dr. Clarence Leslie Starr." *Canad. J.Surg.* 3 (1960):109–111.
18. Report of the Committee on Fellowships and Scholarships (7 April 1922).
19. Fulton, J.F. *Harvey Cushing.* Springfield, Illinois: Charles C. Thomas (1946): 453.
20. Thorburn, W. *A Contribution to the Surgery of the Spinal Cord.* London: Charles Griffin & Co., 1889. Many detailed sensory loss drawings and descriptions of motor loss after injury to the cord, with autopsy correlation, distinguish this book.
21. Brockbank, William. *The Honorary Medical Staff of the Manchester Royal Infirmary 1830–1948.* Manchester University Press (1965).
22. Jefferson, G. *Selected Papers.* London and New York: Pitman Medical Publishing Company (1960): 200 ff. on Thorburn
23. McKenzie, K.G. "Harvey Cushing (1869–1939)." *Am J. Psychiat.* 96 (1940): 1001–1007.
24. Frank Turnbull letter to TPM (23 March 1988).
25. Roy Glenwood Spurling (1894–1968); Raphael Eustace Semmes (1885–1982); Edgar Franklin Fincher (1900–1969).
26. Gallie box. University of Toronto Archives. Sir Heneage Ogilvie (1887–1971) was a leading surgeon in London on the staff of Guy's Hospital. He was elected to the Council of the Royal College of Surgeons of England and became its vice-president from 1945 to 1947. Among his many honours was election in 1943 to an Honorary Fellowship of the Royal College of Physicians and Surgeons of Canada.
27. EHB letter to TPM (28 June 1989). Queen's University archives: Botterell box.

28. C.G. Drake to TPM. Taped interview (March 1987).

29. John Gillingham. Later Professor of Neurosurgery, University of Edinburgh; President of the Royal College of Surgeons of Edinburgh.

30. Gérard Guiot (b.1912). Professor at the Collège de Médecine des Hôpitaux de Paris. A quiet and intensely thoughtful neurosurgeon who made major contributions to stereotaxy for the control of movement disorders, to ventriculostomy and to new approaches to the thoraco-cervical spine. He founded the Department of Neurosurgery at the Hôpital Foch and introduced the first full-time, salaried faculty in France.

31. A. Herbert Olivecrona (1891–1980). Sweden's first neurosurgeon; Professor of Neurosurgery at Karolinska Institutet; Chairman 1935–1960.

32. Drake, C.G. "Perspectives from Dr. Charles Drake: early training in Toronto." *Can. J. Neurol. Sci.* 26 (1999): 331–333.

33. Drake, C.G. "Training under Dr. Kenneth McKenzie." Charles Drake's tape of his life, edited by Stephen P. Lownie (February 1999). Typescript MS. This version of Drake's life was further edited for *Can. J. Neurol. Sci.* (ref. 32 above), and should be consulted for extra information.

34. William M. Lougheed. Emeritus Professor, U of T. Graduated in medicine, Toronto (1947).

35. Lougheed, W.M. and D.S. Kahn. "Circumvention of anoxia during arrest of cerebral circulation for intracranial surgery." *J. Neurosurg.* 12 (1955): 226–239.

36. Lougheed, W.M., W.H. Sweet, J.C. White, and W.R. Brewster. "The use of hypothermia in surgical treatment of cerebral vascular lesions." *J. Neurosurg.* 12 (1955): 240–255.

FOUR

CASE RECORDS AND PUBLICATIONS

*The parenthetical numbering of the
articles in this section refers to the complete list of
McKenzie's published papers found in Appendix D.*

In the first half of the twentieth century TGH archives were largely neglected. True, there had appeared valuable histories of the hospital by C.K. Clarke (1913) and a second by W.G. Cosbie (1975), and the corridors of the hospital administration are hung with portraits of trustees and one or two senior medical and nursing administrators. But the energy of the hospital was concentrated on contemporary and future patient care, teaching and research rather than reflections on the past; in such times, as often happens, archives take second place.

The new College Street building opened in 1913 was justifiably a source of great pride to the city, province and university. A nod of recognition to past European religious and charitable institutions of healing was permitted in the outpatients' hall (Mulock-Larkin wing) with its cloisters. As if embarrassed in the midst of modern splendour by the symbolism of an ancient style, the Florentine arches have been left to make the best of their square, thick supporting pillars, an architectural solecism that not even the beautiful Della Robbia terracotta facsimiles can redeem.

A few, very few, treasures of written medical records survive. At the time of their writing they seemed to their authors so mundane as not to merit preservation once their raison d'être had passed. A few of McKenzie's early patient charts escaped the shredder when, in the 1970s, there was no longer room to store them. Only one or two surviving charts belong to the 1920s, more to the 1930s. Trained by Cushing, McKenzie's written records were more detailed than was the practice elsewhere in the hospital, both in his own hand and type-written by his career-long secretary, Mabel Duthie.

Research was clinically directed. The medical staff of the hospital was not trained to inquire at a more fundamental and "scientific" level. The expanding scope of surgery was the major preoccupation of the curious and adventurous; even the demonstration of the therapeutic value of insulin, reported in 1922, the triumph of the century up to that time, had a closer affiliation to the practice of medicine than to the laboratory. The empirical approach of "trial and error" was as far as clinical research, particularly surgical, had reached.

Most of McKenzie's contributions to the neurosurgical literature were the product of his own thoughts and his own labour. In these, he was the sole author. In some articles, as was the practice of the day, his joint authorship was listed as a courtesy, not, in his case, because he expected or demanded it, but because he was the head of the division and the true authors chose to recognize him in this manner.

In the early twenties, when McKenzie spent his year of residency with Cushing in Boston, neurosurgery consisted mainly in the removal of intracranial and intraspinal tumours, abscesses and blood clots, and the cleaning of open wounds of the head. The operating room itself had to be large enough to accommodate the necessary coming and going of nurses bringing solutions, instruments and sterile towels to the table if the need for them arose unexpectedly. It was a silent room. Audible speech between surgeon, scrub nurse and anaesthetist could not be allowed to be muffled by noisy clashes of wheeled equipment or chatter between staff waiting out of the way in the perimeter of the room. Piped-in music was an intrusion of the future.

The surgical team involved no more members than the responsible surgeon, resident, the scrub nurse and the anaesthetist. The referring physician, medical students and other curious hospital staff could be admitted with the surgeon's approval in a few but unpredictable numbers. Suited in sterile gown, mask and, usually, in cotton cap (outdoor shoes were seldom covered), they added to the congestion and, if order was not strictly enforced, noise. The visiting doctors could be the hardest to silence, but that was the surgeon's decision. A reproachful stare from the surgeon over his mask at the speaker was usually enough to restore peace. McKenzie limited his speech to the scrub nurse and his first assistant, the resident. The head nurse in the operating room led a parallel team, complementary to the surgical. It was a true partnership. Incompatibility between the two teams was a prescription, if not for disaster, for something less than perfection. Histrionics, tantrums, ill-disguised invective muttered behind the surgical mask, are not unknown reactions of a surgeon to a tense turn in an operation. But when the scrub nurse and the surgeon are in harmony, the experience for each is its own reward.

Preliminary laboratory tests and special investigations were hardly more elaborate or informative than plain X-rays of the skull and vertebrae. At William Halsted's urging, Walter Dandy in 1918 and 1919 had outlined the cerebral ventricles and the spinal cord radiographically by injecting air directly into the ventricles or into the lumbar subarachnoid space. For the first time spinal and cerebral masses of whatever nature could be outlined directly or indirectly by displacement of otherwise normal intracranial and intraspinal structures. Dandy's technique held the diagnostic stage for about fifteen years, and neurosurgical operations for the first time could be based on localization more reliable than by interpretation of abnormal neurological signs observed at bedside examination. After Dandy's demonstration, the pursuit of better diagnostic techniques has never stopped, for the injection of air was painful and dangerous, the more so in the presence of a tumour or any other mass. On the other hand, when the diagnosis was in doubt, the failure to demonstrate an abnormality could be equally informative and save the patient from a fruitless exploratory operation.

The development of diagnostic radiological techniques — or imaging, as it is called today — was the most important advance in neurosurgery during the twentieth century. The early techniques of imaging involved the use of fluid material, usually containing an iodine compound, which obstructed the passage of X-rays so that the photographic film was not exposed in the appropriate area and showed up white. The introduction into the ventricles of the brain or subarachnoid space of radio-opaque materials of this nature was not without danger. Their usefulness to the surgeon in the pursuit of accurate anatomical localization had to be balanced against the risk. The danger of complications was not always recognized at first. Lipiodol, an oil-based iodine-containing agent gave excellent imaging for the detection of spinal conditions and even a few cerebral abnormalities, but the inflammatory reaction it induced in the spinal subarachnoid space and even in the outlets of the cerebral ventricles was not recognized until the damage was done. Thorotrast also gave excellent pictures but it contained radioactive thorium, which caused delayed destruction to spinal and cranial nerves, and soon led to the outlawing of its use. Pharmaceutical companies then developed water-soluble contrast media instead of oil-based compounds. Water-soluble media were quickly absorbed without leaving a trail of damage behind them. Contrast angiography, the injection of radio-opaque material into arteries and, sometimes, veins was introduced by Egaz Moniz in 1927 to demonstrate a variety of lesions in the head. It was found to be highly informative and allowed many conditions to come within the scope of the neurosurgeon; but, for many years, the technique brought with it a certain incidence of complications such as stroke, which only justified its use when its benefit outweighed its danger.

The contemporary scene, thanks to a revolution in the technology of imaging, has drastically changed over the last forty years or so to one of then undreamed of safety and information. New imaging techniques have not simplified surgical management of lesions of the brain and spinal cord, but they have brought a greater variety of conditions within surgical reach. McKenzie, and those of his era, of necessity became skilled in the interpretation of clinical neurological signs revealed by bedside examination. To some extent those clinical skills have become redundant and have been replaced by technologically derived information which, to be used appropriately rather than wastefully (or not used at all), requires as much experience and thoughtfulness as McKenzie displayed in his day.

When McKenzie started with Cushing, patient mortality was high, with or without operation. General anaesthesia was not uncommonly a contribution to operative complications and death; it was often less dangerous to operate on the brain under local anaesthesia with moderate sedation. Imaging techniques were new and crude or not available. Antibiotics were at least ten years in the future. Sophisticated monitoring and control of water and electrolytes in tissue fluid was not understood and accurate control of blood volume, oxygenation and blood pressure did not exist. Volume and concentration of administered anaesthetic was unmeasured, haphazard and dependant on clinical observation: colour of the lips — red for safety, blue for danger — the size of pupils, pattern of breathing and absence or presence of movement in response to a pinch or the knife's insertion. Nitrous oxide (laughing gas), ether and chloroform were the standard inhalation anaesthetics.

Two notable figures were responsible for converting a crude skill into a sophisticated art that finally elevated the anaesthetist, in the opinion of many, to the most important member of the surgical team. In 1936 Lord Nuffield, the automobile magnate who founded Morris Motors, endowed four chairs at the University of Oxford: medicine, surgery, obstetrics and anaesthesia. The university protested the choice of anaesthesia, but Nuffield's decision (backed up by the size of his munificence) prevailed with the appointment of Robert Macintosh as the first Professor of Anaesthesia in the western world. Then in 1942 in Montreal, Harold Griffith (1894–1985),[1] in the face of stern disapproval from the leading anaesthetists of the day in both the United States and Britain, convinced the medical world of the advantages of curare as a necessary component in general anaesthesia.[2] To the anaesthetist the use of curare allowed a shallower depth of unconsciousness without restless, struggling breathing which swells the exposed brain, increasing the danger of the operation or rendering it impossible to continue. It was a brave man who embarked on a career in 1921 in what came to be known as neurosurgery.

McKenzie's output of articles from the beginning to the end of his active career was appropriate in numbers and topics for a clinician with academic responsibility and obligations. Without exception the articles were clinical, derived from his personal experience. He was not trained in other, allied neurological specialties and, at the time, the drawing into co-authorship of basic scientists to share in the solving of problems facing the neurosurgeon was not as necessary as it is today. Neither he, nor others in a similar position on the active staff, received any financial reward in support of publications. "Grantsmanship" had not taken hold of medical academicians as a necessary skill; indeed, the very word was not coined until well after World War II. Neurosurgery was an exploration centred in the operating theatre, a discovery of its capabilities; its mission was to convince the medical world to take it seriously. When McKenzie studied under Cushing in the early 1920s, Sir Victor Horsley (1857–1916), one of the very first neurosurgeons and the standard-bearer of the new specialty, had been dead only a few years. The medical profession, in its conservative and cautious wisdom, was suspicious of operations on the brain, and in most institutions — including the Toronto General Hospital — physicians, not surgeons, decided when it was appropriate to release a patient to a neurosurgeon and to the danger of a brain operation.

At TGH senior general surgeons were responsible for the treatment of acute head injuries: scalp lacerations, skull fractures and traumatic intracranial haemorrhage. Surgical invasion was seldom carried deeper than the dura mater (the outermost membrane covering the brain and spinal cord and lining the inner surface of the skull) for when it was, the outcome was frequently fatal. About the only exception was evacuation of traumatic chronic subdural haematoma (a localized collection of blood over the surface of the brain), which could be undertaken with a good result.

McKenzie intended some of his publications, particularly among his earlier articles, to inform the profession in Canada of what could be accomplished in the new branch of surgery. He wrote from his own experience, placing before his readers the results of his handling of certain conditions. The diagnosis and treatment of brain tumours (no.3), the surgical treatment of trigeminal neuralgia (no.4), and the diagnosis of spinal cord tumours (no.10) were aimed at a local readership for which Ontario and Canadian journals were the appropriate media. Similarly, the *University of Toronto Medical Journal*, directed at medical students, published "Some Remarks Concerning Neurosurgical Cases" (no.7) and a lecture on the management of head injuries (no.9), a topic for students he considered important above all others and to which he returned ten years later with the student audience in mind (nos.22, 23).

Most of his articles were for the benefit of an informed, neurosurgical audience. He wasted no time getting into print. The first article (no.1) was prepared while he was still in Boston. It described the radiological features of cranio-pharyngeal pouch tumours. In 1924 the article was one of the few examples of detection of intracranial pathology by plain X-rays; in this case it clinched the diagnosis of craniopharyngioma through the appearance of calcification in the region of the pituitary fossa and deformity of the fossa. Cushing's hand in the paper is apparent from the clinical and pathological description of the lesion. It is the sort of straightforward, descriptive paper he would have urged a resident to sharpen his pencil on.

Spasmodic Torticollis (nos. 2, 41)

An article on the surgical treatment of spasmodic torticollis also appeared in 1924. McKenzie's detailed knowledge of neurological anatomy, acquired before he left for Boston, is clear from this and later articles. His interest in the treatment of spasmodic torticollis, begun at the Brigham while he was Cushing's resident, lasted all his life.

Spasmodic torticollis is a dyskinesia, an abnormal, intermittent, involuntary muscle spasm which distorts the neck's natural alignment into grotesque positions as though the patient is determined to touch the shoulder with his ear, the chest with his chin, or to force back his head between the shoulder blades. The condition is resistant to the many medications that have been offered as specifics over the decades.

First page of McKenzie's draft paper on torticollis with editing by Cushing

It can drive the sufferer to take refuge in his home rather than face the puzzled and embarrassed stares of curious passers-by.

The draft of this substantial article is in McKenzie's handwriting with proofing changes in Cushing's hand.[3] The form of McKenzie's title in the draft he submitted to Cushing was, "Intrameningeal root division for the treatment of spasmodic torticollis," to which Cushing inserted, "[division] of the spinal accessory and roots of the upper cervical nerves [for etc.]," and "By Harvey Cushing MD, Boston and K.G. McKenzie MB (Tor)." McKenzie clearly assisted at the operation since he wrote it up and suggested how the operation could be modified to improve the result. Cushing was more than tolerant of his pupil's uninvited contribution. He limited his own intrusion to minor copy edits and a short trenchant explanatory addition. The manuscript was otherwise little changed for the published version.

In the article there is no inquiry as to the underlying cause of the disabling movements. In some quarters psychological influences were held responsible, but even at that time the condition was generally believed to be an "organic" dysfunction of the brain beyond the patient's control. The psychogenic possibility could not be entirely discredited because it was a matter of ordinary observation that the abnormal movements could often be inhibited by the patient's laying a finger softly on the side of the chin. Since the success of this manoeuvre could not be attributed to forcible opposition to the pull of the involved muscles, a psychological explanation won some support. Today it is accepted that, like certain other involuntary movements, the source in the brain of disturbed muscular activity bears no connection to purely psychological or emotional factors. Cushing and McKenzie, as pragmatists, focused their attention on the most effective way of paralyzing the involved muscles rather than hunting in the dark for the cause of the condition. A degree of impairment of voluntary movement of the neck would be a small price for a patient to pay in exchange for a rest from the spasms.

The principle was not new; Cushing, the year before, denervated the affected muscles in a case of torticollis. But McKenzie, after studying the anatomy of the nerve supply of the involved muscles as closely as his mentor, concluded he could do a little better by more effectively arresting muscle spasm without increasing weakness in the neck — a compromise between doing too little and too much. "It is the main purpose of this paper to describe what we believe to be a *hitherto untried operative procedure*, [emphasis added] which has given a large measure of relief to a patient afflicted with spasmodic torticollis."

Having demonstrated human anatomy to medical students in Professor Playfair McMurrich's anatomy department in Toronto, McKenzie knew what he was talking about when it came to muscles, their attachments, action and nerve supply. The article shows his persistence in seeking a mechanical solution to treatment by a precise analysis of the complex abnormal movements and identification of the muscles responsible for them. He devised a simple diagram to demonstrate the resultant force on head movements of the combined action of the sternomastoid and suboccipital muscles. In the operation as reported by McKenzie, but performed by Cushing, the intradural portion of the accessory nerve and the motor and sensory roots of the upper three cervical spinal nerves on the right side were divided. McKenzie's suggestion for *future* cases was to divide only the sensory roots in order to break the reflex arc while retaining a degree of voluntary movement. He speculated the reflex arc of the fourth and fifth cervical segments could thus be interrupted with benefit but without danger to the main motor supply of the diaphragm. The loss of sensation down to and including the skin supplied by the fifth spinal nerve would not be a serious infliction, since it would affect only the side of the neck, the tip of the shoulder and the back of the scalp on the one side.

Cushing may have been a slave driver but he did his best to support his juniors. On this occasion he listened to McKenzie and allowed his assistant's idea to be aired in the article to which they had, at first, both put their names. But Cushing was not entirely at ease with McKenzie's proposal to sacrifice only the dorsal roots. As a postscript by Cushing in the handwritten MS (which he enlarged in the published version), Cushing gently but firmly suggested his junior should pay more attention to the spinal accessory nerve: "Both Dr. Taylor [who had also carried out denervating operations for torticollis] and Dr. McKenzie fail, I think, to take the spinal accessory nerve sufficiently into consideration," an admonition McKenzie later heeded.

The sternomastoid muscle, prominent in the dyskinesia, can be surgically paralyzed by destruction of its branch supply from the spinal accessory nerve with benefit and without disability, other than cosmetic from wasting of the muscle. The trapezius muscle, which is supplied by the accessory nerve and which contributes to the involuntary movements, can also be denervated, but only at the cost of a drooping shoulder. Cushing didn't flatly disagree with McKenzie's suggestion but, to be on the safe side, he withdrew his name as co-author when it came to publication, identifying his contribution only by the postscript. It seems that Cushing assumed the "hitherto untried operative procedure" was his intradural cutting of the spinal accessory nerve and the spinal nerves in both their motor and sensory components, while McKenzie in the "discussion" section was anxious to air *his* suggestion of destroying sensory roots while sparing important motor ones.

As to McKenzie's hope that perhaps section of the dorsal roots was all that might be required, he confessed in 1955 it "proved to be a poor idea as I tried it in 1927, as did Dowman[4] in 1931. Both cases were failures."[5]

The original case records at the Brigham of this patient were reviewed by Rossitch et al. in 1991.[6] The first longhand draft of the paper in TGH archives is clearly McKenzie's own composition and in large measure retains its character in the final published version. Cushing's additions, deletions, syntactical and stylistic changes to McKenzie's MS, together with Rossitch's examination of the patient's case records, reveal the talents and partnership shared by two great neurosurgeons, mentor and acolyte. Most of Cushing's changes in McKenzie's original draft are to the passages that refer directly to the clinical features of the case. The longer "discussion" section in the published article of 1924 is McKenzie's, left largely untouched by Cushing except for a few strictly copy edits.

Spinal Tumour

On his return from Boston to TGH in 1923, McKenzie was appointed resident to C.L. Starr, the Professor of Surgery. His promotion to staff neurosurgeon was delayed until the following year. The established surgical staff was in no hurry to hand over to McKenzie the cases they felt competent to look after themselves. Furthermore, McKenzie's first year back in Toronto gave the hospital and university an opportunity to keep an eye on his performance before irrevocably appointing him to the attending staff.

During the preliminary year of his appointment to the Toronto General Hospital, McKenzie took charge of one of the most important cases of his career. Success in diagnosis and treatment of the patient's condition established his reputation and weighed heavily in favour of a permanent appointment. No other staff member matched McKenzie's refinement in neurological diagnosis and none had his surgical ability or experience when it came to operations on the brain and spinal cord. His extensive notes on this case covered twenty-four pages, including original history and examinations, discussion of diagnostic possibilities, operation notes and a series of neurological diagrams marking the changing signs in minute detail before and after the operation. He saw this as the opportunity to prove himself. The record, mainly in his own hand but partially typewritten, was in detail, continuity and clinical judgment like none other in the records department of the hospital. Here was the hallmark of a Cushing trainee.

The patient (A.K., no. 58804)[7] was a man of thirty who arrived at the outpatient clinic on January 24, 1924 with a history of four weeks' pain in the back and the outside of both thighs. McKenzie, as resident surgeon to Dr. Starr, saw the patient from the time of his admission. He was uncertain whether he was confronted by a tumour or some other condition not treatable by operation. Myelographic imaging had not yet been developed to localize a spinal tumour. He followed the deteriorating neurological picture over the ensuing three weeks until the degree of sensory and motor impairment made exploration desirable to establish the diagnosis and, if possible, to treat the lesion. The delay in operating was, under the conditions of the day, only prudent. But with paraplegia threatening, if operation was the right move it had to be undertaken at once. The only special examination to support the diagnosis of spinal tumour was lumbar puncture: the cerebrospinal fluid was deep yellow and it clotted after withdrawal, strong evidence of a tumour compressing the spinal cord. He had to operate before it was too late, but the exact site of the tumour was a haunting uncertainty.

Careful attention to the patient's account of his symptoms and the abnormal signs uncovered during repeated physical examinations led McKenzie to expose the cord at the right level and then to remove the tumour. He could have had no knowledge beforehand of the type of tumour responsible for compression of the cord, nor whether it originated within the cord or on the surface. Fortunately it was only lightly attached in one place to the cord and it could be removed completely. The symptoms rapidly regressed up to the patient's discharge on April 13, 1924, by which time he was walking and standing "with difficulty" due to "a loss of position sense more than anything else as strength of legs is good."

Microscopic examination of the tumour failed to show any evidence of malignancy and the pathologist's (Dr. W.L. Robinson) first diagnosis was a benign dural endothelioma.

The same patient was readmitted less than two months later with dizziness, severe suboccipital headaches and vomiting. McKenzie's recorded opinion before he operated was of a tumour in the upper cervical region or "involving inferior peduncle to account for dizziness."

There was no papilloedema to indicate raised intracranial pressure. "I asked Dr. McGarry to do a lumbar puncture and drain him dry in the hope that it would relieve his pain as it had done three or four days previously ... There was no relief of pain; if anything it was worse ...

> I then ordered a 1/4 of morphia but as the nurse went to give it to him he stopped breathing. Artificial respirations were kept up for about three quarters of an hour and with very little effort his pulse could be kept good. We then did a ventricular puncture and about 75 cc of clear fluid under great pressure was removed. I then definitely realized that we were dealing with a posterior block and that the respiratory failure was almost certainly due to herniation following the lumbar puncture. The ventricular puncture was of no value in starting respirations. Finally after having continued artificial respirations for about 2 hours, there was no sign of the heart giving out, I decided that the only possible chance that this man had was to take out the posterior arc of the foramen magnum. This was done. Marked herniation could be seen. In succession the 1st, 2nd, 3rd arcs of the cervical vertebrae were removed and only then could the spinal cord be seen. This herniation appeared to be one lobe of the cerebellum only. Despite this decompression there was no evidence of respiration. Pulse by this time was getting somewhat feeble — artificial respirations discontinued, that is the patient lived about 4 1/2 hours with artificial respiration.
>
> Autopsy was obtained and although complete examination has not yet been made, there is evidently a tumor in the upper part of that lobe of the cerebellum which was herniated.
>
> K.G. McK.
>
> 14 June 1924

McKenzie failed to diagnose the cerebellar tumour because the signs of the spinal tumour when he first examined the patient overshadowed its presence. Post-mortem review of the specimens, spinal and cerebellar, proved both to be medulloblastoma, the cerebellar component, as is its tendency, having shed cells into the cerebrospinal fluid, which then took root on the surface of the cord to grow into the spinal tumour McKenzie removed. McKenzie's correct localization of the tumour without radiological confirmation was nothing less than a surgical *tour de force*. He was still under scrutiny in his first year on the house staff at TGH as surgical resident. The reversal of the patient's symptom of absolute inability even to bear weight on his legs to unaided, if unsteady, walking would have been the talk of the hospital. The fact that there

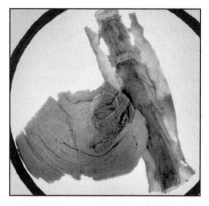

Autopsy specimen of McKenzie's first spinal tumour, 1924 (no. 58804). The site of tumour is in the centre of the length of spinal cord and may represent recurrence. The cerebellar tumour (medulloblastoma) is clearly seen as the darkened area adjacent to the cord. Photo taken through the cover glass. The circle over part of the cerebellar tumour is an air bubble. From the William Boyd Pathology Museum, University of Toronto.

— Courtesy Professor William Halliday

were two tumours of the same type and that the remaining cerebellar tumour was responsible for the patient's death does not detract from McKenzie's achievement in accurate spinal tumour localization based solely on his neurological examination at the bedside. True, his request to his assistant, Dr. McGarry, to perform a lumbar puncture "and drain him dry" makes a neurosurgeon shudder today. But at the time, the presence of the cerebellar tumour was not suspected and the spinal tumour was incorrectly identified as non-malignant. All the same, McKenzie was candid in the recording of his eventual appreciation of the part the puncture played in the patient's death.

This is the only detailed record that has survived of a spinal tumour McKenzie removed before myelography became available. Thirty-five years later, on the occasion of the opening of the new neurosurgical/ neurological unit in the Norman Urquhart wing of the TGH, he referred to the case and his success at the time of the first operation:

> Some of the early cases during this year [1923–24] are still vivid in my memory. Perhaps one of the most fortunate for me was a patient of Dr. C.L. Starr's, with progressive paralysis of the legs. I think I must have put myself in Dr. Starr's good books when a benign spinal cord tumour was localized and successfully removed. These were the days when a localization and diagnosis was made entirely by clinical examination without the aid of X-rays and contrast media.

His recollection many years later that the tumour was benign was no doubt a lapse of memory.

As McKenzie's first year drew to a close, senior surgeons were becoming more inclined to loosen their grip on cases demonstrably neurosurgical. A skillful general surgeon selected by Professor Starr to join the staff of the hospital and university operated on a woman of fifty-nine in 1924 with a suspected spinal tumour (no. 59600). Myelography was still not available and the level of cord exposure at operation depended upon the interpretation of neurological findings. At the apparently appropriate level the surgeon exposed the cord, which showed no sign of a tumour. McKenzie was then asked to see the patient and agreed on the diagnosis of tumour but favoured a lower anatomical level. The patient did not return for the arranged operation by McKenzie so the diagnosis was therefore never established — but at least he had been consulted.

In August 1924, a patient was admitted under McKenzie (no. 59599) with a diagnosis of "Spinal Cord tumour suspect, Cervical 4th or 5th." Apart from the information on the front sheet of the chart, there are no other pages of notes. The front sheet records a partial removal of the bone to expose the spinal canal (cervical laminectomy) on August 22, 1924, and "laminectomy completed" on the 25th of August *after a transfusion*. McKenzie's lost office files could have revealed secrets so tantalizingly withheld in this and other cases like it.

Spinothalamic Tractotomy

A patient (D.J. no. 59597) whose treatment at McKenzie's hands foreshadowed his life-long interest in surgery for intractable pain, was referred to him by Dr. Charles Shuttleworth, senior surgeon and head of one of the three surgical divisions. Shuttleworth had just confirmed McKenzie as a permanent member of his staff. The probationary period was behind him but his reputation as a neurosurgeon was still on the line. McKenzie recorded the case in great detail, adding his thoughts on several problems as they unfolded, and appending his reflections after it was all over.

For ten years, the sixty-year-old man had had unremitting pain in the lower back spreading down the back of the right leg. The commonest cause of sciatica, compression of a lumbar nerve root by a prolapsed intervertebral disc, had not yet been discovered. J.E. Goldthwait in the United States had suggested it and so had G.E. Middleton in Scotland, each in separate publications in 1911. But the syndrome of the prolapsed disc and its successful surgical treatment was not widely accepted until Mixter and Barr published their classic paper in 1934.[8] The patient had been in and out of different hospitals seeking relief from sciatica. He received a number of operations, including laminectomy and injections around the sciatic nerve without relief. At one point during his peripatetic search for help, he consented in desperation to a below-knee amputation. At the time, the maximum site of pain was in the foot, ankle and lower leg. After the amputation, the patient's attention was drawn more to pain in the back of the thigh than to any pain, phantom or other, at the site of the now amputated member.

Eventually he consulted McKenzie. Ahead of his time, K.G.'s resident (whose identity is indecipherable from the signature) made out a good case for the first sacral root as the site of the lesion, but instead of exploring the root, McKenzie decided to expose the sciatic nerve between the gluteus maximus and the biceps femoris and to inject the nerve under direct vision with 2cc 75% alcohol, a treatment not unconventional for sciatica at the time, but now regarded as worthless and even harmful. He wrote:

OPERATION — Sep. 6th 1924.
This patient has caused us a good deal of thought the past week or so. A few days ago I injected 50 cc of 1/2% novocaine in and about the nerve without any relief from the pain. Yesterday I attempted to inject the nerve with alcohol but was unable to satisfy myself that I was in so to-day we cut down and exposed that portion of the nerve. There we found some adhesions upon the sheath of the nerve and the previous operation scar. The nerve was injected with 2cc 75% alcohol. No attempt was made to expose the nerve below the biceps. This will probably give him a motor paralysis and may or may not stop his pain. If the pain is not stopped it would seem that further operative procedure on the sciatic nerve is not worth while.

As McKenzie feared, the procedure was a failure. Nine days later, under local anaesthesia, he carried out an anterior spinothalamic tractotomy, the first at the Toronto General. The purpose of the operation is to incise the nerve pathway in the cord responsible for the transmission of sensory impulses which, on arrival in the brain, are interpreted as pain.

Sep. 15th [1924]
Laminectomy — para-vertebral block — section of pain tract.
After a good deal of hesitation, as none of us could feel sure that the man's pain was not entirely functional [jargon for psychogenic], we

decided to section the pain tract. Section of the posterior root was out
of question and a previous laminectomy had been done in the lumbar
region.* Excellent anaesthesia was obtained in the mid thoracic region
by para-vertebral block and infiltration. One per cent novocain with
3 drops of adrenalin to the ounce was used. Patient's pulse at the
commence of the operation was 140 — his blood pressure was not
over 98. This was disturbing and due, I believe, to too much novocain.
However, we went ahead with the operation and no pain was experienced
by the patient until we manipulated the sensory root. The dentate
ligament was easily seen and severed from its dural connection. This
ligament was then used as a retractor and the cord rotated so that the
antero-lateral column could be seen. Special knife[9] was then inserted
which caused the patient no pain. He was then asked to move his toes
on that side so that we knew that the pyramidal tract was alright.
Antero-lateral column was then cut and deep pin pricks immediately
tried in the stump. These were certainly felt but apparently not painful.
Closure was made with interrupted silk in the dura and continuous
catgut in the muscles. Towards the end of the operation the patient
was commencing to feel some pain but was returned to bed however,
with his pulse somewhat lower and pressure higher than at the
commencement of the operation.

Examination 3 hours later — Patient states that all pain has
disappeared from his leg — says that it is the first time that he has
been free from it for years. However some pinpricks appear to produce
pain and it is certainly going to take a few days to interpret the outcome
of this operation. I feel that possibly I did not cut deep enough.

Dr. K.G. McKenzie.

On the day of the patient's discharge, McKenzie recorded in the chart:

October 4th, 1924

As will be seen from the study of sensation charts on this pt. only part
of the pain tract was severed in this case. On discharge pt. tells me that
there is some return of the old pain in his leg but not nearly so severe
and nothing that he cannot put up with. If this continues we may
feel that the operation has been worth while, and also that if the
pain tract had been completely cut probably there would have been
no recurrence at all of the old trouble; that is, we would interpret it,
as real pain and not a functional pain and also in spite of 15 yr's

---

*No operation record discovered, nor the identity of the surgeon.

duration, it is not represented in the optic thalamus, as has been suggested in some of these cases where the pain has persisted for a number of years and section of posterior root and various other operative measures have not given relief.

Dr. K.G. McKenzie.

McKenzie's reflections in this last entry showed he was well aware of the type of pain that had no discoverable physical or structural cause, and of the pitfall of operating on a patient whose symptoms are psychogenic. But the immediate relief to the patient makes it probable that the pain was due to nerve root compression, as from a prolapsed disc, a condition not recognized or understood at the time except, possibly, by his anonymous resident! Unfortunately, later follow-up notes are not included in the chart; equally unfortunate is McKenzie's admitted failure to have made the cut in the spino-thalamic tract deeper — an excess of caution neurosurgeons the world over have experienced from time to time with this operation. But the case stands as a landmark in his early career as neurosurgeon while he was under the watchful eyes of some still skeptical colleagues.

Trigeminal Neuralgia (*Tic Douloureux*)

McKenzie's first article (no.3) from Toronto was on trigeminal neuralgia. Its purpose was to inform Canadian practitioners what neurosurgery had to offer for the relief of the most painful affliction known to humans. John Fothergill's (1712–1780) description of the condition has not been bettered:[10]

> The pain comes suddenly, and is excruciating: it lasts but a short
> time, perhaps a quarter or half a minute, and then goes off; it returns
> at irregular intervals, sometimes in half an hour, sometimes there are
> two or three repetitions in a few minutes … Eating will bring it on
> some persons. Talking, or the least motion of the muscles of the face,
> affect others; the gentlest touch of a hand or handkerchief will sometimes
> bring on the pain, whilst a strong pressure on the part has no effect …
> The disease which is the subject of this essay is seldom observed till
> between forty and fifty and through the later stages of life … The
> affection I am treating is most commonly severer in the day than
> in the night … [Concerning one patient] in a moment she would be
> seized with the most excruciating pain, affecting the inner canthus of
> the eye: it lasted but a few seconds, forced out the tears, and gradually

went off. In a few minutes the same thing happened, and in like manner at unequal distances during the day, so as to occasion a life of great misery ...

The remedies administered in the past are too numerous to dwell on. Remedies touted and published in medical journals in modern times for the relief of trigeminal neuralgia have included: cutaneous faradic stimulation, X-ray therapy, aconitine ionization, tonsillectomy, short-wave therapy, ergotamine, calcium, procaine with caffeine injections to the pain areas, antisyphilitic therapy (bismuth and acetarsone), fever therapy and other well-intentioned therapies. Within recent memory equally outlandish remedies have been recommended: vitamin B_1, B complex, huge and expensive doses of vitamin B_{12}, injections (not in the face) of colloidal copper, manipulation of the cervical spine, and acupuncture. The administration of neurotoxins (trichlorethylene, stilbamidine) was more rational but ill-advised; impaired conduction in the (sensory) trigeminal nerve from the toxic effect of the medicaments often arrested the painful attacks but as often left in its wake severe, unrelenting tingling and distorted sensation; worse, the sensory impairment did not stop with the affected trigeminal nerve but involved the nerve supplying the other side of the face, not to mention other nerves in the body.

Modern treatment, medical or surgical, or a combination of each, can at last be effective. Before the arrival of carbamazepine (Tegretol), partial or complete interruption of trigeminal pathways, peripheral or central, was the only sure method of relief. In McKenzie's time Tegretol had not reached the marketplace and no other drug touched even its uncertain specificity. For some forty years, from the time Cushing and Frazier had perfected the difficult operation on the trigeminal ganglion or its sensory root, to the Tegretol era and to P.J. Janetta's operation[11], McKenzie concentrated on improving the results of Charles H. Frazier. Although the Frazier operation removed the agonizing shocks of pain, one of its disadvantages was to leave part or all of the face and tongue, teeth and cornea completely numb on the side of operation. Most patients were happy at the exchange, others failed to look after the numb skin and cornea which normal sensation had protected. Painless corneal damage and scarring, skin ulceration around the nostril and lips from scratching and picking were serious complications. Surgically-induced anaesthesia abolished the tic pain but it sometimes gave place to insufferable itching or a different pain, constant, tolerable at first but after a while unbearable, for which there was no remedy other than excessive medication. Most patients set their minds to putting up with it, like amputees with phantom limb pain, but they had to round that corner of their own will.

Before McKenzie could turn his attention to improvements in the Frazier operation, he had to learn how to do it. He never performed the operation while he was with Cushing, nor was he able to see exactly how his teacher carried it out. The approach to the trigeminal nerve is down a deep hole surgically created as the brain is retracted upwards from the floor of the skull. Cushing was too preoccupied with the essential steps to shift his head or his hand to allow his assistant to see exactly what he was doing. A visit by McKenzie to Alfred W. Adson[12] at the Mayo Clinic, on his return to Toronto

> proved most helpful. He had been through the fire and took me under his wing. For the first time I could see what was being done and felt that his particular technique could be duplicated. The underlying principle, of course, was the sitting-up position with the patient positioned so that blood ran out of the field and did not continuously obstruct the surgeon's vision. With a kitchen chair and attached dental head rest I became reasonably adept with this procedure. (see Appendix G)

In 1950, when Charles Drake went to Stockholm at McKenzie's behest, he watched Herbert Olivecrona's assistant, Peter Taarnhøj, operate on a patient with tic douloureux, using Olivecrona's technique to spare the facial nerve while removing an acoustic neuroma. McKenzie didn't think it was possible to do so without leaving some tumour behind. Olivecrona's technique, Taarnhøj assured Drake, was not always successful. Drake recalled in 1987[13]:

> Olivecrona had said to Taarnhøj, tic douloureux in a young person [must mean there] is a tumour in the angle and you must go and look for it. When I was there Taarnhøj had picked off a tiny little pearly tumour and the Professor had said that if you take the tumour out you must cut the nerve at the same time otherwise the pain won't be cured. Taarnhøj did not [cut it], in the absence of the Professor, and the tic was gone. The Professor wouldn't believe him, but then when I was there he did another one. And the man woke up without pain. And that interested me. I think that's where [Hunter] Sheldon got the idea [to relieve tic pain by enlarging the foramen ovale to decompress the third division]. Because then Taarnhøj went on to cut the superior

petrosal sinus above the root at the entrance to the [Meckel's] cave [to relieve supposed pressure on the nerve].

The cause of trigeminal neuralgia still engaged the interest of most neurosurgeons. Even moderately effective medicinal treatment had not yet been discovered, and the proposal of Gardner and, particularly, Jannetta that the cause of the neuralgia was usually distortion or compression of the trigeminal root by a blood vessel was still in the future. (see also p. 107 et seq.)

Trigeminal tractotomy (no. 41)

Surgical treatment for trigeminal neuralgia had for the first time given relief from its agonies. Removal of the Gasserian (trigeminal) ganglion was reported by Victor Horsley (1857–1916) in 1891[14] but acceptable safety of intracranial operations on the fifth nerve had to await the Cushing era before the Frazier operation on the sensory root became a standard procedure.[15] It was, and is, a major operation with risk of complications, but the great drawback was a total loss of sensation in the denervated area of the face. To overcome this disadvantage, O. Sjöqvist[16] preserved the sensation of touch in the affected areas of the face yet eliminated the sense of pain. The operation was based on a well-known anatomical fact (as in the case of D.J.; see p. 74) that sensory nerve impulses from periphery to brain are conducted along several separate tracts in the spinal cord. Pain gives rise to impulses carried mainly in the anterior spino-thalamic tract. By an incision of a few millimetres in the cord across the tract, the sensation of pain and temperature below and on the opposite side of the body is abolished. Touch, pressure and the sense of position, so important in the normal function of arms and legs, is preserved. But an incision in the upper reaches of the spinal cord, the medulla oblongata, necessary if pain in parts as high as the face is to be relieved, needed careful planning to avoid damage to motor and other vital functions dependant on the medulla.

After Sjöqvist's article appeared in 1938 the operation was taken up over the next decade in a number of centres. It seemed to be the perfect answer: abolition of pain without total loss of sensation. A number of surgeons, including McKenzie, reported their experience with the operation. His first case was in 1949; by the time he published his series in 1955 he had operated on 42 patients, of which two had had severe bilateral trigeminal neuralgia and two suffered from painful cancer of the mouth. McKenzie knew that he should not perform the Frazier operation on both sides; the disability from total bilateral facial and mouth numbness was not to be borne. The trigeminal tractotomy operation of Sjöqvist seemed to be the best solution.

McKenzie followed his patients from two to five years after operation. It was a procedure well suited to his interest in neuroanatomy, to his patience and his dexterity. He examined all patients himself regularly after the operation. Patients in whom the pathway for pain in the medulla was not completely interrupted by the operation, as proved by pin-prick testing on the skin of what had been the painful area, were free from pain for at least six months —

> but now (2 to 5 years after operation) practically all have complained of recurring pain and 5 have submitted to a partial section of the sensory root. Before we are finished with this group I suspect that further operation will be necessary on most of them.

All patients who were fortunate to have remained free from recurrent neuralgia were assumed to have received complete interruption of the "pain pathway."

The article demonstrated McKenzie's meticulous attention to detail in preparation, execution and assessment of an operation. It is one of his finest publications. He presented the paper as part of the Fourth Max Peet Lecture delivered at the University of Michigan, Ann Arbor, in 1952 and again in 1954 before the Congress of Neurological Surgeons in New York when he brought the results up to date. He published this latter version.

The operation of trigeminal tractotomy is seldom if ever performed for trigeminal neuralgia today. It has been superseded by better drug control (carbamazepine, the generic name for Tegretol), and by Jannetta's operation which, when successful (it usually is), cures the tic and saves all modalities of facial sensation. The first steps taken towards the perfection of the operation by Jannetta were in the 1960s. He held that the cause of trigeminal neuralgia could be explained by contact between the nerve root and an otherwise normally situated artery or vein. Physical separation of blood vessel from nerve was the key to a successful operation, an assertion at first received with skepticism, but which eventually won wide approval. Its great merit was the high incidence of pain relief with no loss of sensation. McKenzie had retired before Jannetta's publications appeared. There is still a place for safe minor operations that destroy peripheral branches of the nerve in the face where the pain is located and where the small resultant area of anaesthesia is easily tolerated.

Mesencephalic tractotomy for pain (No. 40)

In 1942 A. Earl Walker recommended a yet higher incision of the spino-thalamic tract, this time in the mid-brain, for the relief of unremitting pain on one side of the body.[17] Attracted by the prospect of an operation in the mid brain remote from the danger zone of the medulla, Drake[18] and McKenzie operated on six patients with intractable pain from a variety of conditions other than trigeminal neuralgia — cancer, phantom arm pain following traumatic disarticulation, and hypersensitivity after intercostal neurectomy. (Destruction of the sensory component of an intercostal nerve by virus [shingles] or surgical necessity in chest opera-tions, may lead to a pain in the area of the nerve's distribution which is unrelieved by medication.) The operation was well conceived to cover, more certainly than medullary tractotomy, pain in the upper trunk, arms, head and neck. At first, as with the medullary (trigeminal) tractotomy, relief from pain was absolute, but after some months an intolerable distortion of sensation crept into the otherwise pain-free area:

> This postoperative dysesthesia has profoundly influenced our thoughts about the operation; so much so that we are unlikely to carry out the procedure again.

Why an incision at these upper levels should be followed after several months by the old pain, as in trigeminal neuralgia, or new ones (unbear-able distortions of sensation following a mere touch on the skin, for example) is unknown, although there is no lack of hypotheses. Neither Cushing nor McKenzie nor Charles Drake were themselves equipped to investigate these and other conundrums by the methods of neuro-physiological research. Their studies had to come hand-in-hand with the practice of neurological surgery; there was no time in their clinical lives to add the acquisition and interpretation of sophisticated research techniques in fundamental neurophysiology.

Pain — Surgeon and Patient (no. 39)

The Royal College of Physicians and Surgeons of Canada invited McKenzie to give the annual Lecture in Surgery at the 1952 meeting of the College at the Royal York Hotel in Toronto. He took the opportunity to put together his thoughts on pain, the part a neurosurgeon might play in its relief and when surgical interference should be avoided.

Most neurosurgeons at one time or another have fallen for the desperate pleadings of a patient in pain by interrupting, at one of several sites along its way, the pathway from the painful area to the brain, only to be rewarded by bitter recrimination from the sufferer whose pain is unchanged or worsened. McKenzie had his share in his early career of resorting to surgery when what the patient really needed was the ministration of a neurologist, psychiatrist or a compassionate partner. At the meeting, he lectured as an interpreter exchanging the sometimes obscure language of psychiatry for the clarity of common usage:

> "Pain causes more patients to seek medical help than any other symptoms." So said Dr. Van Wart of Fredericton while we were fishing on the Nipisiquit in New Brunswick. At the time I was only psychologically pained, having just lost the one and only salmon rising to the fly after several days' fishing. Although losing a salmon may not bear directly on the problem at hand, the experience encouraged me to think of an aspect of pain that has not been given sufficient attention by surgeons. I refer to the patient complaining of pain which cannot adequately be explained by any stimulus of the central or peripheral nervous system and in whom there is quite possibly a minor or major emotional factor.

McKenzie had no formal training in psychiatry but his close association with Aldwyn Stokes over the lobotomy programme and with Allan Walters in the TGH was a fair substitute for a neurosurgeon called on to handle patients in pain (see p. 119 et seq.).

Neurologist and psychiatrist, James Allan Walters (1906–1986),[19] mercurial, nimble in body and mind, made the study of bodily pain his specialty. He wrote "Psychogenic regional pain alias hysterical pain" (*Brain*, 84 [1961]: 1–18,), which firmly established his reputation abroad, particularly in Great Britain. During his time in the army in World War II, he was appointed neuropsychiatrist to No. 1 Canadian Neurological and Psychiatric Hospital in Basingstoke, England, and in 1944 he was posted to northwest continental Europe after the Normandy landings. He later expanded his knowledge and beliefs in "Psychiatric Considerations of Pain" in the first edition (1973) of J. Youmans's encyclopaedic *Neurological Surgery* (Philadelphia: W.B. Saunders Co. Vol. 3. chap. 86: 1615–1645).

To the neurosurgeon and neurologist his advice, when sought and taken, was precious. He coined the diagnostic term "psychogenic regional pain" for pain perceived after industrial or other civilian accidents, domestic strife or overwhelming misfortune when there was no accounting for it on physical grounds alone. He was of the breed of psychiatrist, now almost extinct, firmly grounded in organic neurology. McKenzie and his colleagues trusted his judgment even when they lost his drift as he broke into a rapid-fire psychiatric exposition of a case, in language they could only intermittently understand. At the termination of a consultation, he darted out of the room as quickly as he came in and, poking his head round the closing door, he whispered, "You gotter love 'em!" and was gone.

For the benefit of his general surgical audience, on this occasion McKenzie dealt at some length with psychogenic regional pain, acknowledging his debt to Allan Walters, who helped him to understand the phenomenon. He admitted he hadn't known much about the condition when he was young, but he demonstrated in the lecture he knew a great deal about it now that his experience was behind him.

> Man, [he writes] is constantly wavering between ease and comfort on the one hand and uneasiness and discomfort on the other. All this is normal and a certain degree of uneasiness and discomfort provides many necessary drives in life.

Not, perhaps, stated in the psychiatric vernacular, but the meaning, as in the rest of the article, is crystal clear.

> I now wish [he writes in 1952] that, in my younger years ... I had appreciated what I now know to be true; namely, many patients must be made to understand that the cause of their pain cannot be cured by surgery or drugs ... For long I had little or no appreciation that a state of mind could so lower the threshold for discomfort and bring about a situation where the patient interpreted discomfort as severe pain.

Such frankness from an Olympian is solace for any practitioner who has dragged himself through the same mill of misunderstanding and failure.

Turning to pain of "organic" or physical origin, McKenzie chose as an example trigeminal tractotomy, that is to say treatment by incision of the descending tract in the medulla of the fifth (trigeminal) nerve in cases of carcinoma of the face, mouth, throat and ear, where the cancer can cause great pain (see p. 80 et seq.). He confirmed the benefit (no. 41) two years later after bringing the follow-up information up-to-date. He was emphatic the operation relieved cancer pain in this area where otherwise its intensity went unrelieved. Freedom from the pain could be expected for the rest of the patient's life, shortened by the cancer that caused it. By contrast, relief from tractotomy for trigeminal neuralgia failed to outlast the patient's normal life expectancy.

> Such a procedure [for relief from the pain of cancer] interrupts pain fibres from the face and often as well from the nasopharynx. Light touch is not interfered with, so eye complications and complete numbness are not added to the misery of these patients. The operative exposure also makes it possible to section the upper cervical nerves and the ninth and upper filaments of the vagus. Bilateral section of the descending tract may be done at one operation. The whole procedure is relatively safe, free from shock and complications and takes about one hour.

The exhortation was no idle boast (McKenzie was not given to boasting in any guise). It took him little time to work through muscle and bone and to incise the tract at the junction of medulla and cord and to divide the appropriate nerves. All the same, confidence, experience and deftness were the necessary ingredients for a one-hour operation.

Scoliosis with Paraplegia (nos. 5, 34)

Within the vertebral canal the spinal cord lies ensheathed in the dura mater, a tube with no elasticity in its wall. Congenital abnormality of the thoracic segment of the spinal column leads to the deformity of scoliosis. When the angulation of the deformity is severe, the spinal cord becomes stretched over the protruding gibbus of the hunched back and its function can be impaired even to the point of paraplegia. Congenital (or juvenile) scoliosis by itself is not uncommon, but spinal cord impairment is an unusual complication.

In 1949 McKenzie and F.P. (Ted) Dewar[20] reported their experience with five patients and reviewed another thirty-six from the literature. They made a strong case for early laminectomy and wide opening of the dura as soon as signs of spinal cord impairment developed.

McKenzie published his first case of the condition (no. 5) in 1927. It was titled "Paraplegia associated with congenital scoliosis. Report of a case." The subtitle ran, "With comments by Professor Clarence L. Starr." McKenzie's part in the article was to record in detail the history, neurological examination, the operation and the patient's steady neurological improvement over the succeeding months. He stated what he believed was the explanation for the cord compression which in turn dictated what the crucial step in the operation should be. Starr was impressed with McKenzie's handling of the matter, his neurological competence and the correctness of the operation. His "comment" was a valuable review of the literature on congenital scoliosis complicated by paraplegia, of which, he says, this was the first case he had seen. Starr could, with justice, have listed himself as co-author, but by labelling his contribution as a mere comment he promoted his young colleague and by his authority made it clear the article was important.

From the purely mechanistic point of view, it would be desirable to remove the apex of the bone deformity over which the cord was stretched; the cord would then lie comfortably in the natural configuration of the vertebral canal without compression or tension. An operation of such magnitude was held at the time to be unjustified, but since the 1960s the specialty of orthopaedics has shown it is the procedure of choice.

The crucial step in the operation, first demonstrated by McKenzie in 1927, was to expose the cord simply by opening the dural tube widely throughout the length of the deformity. The opening of dura over the convexity of the angulation relieved pressure on the cord. He showed that the dural tube, being inelastic and unyielding, narrowed as it lay over the apex of the deformity like a kinked garden hose. By a generous opening of the exposed dura throughout the length of the convexity, the cord, formerly compressed from behind by the kinked dural tube, was relieved even while the bone deformity remained.

McKenzie and Dewar, in their later publication, upheld McKenzie's original theory that dural compression rather than bone deformity was the ultimate cause of cord impairment. "The paucity of case reports of scoliosis with paraplegia, and the fact that surgeons who see many patients with severe scoliosis have never seen one with paraplegia, indicates the rarity of the syndrome. It seems that there must be some factor other than the [bone] deformity itself that accounts for paralysis."

The results of their operations vindicated McKenzie. In 1927 the first patient, a young man of eighteen, was almost completely paraplegic before operation. When McKenzie examined him twenty-two years later he could not demonstrate any neurological abnormality. A girl of twelve with "profound paraplegia with sensory loss coming on over a period of three months [was] discharged, walking two months after operation. Five months later able to run ... Sensation practically normal." Two other males of sixteen and seventeen, one "barely able to walk" and the other with an "unsteady, spastic gait," recovered the ability to walk "well," or for "several miles" with minimal abnormality when examined. Only one patient, a man of twenty-nine, failed to improve. Seven years after the operation, a cystic cavity (syringomyelia) was discovered in the cord. McKenzie gave his reasons for his belief that this case was of a different pathological nature from the others and that he should not have treated the patient in the same way.

A Silver Clip Outfit (no. 6)

McKenzie had long been interested in the mechanics of surgery and was always looking for ways to improve both surgical techniques and the instruments associated with them. Of the several innovations Cushing introduced to the instrumentation of central nervous system surgery, none was more important than the wire clip.[21] It is a small piece of silver wire doubled on itself over a blood vessel to close it off to stop the bleeding. Malleable, fine silver wire was cut into lengths of approximately 8mm and bent into a V. The V-shaped piece was placed astride the bleeding vessel so that when the legs of the V were pinched together the vessel was obliterated.

As Cushing's assistant at operations, McKenzie had great difficulty cutting, preparing and handing the little clips to Cushing without fumbling, so he set about designing an improved version. Being round in cross-section, the arms of the original clip slipped over one another as the clip was closed on the vessel, with the result it failed to shut off the bleeding vessel completely, or the crossed legs of the clip tore it like blunt scissors. The length of each clip varied since the length of wire cut by an assistant to form a clip was not always the same; it required two hands to load each clip into the clip holder before it was handed to the surgeon; and the grooves for the clip stopped short of the tip of the jaws of the holder. In the 1927 paper deferentially entitled "Some minor modifications of Harvey Cushing's silver clip outfit," McKenzie converted a device that was almost unusable into an "outfit" that became widely adopted.

McKenzie dealt with these technical difficulties in the first place by using wire that was square instead of round in cross-section, to prevent the arms overlapping as the clip closed. The grooves were extended to the tip of the jaws for greater precision in clip application. A spring held the jaws of the holder apart at the correct distance once the clip was loaded. A special tool cut the wire to the right length and at the same time bent it to the proper angle. A magazine stored a large number of clips ready for loading into the holder. The magazine sat on a heavy metal base to prevent its sliding on the instrument tray during clip-loading, which could then be done with one hand. The assisting nurse loaded the holder simply by pressing the tips of the jaws on to a clip in the magazine. Finally, the magazine was given a sliding cover to keep the rack of clips in place until required.

The J.F. Hartz Co. on Grenville Street was only minutes from the hospital. Eugen Scheerle, whose fingers had the precision of a watchmaker's, was employed by the company for a long time as surgical instrument maker. He caught on at once to whatever McKenzie was after. If something wasn't exactly right, Eugen gladly corrected it. The two men worked in happy harmony over the design of new instruments and refinements to existing items in the catalogue. Eugen was never more content than when putting K.G.'s ideas to the test. After K.G.'s retirement he continued working for a few years with the hospital's neurosurgical staff,

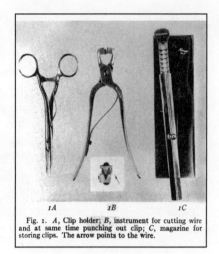

1A   1B   1C

Fig. 1. *A*, Clip holder; *B*, instrument for cutting wire and at same time punching out clip; *C*, magazine for storing clips. The arrow points to the wire.

Haemostatic clip equipment

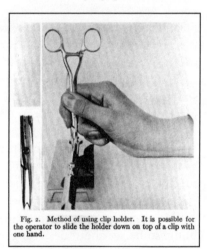

Fig. 2. Method of using clip holder. It is possible for the operator to slide the holder down on top of a clip with one hand.

Loading the clip holder
— COURTESY JOURNAL OF NEUROSURGERY

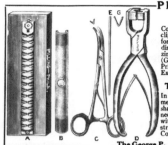

A contemporary advertisement for the McKenzie Brain Clip Suture Set

but he was approaching his own retirement and had become something of a financial liability to the company. He began to lose interest in other assignments expected of him by the company, not all of which required his creative skill. The day of the craftsman with Eugen's particular skills was ending, to be replaced by new materials and manufacturing techniques.

The "Silver Clip Outfit" spread the young McKenzie's name throughout the neurosurgical world. All neurosurgeons and some in other specialties adopted it. Surgeons will continue to use it so long as open operations are undertaken. If McKenzie had been asked, as Cushing was, what *his* greatest contribution had been to neurosurgery, he could well have answered, "My Silver Clip Outfit." He may have been surprised — and perhaps a little disappointed — to discover, seventy years later, that his name is on the lips of neurosurgeons only because of his hardware. But he need have had no regrets. Almost all written clinical articles are obsolescent before the ink is dry; this one, of less than 600 words, is of an instrument that outlived him.

Brain Abscess (nos. 8, 31, 35)

The first publication in modern times on cerebral abscess can be found in Sir William Macewen's monograph from Glasgow that appeared in 1893.[22] Macewen astonished the medical world at the 1884 International Medical Congress in Copenhagen by reporting his series of 1,800 femoral osteotomies* without a single case of postoperative infection. His success followed the application of asepsic operating techniques his mentor

---

*Operation for realignment of femur in hip joint deformity.

Lister showed to be essential to avoiding wound infection.[23] He followed this up with a hardly less remarkable triumph with brain abscess: nineteen operations with eighteen recoveries. Even allowing for a confusing statistical analysis of his results (of eleven cerebral abscesses, ten were "cured" but three died, cause not stated), his operative success rate was not equalled by the time the 1960s arrived.[24] Geoffrey Jefferson,[25] and others inclined to incredulity, argued that to achieve such remarkably good results Macewen must have refused to operate on patients he saw little hope of recovering, which left the "good" cases for surgical treatment and survival. G.K. Tutton, who could not gain access to Macewen's case records[26] when he was preparing his Hunterian Lecture on "the present position,"[27] was of the same opinion.

For many later surgeons, including McKenzie, simple aspiration [removal with suction] was the chosen operation, repeated as required; but of the four surgical methods in common use, tube drainage, marsupialization, aspiration and excision—excision had the lowest mortality rate (18%) up to the time of S. Stephanov's review of the medical literature on the subject in 1988.[24]

McKenzie brings his experience up to date in his 1950 article (no. 35) based on 105 consecutive cases he treated by operation and forty-seven consecutive necropsy cases who died without benefit of surgery. "In truth," he wrote, "there are several ways of dealing with a brain abscess. The radical treatment [excision] carried out by Le Beau[28] is definitely the method of choice in certain cases, but it will not likely be adopted as a routine measure." McKenzie, before the "penicillin era," operated on 105 patients for brain abscess with a mortality of 53%. The mortality rate is now much lower, but no better than Macewen's *published* rate which can be disregarded for statistical comparison with subsequent reports. Cerebral abscess remains, as McKenzie felt, "a grievous experience" for a neurosurgeon. Today, with improved antibiotics and better control of cerebral oedema and swelling, the mortality rate should be in single figures.

By 1929, when McKenzie published his first article (no. 8) on brain abscess, he had gained in self-confidence and spoke with an authority on neurosurgical practice none of his Toronto colleagues in "general" surgery could match. Deference to his seniors was no longer necessary nor expected. In this article of twenty-seven pages he discussed his failures, their cause and correction at greater length than his successes. "The preparation of a paper based on this material has not been easy.

There are so many controversial points ... Increasing experience with cases finally classified as 'brain tumour suspect' [i.e. unproven] has made one conservative in advising surgical intervention." He was advising (in 1929) caution until a diagnosis of abscess was almost certain. Operation before the abscess developed a firm capsule could result in death from spread of the infection. This was a principle well understood by surgeons as applying to local infection and abscess anywhere in the body.

He describes an experience with one of his patients. A boy developed suppuration in the frontal sinus complicated by a frontal lobe brain abscess. For a year before his first admission to hospital, the patient's mother said her son had been having trouble in schoolwork, especially with algebra.

McKenzie first drained the abscess externally through a burr hole in the skull but the abscess persisted. A more extensive exposure provided by a bone flap was required to locate and remove the abscess. "Then commenced a harrowing experience." He couldn't find the abscess by probing the frontal lobe with a brain cannula. "Considerable trauma to the frontal lobe resulted." Under increasing pressure from swelling during the operation, the brain herniated through the opening in the skull. Over the next ten days on several occasions the ever-recurring brain hernia was removed by the cutting cautery until the abscess itself presented in the extruded brain and was removed. Recovery was then rapid, and McKenzie could report, "Despite the loss of a considerable amount of the right frontal lobe from herniation, the patient has a pleasing disposition and stood fourth in his class at school this past year, making nearly 90 per cent in algebra." Later, when the risk of further wound infection had passed, the opening in the skull was repaired "with a piece of celluloid soap box."

A similar experience today of acute, severe brain swelling during an operation, though very unusual, is harrowing enough. In 1929, without the help of modern anaesthesia (or the extra security of antibiotics), it needed a cool head indeed to rescue the brain from prolapse during operation and to bring the patient through to safety. McKenzie's decision to allow the abscess to extrude itself under increased intracranial pressure was a necessity rather than a plan. Perhaps his old friend Edgar Kahn listened to Ken's alarming account with its happy ending, for he published his experience with four patients (one died) in whom he adopted intentionally the "migration" method for which Ken unwittingly showed the way.[29]

On the timing of operation, McKenzie gives advice as commendable today as when he wrote a comprehensive article (1948) on brain abscess in British Surgical Practice (no. 31). Wait, he said, until

> the history suggests intracranial trouble for a matter of weeks, that is at a time when good capsule formation may be expected. The surgeon's hand may be forced in the presence of a short history by serious stupor or coma ... I am willing to postpone operation until some time in the future if the patient will respond actively in conversation.

Advice especially pertinent in these days of previously undreamed of imaging techniques, which by displaying the earliest stages of abscess formation, may trap the unwary into premature operation.

Head Injury

McKenzie saw head injury as the most important neurosurgical topic to teach students and practitioners. The frequency and severity of skull and brain injury was on the rise, and while the most severe cases were beyond saving, the less severe were all too often unnecessarily lost. The signs of gathering pressure in the head from a clot were not fully appreciated or, if they were, surgeons and general practitioners, like their professional forebears, were afraid to enter the cranium.

In an early article (1929) for medical students (no. 9) it was McKenzie's conviction that since the drilling of a hole in the skull to let out surface blood from compressing the brain was one of the simplest and safest of emergency surgical procedures, every practitioner should be competent in its performance. Furthermore, of all the possible neurological signs pointing to danger, the earliest and the easiest to recognize was deterioration of consciousness or a deepening level of coma. For that reason he pleaded for the opportunity for all surgeons-in-training in the country to be required to spend a short time on a neurosurgical service to become adept at the procedure. His advice has only partly been taken.

Cushing advised a wide skull opening for the removal of surface blood, liquid or clotted. McKenzie resorted to the more extensive exposure only when one or more burr holes were found to be inadequate. He made the drilling of a hole in the skull easier than it had been. Until 1944 neurosurgeons used a drill bit from the nineteenth century, the Hudson perforator. Like many a surgeon with a flair for mechanical devices, McKenzie adapted carpenters' and metal workers' tools for neurosurgical use (no.29). Electric motors and compressed air turbines had not yet replaced the manual brace and bit of the neurosurgeon. The disadvantage of the manual brace and bit was the constant danger of the bit's plunging into the brain under the pressure of the operator as it penetrated the inner table of the skull. Serious brain damage and even death could be the consequence. McKenzie had a perforator bit so designed that as soon as the sharp, pointed tip had penetrated the inner table of the skull it became jammed and further rotation of the brace was impossible. To complete the hole in the skull, the perforation of the skull was exploited by a burr to enlarge the hole to a 1–2 cm diameter. The burr was a spherical bit that was effective only after the preliminary perforation. Its disadvantage, which McKenzie did not correct, was that once the diameter of the burr passed through the inner table, there was nothing to stop its plunge. Judicious use was required to anticipate such a disaster. Subsequently, cone-shaped burrs were manufactured which, in their turn, jam like a wedge in the hole to prevent a plunge.

McKenzie pursued the theme of the advantage of a small rather than a large skull opening to drain fluid in a 1932 study of nine cases of chronic subdural haematoma (no.12).

> In the light of our experience with 9 cases I am convinced that the wrong surgical procedure was used when we operated upon our earlier cases by using a large osteoplastic exposure in preference to a small bone opening.

He marshalled his argument from the example of the nine cases he reported. All were "chronic" haematomas and therefore liquid, encysted collections of fluid. "If in the future I meet with a case in which the clot is so well organized that it cannot be removed by a sucker through a small opening, a bone flap will be turned down." He was not concerned, as some were and still are, to remove the fibrin membrane enclosing the fluid collection. He did not believe its presence delayed expansion of the brain after removal of the fluid; any delay in expansion was due to the surgeon's failure to leave a drainage tube in the cavity for a day. Today the topic stirs little debate now that common practice follows McKenzie's advice and neurosurgical enthusiasm has turned to new possibilities undreamed of in the thirties. Besides, a postoperative brain scan is always available when the thoroughness of the evacuation is in doubt.

As time passed, McKenzie became increasingly aware of the importance of psychological and emotional influences in recovery from head injury. Much of his attention was taken up by looking into irregularities of anatomy and neurophysiology to explain disturbed function of the nervous system. Given the correct diagnosis, such conditions could be treated successfully without much concern for the intangibles of emotional reaction. Surgical relief from intolerable symptoms was its own successful therapy. In his article (no.28) in 1943, "One Aspect of the Posttraumatic Syndrome in Craniocerebral Injuries," he tried to straddle the physiological and the psychological divide.

> Briefly the hypothesis is this: An injured and therefore unstable vasomotor system, incapable of quickly supplying blood to the brain, is the cause of the symptoms of dizziness, light headedness, blackouts, headaches, and mental and physical fatigue in at least some patients. If this be true one should take steps to restore the function of the vasomotor centres as soon as possible and so prevent a train of symptoms, which have an organic basis, but may, as the weeks go by, become clouded by a functional superstructure. This idea developed and became useful to us some 6 years ago after observing

a young man who had been knocked out for half an hour some six months before he came to McKenzie's attention. Up to that time the hallowed treatment for loss of consciousness after head injury was bed rest, a shaded or darkened room and greatly reduced aural, visual and intellectual stimulation. Unsure, perhaps, of his physiological ground, McKenzie did not go into any details of the "organic basis" of vasomotor disturbance but accepted the hypothesis as he moved to discuss its correction. The patient was kept flat in bed at home for eight or ten weeks by which time he fainted every time he got up, an alarming symptom which brought him to McKenzie. The symptomatology would today indicate that prolonged bed rest is apt to cause transient fainting on rising. But

> our interpretation of this case was somewhat as follows: The man's vasomotor centres had been injured along with the rest of the brain and he had been kept flat on his back for some 10 weeks and during this period his injured vasomotor system had adjusted itself to supply blood to the brain in adequate amounts only in the horizontal position — the patient found himself comfortable when lying flat and so spent

almost all his time in that position, in this manner never stimulating the vasomotor system to function adequately in the upright position.

In the rest of the short article, the mystique of injury to the vasomotor centre is not entirely rejected, as it would be today, but he dismisses the contemporary rule of treatment by prolonged and absolute bed rest as unnecessary, as in a patient who appeared to have a definite interest in financial compensation for his injury. "It is quite definite that the Compensation Board of Ontario is not now having nearly the number of post-traumatic syndromes as they had in hard times; this of course we always suspected but it has been clearly demonstrated during this unusually remunerative period[30] for the manual worker." At the end of the article he begins to remove himself from dependence on a harmful lowering of "vasomotor tone" as the main cause of post-traumatic symptoms in favour of greater emphasis on psychologically prompted disability. He urges early vigorous physical and intellectual rehabilitation. He also recognizes that facilities for rehabilitation in civilian life are lacking, in contrast to life in the armed forces where "the problem may be more efficiently approached and developed." As a postscript, he adds in small print:

> ... early attention to the restoration of vasomotor tone is important; but probably more important is an active regimen instituted by the surgeon to prevent a functional syndrome — so difficult to deal with when once established. Surgeons are prone to pay little attention to this problem which is so important in the case of the patient with a craniocerebral injury.

Malignant Brain Tumours (no. 20)

There is an intimacy in McKenzie's clinical papers seldom seen in current journals. He speaks directly to the reader with an ingenuousness that commands the attention and sympathy of his fellow neurosurgeons today. In discussing the implications of his findings he may lapse into the first person singular rather than the commoner, less forceful, third. The contrast from current medical writing is understandable. The mathematics of statistical method and analysis, the intrusion of basic science, the construction of controlled therapeutic clinical trials, the enlistment of biochemical, physical and molecular knowledge to solve the mysteries of disease, all have little place for expressions of personal opinion even when based on personal experience. Of course there is and always will be a need for the doctor's voice. The nature of human medical practice rests on the practitioner giving an informed opinion after the scientific facts have been weighed against those intangibles that are the heart and soul of the patient. In his writings McKenzie shows, time and again, he has not lost sight of this enduring foundation. Nowhere is this more eloquently stated than in his writings on malignant brain tumours or in severe head injuries.

In the surgical management of gliomas and metastatic brain tumours, most of his colleagues, including Cushing himself and that other prolific writer, Walter Dandy, advocated reliance on the external cranial decompression for the temporary relief of headache (the commonest symptom of malignant tumour). By discarding the bone flap and leaving the underlying dural membrane open, pressure inside the head could be kept down as the brain swelled from the growing tumour. The swelling brain was then held back only by the flap of skin which itself stretched to accommodate the ever-increasing bulge. The operation gave the patient a few extra weeks or months of life.

In his autobiography, *No Man Alone*, Penfield quotes an exchange of letters in 1931 between himself and the brilliant if acerbic F.M.R. Walshe, neurologist at the National Hospital for Nervous and Mental Diseases, Queen Square, London. Walshe, riding his hobbyhorse of criticism of what he believed to be the philosophy of neurosurgeons, wrote to his friend Penfield on January 6, 1931, on the importance of neurologist and neurosurgeon each embracing the knowledge of the other. It should be said, however, Walshe's emphasis was on the superiority of the neurologist from whose example the neurosurgeon could benefit:

> ... I had an opportunity of seeing a few years ago in America (not in
> Boston, let it be said) the way this admirable notion of the surgeon-
> neurologist actually works out ... If the unhappy patient happened to
> have paralysis agitans or epilepsy, that was his misfortune. If he had
> a vast glioma filling one hemisphere, then the hemisphere came out.
> I must admit that it was so skillfully removed that the wretched victim
> of this surgical ecstasy survived — a bedridden, demented hemiplegic
> with a head like three-quarters of a watermelon, draped with a sagging
> scalp. Nevertheless, he continued to breathe, eat, make noises, and
> wet his bed for many months longer than life would have been
> possible had he not been mutilated, and he was therefore a
> neurological success ...

In his good-natured rebuttal to Walshe's tirade that he, Penfield, put neurosurgery above neurology, Penfield replied:

> ... I had intended [in my article] that my thesis should be interpreted as an attack upon the tendency in the United States for neurosurgeons to ignore neurology and the tendency elsewhere to *reverse the process.* I intended to point out that the neurosurgeon should no longer spring from the ranks of simple surgeons, but I was entirely incapable of that lovely phrase [of yours], "he expects with no preliminary training to spring Minerva-like from the head of Cushing."

It is certain Walshe would have approved of McKenzie's rejection of malignant glioma management by external decompression; it is equally certain McKenzie would have applauded Penfield's style in his rebuttal of Walshe. Walshe continued the neurology/neurosurgery debate though on a more objective and scientific plane twenty-five years later, in a critical article, "The brain stem conceived as the 'highest level' of function in the nervous system; with particular reference to the 'autonomic apparatus' of Carpenter and to the 'centrencephalic integrating system' of Penfield" (*Brain* 80 [1957]: 510–539). This time Walshe's disagreement with Penfield was serious and without flippancy. Penfield was arguing against Walshe's adverse criticism over a hypothesis he, Penfield, had put forward. One sensed, however, that Walshe's comments did not entirely reveal scientific detachment, but rather that he had found another opportunity to ride his hobbyhorse.

At a meeting in London of the Society of British Neurological Surgeons in 1935, McKenzie gave his point of view concerning the treatment of glioblastoma, the malignant brain tumour for which, now as then, there is no lasting cure.

> ... The conclusion which I have reached in regard to surgical treatment is at variance with the view held by some neurosurgeons in America and probably also by some in England. A few years ago I formed the opinion that operation was futile and better left undone ... I think otherwise at the present time ...
>
> In most cases I believe it is worth while to advise operation on the understanding [an operation] will probably enable the patient to carry on in a satisfactory manner with little or no disability and without deformity for several months ... Usually this involves the removal of a mass of tumor and overlying brain, approximately the size of a small orange ... The dura is then carefully sutured. When the space left after

this resection fills with tumor, symptoms return, but life is not then unduly prolonged because the dura has been closed tightly ... This may be termed an internal decompression in contrast to the other procedure, in which intracranial pressure is largely controlled by an external decompression, a procedure which I thoroughly condemn as a treatment for glioblastoma because of the resulting deformity [a grotesque bulge on the side of the head] and the prolongation of life long after the time when death would be a relief.

McKenzie's philosophy and operative technique of dealing surgically with malignant tumours is generally accepted, but treatment today is combined with a number of complementary methods (including radiation and chemotherapy) directed at the cancer cell and the enhancement of the body's defences, approaches not then available.

McKenzie also reported in 1955 his life's experience with intracranial astrocytomas (nos. 41, 42). Some of these are slow-growing tumours and on that account sometimes referred to as benign. But if by "malignant" we mean incurable by resection and ultimately deadly, then the astrocytoma qualifies for inclusion with glioblastoma, each occupying the two extremes of the pathological spectrum and places between. McKenzie allowed that "an individual study of results following surgery on a particular brain tumour can only show a trend," but "an aggregate of such papers from various surgeons will have statistical value." He studied intracranial tumours he had resected and which had been reported by Eric Linell to have the microscopic appearance of astrocytoma of varying degree of malignancy. He chose as his title "Survival Periods Following Operation on 61 Intracranial Astrocytomas." He grouped the tumours according to the location they occupied in the brain: fronto-temporal, parietal, occipital, optic chiasma, central cerebellar and cerebellar hemisphere. Excluding the immediate postoperative deaths (eight cases), survival ranged from twenty-one years in patients still alive at the time McKenzie was preparing his report, down to death at six months. His detailed analysis confirmed ("crystallized") impressions "long held by neurosurgeons": the cerebellar tumours are a favourable group and long, useful survival can be expected in the majority; the cerebral tumours are more aggressive but long survival occurs in a few; a benign astrocytoma "may take on malignant characteristics." This last finding made him "much more cautious about a diagnosis of benign astrocytoma, particularly in the supratentorial [i.e. cerebral] region, than we have been in the past."

McKenzie was sure of his ground and his contemporaries respected him for his openness in success and failure. In the discussion that followed the paper on astrocytomas, Leo Davidoff, professor in neurosurgery at The Albert Einstein College of Medicine in New York City, said the paper "was given by one of the philosophers in neurological surgery and perhaps the most thoughtful man in our field on the North American continent."

Frank Turnbull, Resident in 1932 to Ken McKenzie, "to whom I am so greatly indebted for a good start in neurosurgery."

Certainly McKenzie had depressed moods, usually related to administrative frustrations, but often resulting from complications of operations for which, in silence, he blamed himself. Frank Turnbull, McKenzie's assistant in 1932, believed K.G. was a "mild manic-depressive,"[31] a belief confirmed by K.G.'s son, Dr. Fred McKenzie, Director of Adolescence of the Children's Psychiatric Research Institute, London, Ontario.[32] The episodes of depression he experienced were not severe enough to produce the physical and behavioural symptoms that deserved a pathological label. They were simply somewhat more pronounced than the usual mood swings of universal experience.

Jean Yuill, the Scottish nursing night supervisor at TGH from 1915 to 1935, on one of her usual night rounds of the hospital, says she met K.G. outside the operating room wandering along the basement corridor, deep in meditation and in his combination woollen underwear. A smouldering cigarette hung from his lips. She gently turned him round and pointed him back to the OR. He had had a difficult case that had not gone well. In those days the hospital was normally quiet by night. Surgical emergencies were few and Miss Yuill, like her successor Miss Woolford, kept the night watch unassisted. Of course Dr. McKenzie was moody after a case that had not gone well; it was no surprise to her that he chose to mull over the case imperfectly dressed. He learned from patients' misfortunes. It is unlikely that Miss Yuill or Mabel Duthie, Kenneth's life-long secretary, or Irene would have seen in his moods anything more than the effect of weariness or disappointment.[33] Turnbull writes:

"During his [McKenzie's] depressed moods, usually despairing about the limitations of neurosurgery, a triumvirate of females sustained and boosted his morale: the faithful Miss Duthie, his wife Irene ('Poor Ken, he's had another of those operations,' she would say), and an elderly Scottish nursing supervisor [Miss Yuill] who had been 'on nights' for years at TGH and had consoled him since his early years when so many of the operations for brain tumour ended fatally."

Harry Botterell said, "I would disagree, unequivocally, that Ken was a manic-depressive. A 'run' of several disappointing cases, e.g., brain tumours, malignant instead of benign, a death from a technical error (he had them too) would deplete his reserves of energy and emotion and he would run away for a long week-end, or a few days."[34]

Acoustic Neuroma (no. 41)

Cushing's classic monograph on tumours of the auditory nerve[35] came out only five years before McKenzie's time with him in Boston. The book was a detailed report (296 pages) of 30 patients on whom Cushing had operated. Some tumours were totally removed, others were gutted to reduce their bulk. The operation was easier and there-fore safer if the capsule was left in place, but some patients had to return for a second operation when symptoms recurred. While the sub-capsular operations lowered the mortality, the operation was still a most serious undertaking. Between 1910 and 1915 there was a 68.7% mortality according to the reported figures from other clinics cited by Cushing. His own experience in the first 10 cases was a mortality of 40%, but by the time his monograph was published in 1917, the mor-tality rate of the whole series of 30 was 20%. He thought it "must" drop further "to 10 or to 5 per cent or better."

By 1954, when McKenzie reported his life's experience, the operation was still a challenging undertaking for the surgeon and a dangerous adventure for the patient. It was then regarded as the most demanding in the neurosurgical repertoire. Injury to the brainstem and its arteries adherent to the tumour were — and are — the main surgical risks of the operation. Their avoidance is the surgeon's responsibility alone. Today properly trained neurosurgeons, with or without cooperation with otologists, take it in their stride supported by superior skill from anaesthetists and the use of magnification provided by the operating microscope. McKenzie doubted the attempt to save the contiguous facial nerve should ever be made if the surgical intent was complete tumour removal. The neurosurgeon today is distressed if he cannot save the nerve during total tumour removal.

Towards the end of his career in the early 1950s, McKenzie lowered the mortality rate following total removal to 12% in 66 consecutive patients. This compared with the remarkable 1965 report by Hullay and Tomits of one death in fifty consecutive cases of total removal.[36] Since then, operative mortality in otherwise healthy patients has dropped to around 1.0%. However, a bald statement comparing operative mortality amongst different authors does not necessarily redound to the credit of one, nor to the discredit of another. Diverse factors influence results, in particular size of tumour and the patient's age and state of health. In the context of the difficult operation of total acoustic neuroma removal, McKenzie and Alexander warned against a surfeit of neurosurgeons: "... brain tumours do not now concentrate in a few clinics as they did some years ago and it is difficult for any one surgeon to gain sufficient personal experience to establish with any degree of certainty, the correct operative procedure in the various age groups,"[37] a situation in all branches of surgery that has been only partly remedied by "superspecialization." The warning still applies.

Brain Lesions and Mental Disorder (no. 18)

McKenzie's 1935 paper, delivered to a predominantly psychiatric audience in Toronto, was somewhat superficial in psychiatric terms. But he was at pains to warn psychiatrists, whose specialty was increasingly drifting away from the fold of organic neurology, to look for physical brain disease before arriving at a diagnosis of primary "mental disorder." Chronic subdural haematoma and frontal brain tumour for example, were well known to masquerade as purely psychological disturbances. The title of his paper was "Mental Disorders with Relation to Trauma." He expanded the topic to include any mass lesion of the frontal lobe: tumour or traumatic disruption of the brain, cerebral or subdural haematoma. It is the mass that causes symptoms, not its pathological nature. He did not speak in the ever-changing jargon of psychiatric hypotheses and diagnostic nomenclature, but delivered his simple message in plain language. He talked, for example, of "lack of restraint" rather than "lack of inhibition," the latter a term with its special meaning to physiologists and psychologists but which to most people, including doctors, is not so immediately informative when it comes to describing social solecisms of disturbed patients. On behaviour of a patient recovering from a head injury he said, "It remains to be seen whether this young man will pull himself together and tackle his responsibilities with normal seriousness and initiative." So much of McKenzie himself is revealed in that refreshing sentence, a patriarch with patience, determination, inquisitiveness and diligence. He doesn't camouflage with mealy-mouthed jargon when straight talk will do.

C.B. Farrar, Professor of Psychiatry in the University, said in the discussion of McKenzie's paper:

> One of the most valuable points in his paper ... [was] his suggestion
> to psychiatrists of the importance of basing their work in the first
> instance upon organic neurology ... In this way the psychiatric structure
> is reared upon a sound and scientific foundation. If one begins with
> psychogenic theories to the neglect of the organic side it is like
> building the roof for a house and then finding that there is no
> house under it.

McKenzie, musing on the changeability of symptoms in psychological disturbances and the difficulty it brings to diagnosis, writes:

> We must admit that any given brain may function in a perfectly
> normal manner one minute and in a pathological way the next.
> I suppose the ordinary nightmare is an example of this. Every
> man, as with metals, has his modulus of elasticity and strain ...

As a commentary on the mystery of human nature the metaphor is at least as enlightening as the unprovable speculations of some psychological hypotheses.

Spinal Cord Lesions (nos. 14, 17, 26)

McKenzie's only published article on vertebral fractures with and without spinal cord injury appeared in 1935 (no. 17). It was directed at general surgeons who carried the load for spinal injuries in every community. He described the principles of care and how he achieved them through his focus on patients who were not immediately rendered completely paraplegic or quadriplegic. Before the war, McKenzie and Botterell discussed the management of spinal injuries at some length. It wasn't until Harry was in military charge of neurosurgery at Basingstoke, England, that he was able to put into practice what he and K.G. had agreed upon. Survival with complete cord lesions after injury before the era of Sir Ludwig Guttmann[38] and Harry Botterell during World War II was so short it must have seemed more profitable to dwell on the other aspect of management — prevention: prevention of further cord damage that can follow improper handling. The principles of treatment, restoration of the fracture to its normal alignment followed by fixation to allow for bone healing, are the same today. The place of non-surgical manipulation to reduce the deformity compared to surgical correction has been debated over the years. But the protection of the cord from the hazards of first-aid handling or later treatment has always been a prime objective.

George Riddoch, neurological consultant to the British Army and Ministry of Pensions hospitals, and consultant to the Peripheral Nerve Committee of the Medical Research Council, "decided to congregate spinal cord casualties in special Spinal Injuries Units ... in Great Britain" in anticipation of civilian and military spinal casualties during World War II. In 1943 the British government told Guttmann to set up a unit at Stoke Mandeville Hospital to prepare to receive casualties following the second front spring offensive (the invasion of Normandy) that was to be launched in 1944. Before the Normandy landing, Guttmann visited Australia, Canada and the United States and found that the results of treatment of spinal cord injury and paraplegia ("the most depressing and neglected [subject] in medicine") were no better than in Britain.

Guttmann's organization depended on concentrating paraplegics (and quadriplegics) in one institution where patients could receive continuing special care not otherwise available. It was the complications of cord injury — bladder and kidney infection, extensive, deep bedsores, lung infection and despair — that killed patients. The survival rate after a complete spinal cord injury was thus extended from a matter of months or a year or two, to almost normal life expectancy. Harry Botterell, aware of Guttmann's work, wasted no time setting up a spinal injuries centre at the Canadian military neurological hospital at Basingstoke with the same transforming results. The newly formed Canadian Paraplegic Association became the socio-political arm to carry through to civilian life the principles of patient management Botterell and Guttmann proved essential to survival.

Skull Calipers

In what is essentially an excellent textbook article of the day (no. 17), McKenzie records another of his innovations:

> My only original contribution to the subject is a description of skeletal traction which I have utilized in the treatment of certain cervical injuries. This method of treatment was suggested to me by Doctor Janes at a time when we were each having trouble with a patient in maintaining satisfactory extension by the halter method. Our experience with this first case, and more recently with two others, has convinced us that skeletal traction is a satisfactory method of maintaining a prolonged forcible pull on the cervical spine.

Forceful, sustained traction is required to disimpact overriding facets and to correct the deformity of a crushed cervical vertebral body. The accepted method at the time was to surround the neck with a canvas or leather halter to which weights could be attached by a cord hung by a pulley over the head of the bed. The disadvantage of this device, though correct in principle, was the patient's intolerance of sustained pressure on the skin over the jaw by the halter from a weight of more than a few pounds. To be effective, a pull of up to twenty pounds for many hours is necessary and the only way this could be done was to attach a device directly to the skull through which painless traction on the neck could be applied.

Frank Turnbull,[39] while McKenzie's resident in 1932, heard him discussing a case with his general surgical colleague and later the professor of surgery, Robert Janes. Janes suggested McKenzie take a leaf out of the orthopaedic book and apply traction directly to the skull to reduce cervical fractures in the same way fractures of the femoral neck were reduced through the application of large ice tongs in the femur. When the neck or shaft of the femur is broken, the thigh muscles contract and cause the ends of the fractured bone to override. To "set" the facture surfaces, they must be restored to their natural position. This is achieved by applying "ice-tong" calipers to the femur below the fracture and exerting traction on the caliper. Once the fracture has thus been "reduced," it is held in position until the bone heals. Similarly a displaced vertebral neck fracture has to be reduced and held in position until bone healing occurs naturally or by bone grafting. McKenzie and Turnbull accomplished reduction by pulling on the head with ice tongs fixed into the outer table of the skull to which about 20 pounds were painlessly applied. Says Turnbull, "Ken turned to me nonchalantly and asked me to go ahead and try them. So I applied the tongs plus traction. The technique worked, but curiously Ken seemed to take no further interest in the procedure."[40]

Two years later Crutchfield reported the technique, and two years after that McKenzie recorded his part in the matter. As an addendum to his article he acknowledges that "just recently" he had become aware of an article in *The Southern Surgeon* by Crutchfield who, in turn, confessed he had no knowledge of McKenzie's then unpublished use of skull calipers for traction.[41] The word must have gone the rounds at the annual neurosurgical meetings. After McKenzie and Crutchfield each modified the design of the domestic ice tongs, there were changes made by other surgeons. But whatever the pattern chosen, skull calipers are universally used today at least in the early stage of treatment of a broken neck.

W. James Gardner of the Cleveland Clinic, in a letter to Harry Botterell (October 4, 1974), wrote, "I am quite sure now that Gayle Crutchfield was not the first to apply skeletal traction ... and I am reasonably sure that this method was suggested to him by Claude Coleman, although Crutchfield denied this ..."

At the time, Gardner was setting up an exhibit for the Smithsonian. It included the "Edmonton [femur traction] tong," an artifact borrowed from A.L. Hepburn, neurosurgeon, in Calgary. Hepburn, writing to Botterell on October 2, 1975, said, "I agree there is some merit in publishing the history of the Edmonton tongs, but I made previous inquiries and find that documentation is lacking. I was previously in correspondence with Dr. James Gardner ... and he, in fact, included my father's tongs in his exhibit at the Smithsonian Institute. At that time I had great difficulty in obtaining documentation. It is my impression that my late father was in personal communication with Dr. W.G. Crutchfield, at the British Medical Association meeting in London in 1932, or perhaps someone from his service might have attended that meeting. The Edmonton tongs bear some resemblance to the original McKenzie tongs, though they lack the calibrated box lock, as I recall the tongs were kept approximated by a piece of bicycle inner tubing ..."

In his letter quoted above to Botterell, Gardner, for the record, reports: "Since it has been definitely established that in two instances during World War II an orthopaedist treated a broken neck by traction on a Steinman pin driven entirely through the skull and brain [and out the other side], I prepared a skull with the Steinman pin for the Smithsonian exhibit." The commercial firm erecting the exhibit unfortunately ran out of space and the macabre specimen was never enjoyed by the public. The story of the pin, however, is established neurosurgical currency in friendly rivalry between nutcracker and orthopod.

Other Afflictions of the Spinal Cord

Article no. 26 (1940) is a report by McKenzie and colleagues of the results of operation in 83 cases of a variety of mass lesions of the spinal cord and cauda equina, all except four (arachnoiditis [2] and cavernous haemangioma & aneurysm [2]) causing cord compression. It is, again, directed at general physicians and surgeons to show what can be expected of operations on the cord. It appeared, like others of its type, in the *Canadian Medical Association Journal* where it would reach a readership unfamiliar with the subject.

> Eighty-three patients were operated upon [no metastatic carcinoma was included in the survey]. An excellent result was obtained in 42, and a result that was worthwhile in twelve ... It is fair to state that 75 percent of patients suffering from interference of function of the spinal cord or cauda equina from the various lesions considered in this report will be benefited by surgery. Laminectomy is a safe procedure. There has been no operative mortality ...

In 1933 Turnbull, H.H. Hyland[42] and McKenzie published a case of spinal cord compression with a "unique feature" (no. 14). The patient came under their care with advanced signs of spinal cord compression that had developed over five weeks. McKenzie removed an inflammatory mass compressing the cord due to a localized staphylococcal infection in the extradural space, an operation which was of itself not particularly remarkable.

> [The patient] had always been well with the exception of a period of three months, nine years [1922] before the onset of his present illness [1931], when he was in hospital in Poland with exactly similar abdominal pain and weakness in the legs, the latter so severe that he was unable to walk for ten weeks. He stated that several samples of his blood were taken and he was told it was "no good." He was given six or seven injections into his arm, but has received none since. The pain subsided and the legs entirely recovered.

McKenzie removed the infected material compressing the cord on October 2, 1931. He believed the symptoms nine years earlier were due to the same staphylococcal infection he removed in 1931. The authors acknowledged that "about" ten cases of a similar inflammatory mass in the vertebral canal had been reported already, notably by Dandy (*Arch. Surg.*, Chicago, 13 [1926]: 447). But the uniqueness of the case was the recurrence of symptoms after nine years of spontaneous remission. Since their report was published, dormant extradural inflammatory masses, particularly staphylococcal, have occasionally been encountered by neurosurgeons. W.S. Keith,[43] in 1944, recorded two similar cases of prolonged symptomatic remission from severe disability until, six years later, signs of cord compression returned which in each case required surgical removal of a granulomatous mass.[44] Keith was evidently unaware of the earlier report of Turnbull et al. As in Turnbull, Hyland and McKenzie's patient, recovery was complete in both of Keith's cases after removal of the infected mass.

Surgical Treatment of Ménière's Disease (nos. 13, 19, 38 and 41)

A disturbance of the vestibular division of the eighth nerve, Ménière's disease inflicts sudden attacks of vomiting and dizziness severe enough to throw the victim to the ground. The syndrome includes tinnitus and progressive deafness in the affected ear due to parallel involvement of the auditory component of the eighth nerve. Once deafness has become complete the function of both components of the eighth (acoustic) nerve has usually been destroyed and symptoms vanish. The attacks can be severe and frequent and when they are unrelieved by either medicinal means or the lapse of time, the patient is prepared, even pleased, to undergo operation for relief. It is more accurately referred to as Ménière's syndrome rather than disease since the intolerable characteristics of the condition are simply symptoms of disturbance of the inner ear but of questionable cause.

In recent years Gardner[45, 46] argued for the strong possibility that trigeminal neuralgia (tic douloureux) is symptomatic of distortion and compression of the trigeminal nerve root by contact between the nerve and a small intracranial artery, a theory pursued by Peter Jannetta to the point of general acceptance.[47] By 1990 Jannetta had taken the theory further.[46]

If contact between nerve and blood vessel is the cause of tic douloureux, why not give the same explanation for the phenomena of dysfunctional conditions of other cranial nerves — hemifacial spasm, glossopharyngeal neuralgia and Ménière's syndrome itself? Jannetta has since been vindicated by the result of his separating the affected nerve from the encroaching artery or vein in all these conditions, operations now widely adopted by others. But, at least in the case of Ménière's syndrome, there are still enough skeptics to keep the proposition at bay.

In McKenzie's day no one thought of the explanation Gardner and, later, Jannetta suggested for the cause of trigeminal neuralgia, much less of Ménière's syndrome — except McKenzie himself. This is curious because the then standard operation, destruction of the nerve supply to the inner ear by section of the whole thickness of the eighth (acoustic) nerve (auditory and vestibular components), was undertaken by neurosurgeons in many hundreds, if not in thousands of patients. Had surgeons not observed at operation any contact between artery and nerve? Or had they simply failed to put two and two together? Contact between cranial nerves and blood vessels in the subarachnoid space was something a neurosurgeon saw almost every time an operation took him to the base of the brain, yet no one seemed to suspect that there lay the clue to the cause of Ménière's syndrome. It just did not occur to anyone that the common cause of "primary" trigeminal neuralgia, glossopharyngeal neuralgia, hemifacial spasm or Ménière's syndrome was before every neurosurgeon's eyes. It was well known that mass lesions (tumours and aneurysms), by compression or distortion of certain sensory nerves (trigeminal and acoustic), could produce neuralgia in the one and paroxysms of dizziness with increasing deafness in the other. If contact by a tumour could produce symptoms, why not contact by an artery? Walter Dandy (1886–1946) of Baltimore, one of the first generation of neurosurgeons from Cushing's stable, like his teacher an obsessed worker and prolific writer of his neurosurgical experiences and innovations, undertook over 800 eighth nerve sections for Ménière's syndrome during his career, yet he apparently attached no clinical importance to the nerve-vessel contacts he must have seen almost every time he operated.

The acoustic nerve looks like a fairly thick strand of string but is made up of two main components, one serving the sense of hearing and the other, the vestibular, responsible for balance. By splitting the nerve longitudinally a surgeon can separate the two components without harming either, and then cut only the vestibular to put the semicircular canals out of action and bring the attacks of Ménière's syndrome to an end, while preserving hearing. On March 10, 1933, Dandy undertook this modification of the standard, total division of the acoustic nerve, emphasizing in his operation note, "This is the first instance in which the vestibular branch of the nerve alone has been sectioned."[48] He could not have known that McKenzie, in the comparative obscurity of the *Transactions of the Toronto Academy of Medicine*, (*Trans. Acad. Med.*, Toronto, 14 [Nov. 15, 1932]. Section of Surgery item no. 5), had already reported two cases of "Intracranial division of the vestibular portion of the auditory nerve for intractable vertigo with two case reports." McKenzie wrote:

> Recent publications by Dandy, Coleman, and Cairns have aroused renewed interest in Ménière's Disease, as these authors have shown that there is dramatic cessation of the severe attacks of vertigo after intracranial section of [the whole of] the eighth nerve. Operation is a particularly suitable treatment for these patients who are prevented from working either on account of the frequency and severity of their attacks or because of danger to themselves or others if an attack should occur while at work.
>
> Following the operation these patients have a total loss of hearing on the side on which the nerve is cut; usually this is of little moment because of the severe impairment of hearing on the involved side before operation; however, this is not always the case so for the past two years I have been interested in the feasibility of splitting the eighth nerve and cutting only the vestibular portion. Such an operation would be highly desirable in patients with considerable preservation of hearing, especially if there were some doubt as to the correct side on which to operate. If unilateral operations should fail to give relief and the disability were great, bilateral sections could be considered as it is a well-established fact that certain individuals who have had both labyrinths [semi-circular canals] destroyed by disease are capable of maintaining their equilibrium ...

After operation in the first case, the vertigo was cured but the hearing "was very badly impaired but was thought to be unchanged" from before the operation. The outcome in the second "has been highly satisfactory; from an individual who had lost his morale he was transformed into a cheerful and grateful patient who has continued to work free from disability."

Both McKenzie and Dandy kept up their interest in Ménière's syndrome, satisfied with the improved benefit from partial section of the acoustic nerve, but neither suspected the true cause of the condition.

Medicine is a slow-moving, conservative profession, resistant to changing the established consensus of the cause of illness. As W.J. Gardner[45] so aptly put it, "Nothing is more likely to mislead an investigator than a preconceived idea."

McKenzie, then, was the first to split the eighth nerve and cut only its vestibular portion in two patients with Ménière's syndrome. He read his paper before the Section of Surgery, Toronto Academy of Medicine on November 15, 1932, and it was published in the *Transactions of the Academy*. An updated account of the operation in twelve patients was presented before the International Neurological Congress in London in August 1935, and appeared in the *Canadian Medical Association Journal* in 1936.

Surgeons like to establish their primacy for innovative operations, a harmless vanity which is, however, sometimes erroneously, if innocently, claimed. Thus Dandy thought he was first off the mark and perhaps Cairns felt the same. But McKenzie set the record straight in the CMAJ article by giving the dates of the first operations of each contestant: McKenzie, September 1931 and July 1932; Cairns, February 1933; Dandy, March 1933. With a sense of fair play ingrained during his school days at St. Andrew's, McKenzie, without further details, added that Dandy had "suggested" the operation in 1928. For his part, Dandy wrote McKenzie a courteous note from Johns Hopkins on April 24, 1936:

> I have just seen your publication on Ménière's disease. It is very
> nicely done. I am so sorry I had not known of your work before.
> I shall, of course, be very happy to give you full credit for priority.
> Trusting you are well, and with all good wishes, I am,
> most sincerely
>
> Walter E. Dandy.[49]

The 1936 article in the CMAJ deals in detail with the anatomy of the seventh and eighth nerve as seen at operation. The line illustrations by Maria Wishart[50] complement the clarity of the text. Case histories of the twelve patients on whom McKenzie had performed the differential section of the eighth nerve are also given.

McKenzie came near to scooping Jannetta by about thirty years:

> The lesion if it is in the nerve itself does not cause a microscopic
> change (Case 8). I suggest that some consideration be given to the

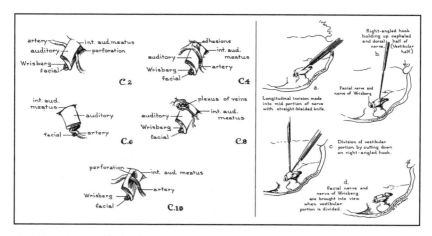

Left: Drawings by Maria Wishart from McKenzie's sketches and notes in five cases of Ménière's syndrome out of twelve reported. Contact between the eighth nerve and a blood vessel (4 arteries and 1 vein). The artery in each instance was considered to be the anterior inferior cerebellar.

Right: Maria Wishart's drawing of right vestibular nerve section for Ménière's syndrome.

— FROM MCKENZIE, K.G. "INTRACRANIAL DIVISION OF THE VESTIBULAR PORTION OF THE AUDITORY NERVE FOR MÉNIÉRE'S DISEASE." *CANAD. MED. ASSOC. J.* 34 [1936]: 369–381.

theory that an abnormal relationship of the anterior inferior cerebellar artery to the [eighth] nerve may be an etiological factor. In Cases 2, 4, 6 and 10 such an artery was seen at operation. In Case 8, there was a large vein in direct contact with the nerve. These observations have not been supported by Dandy, Cairns or Coleman, but the nerve could have an abnormal relationship with the artery close to the brainstem and not be seen at operations … I suggest also that this relationship of artery to nerve may account for nerve deafness in some patients, especially in older individuals where the artery may be thickened and stiff from arteriosclerosis.

The last sentence could have been written by Jannetta, who not only made the same comment on Ménière's syndrome but acted on it. In his article, McKenzie was the first to observe, describe and illustrate the variable relationships between the eighth nerve and a blood vessel. He pondered its significance but took it no further. It remained for Jannetta to prove that contact and distortion of certain cranial nerves by adjacent arteries or veins accounted for the cause of a cluster of conditions — trigeminal neuralgia, glossopharyngeal neuralgia, hemifacial spasm and Ménière's syndrome — and which led to their surgical cure. The inclusion by Jannetta of Ménière's syndrome in the list is not yet accepted by some, particularly otologists, but eventually, like those who once vigorously opposed the same theory of causation in the other conditions, they will be won over. The principle of the operation is the same in all cases: separate the blood vessel from the nerve and the pain, the facial twitching or paroxysms of vertigo will be laid to rest.

McKenzie's last article on the subject of Ménière's syndrome (no. 39) completed his series of 117 patients seen over 20 years from 1931 to 1951. Of this total, McKenzie and E.H. Botterell had between them operated on 103 patients. Their otologist colleagues, Hugh Barber and Percy Ireland, had just reported their findings in the fifty-three patients from McKenzie's series who were available for follow-up examination during 1951 and 1952.[51] All patients were treated by section of only the vestibular division of the eighth nerve. Barber and Ireland proclaimed the operation "very satisfactory" both for the relief from severe vertigo and for the preservation of such hearing as remained, but not for arrest of its seemingly inevitable decline. McKenzie had retired from the university two years earlier when he gave the paper at the 1954 meeting of the Congress of Neurological Surgeons in New York. He did not have any new data of his own, but he drew on the article by Barber and Ireland who had given it at their specialty society, unheard by most neurosurgeons. The advantages of the procedure were recognized as well as its imperfections. The voice of the seasoned elder was heard as McKenzie now advised, "I would caution otologists and physicians to adopt a conservative approach [to the surgical treatment of Ménière's syndrome]. Adequate and straightforward advice will enable many of these patients to accept their attacks with equanimity. Not too many require surgical treatment."

Otologists referred to the syndrome as "hydrops of the labyrinth," a tautology with flimsy justification. There is no agreement that Ménière's syndrome is caused by an excess of fluid or oedema in the inner ear, but the hypothesis, in the absence of any more convincing explanation, had caught on. Most otologists developed the operation of destruction of the labyrinth as their favourite treatment for Ménière's syndrome in spite of the total deafness it inevitably left behind. It involved operating within territory familiar to their specialty. They were as uneasy working inside the cranium as neurosurgeons were within the petrous bone. And since otologists were usually the first to see patients with dizziness and deafness who might require surgical treatment, the referrals to a neurosurgeon dropped as soon as labyrinthectomy became the otologist's stock-in-trade.

In McKenzie's view the results from the two separate approaches at that time were each as good as the other. They brought their own complications with them in a few cases, but either operation was well received by the patient. Had McKenzie lived to see the results of Jannetta's operation he would have applauded him. He would have smiled ruefully at his own missed opportunity of four decades earlier to separate artery from nerve to relieve the vertigo and halt the gradual onset of deafness.

The First Hemispherectomy for Epilepsy

The first surgeon to remove half the brain was Walter Dandy in 1928. It was a desperate, doomed gesture but approved by patient and family to save the patient from imminent death from a deep, malignant brain tumour.[52] The attempt was made in the hope that if the tumour could be removed, complete with enveloping brain tissue, a permanent cure could be expected. Intrinsic brain tumours of the glioma group virtually never metastasize outside the brain. Their behaviour is different from malignant tumours elsewhere in the body, which spread to other parts by the bloodstream or the lymphatic system. The question had to be asked and Dandy attempted to answer it by radical removal, but it failed. He reported five patients from whom he removed the right cerebral hemisphere in which lay a deep glioblastoma. Three patients died postoperatively from infection and a fourth died from recurrent tumour three and a half years later, but it was known at the time of operation that "in the region of the carotid artery the tumour had invaded the dura and this small portion could not be excised."

Unfortunately Dandy didn't wait to follow a fifth surviving patient long enough before he reported the case (it was subtitled "a preliminary report"); he simply said the patient was "still under observation," but did not state for how long. The question therefore remained unanswered, although the impossibility of eradicating primary malignant brain tumours by surgical removal is now generally admitted. McKenzie's operation of hemispherectory in 1936 was for a very different and more amenable condition.

In 1938 McKenzie delivered his paper to the Section on Nervous and Mental Disease of the American Medical Association annual meeting in San Francisco. The title was "Present status of a patient who has had the right cerebral hemisphere removed."[53] McKenzie's draft typescript tells the story.

When Betty was born prematurely after an obstetrical version she weighed three pounds. At fourteen days she fell from a table and struck the back of her head but did not lose consciousness. "Blue spells" and epileptic convulsions occurred frequently after the accident and at twenty-one days she was not moving the left arm as well as the right, and the left thumb was permanently flexed. By six months it was clear the left arm and leg were paralyzed in a manner typical of a cerebral hemisphere lesion, that is, the arm was immobile while the leg retained enough movement to walk lamely. Worst of all, the grand mal epileptic seizures were not only undiminished in frequency by appropriate medication, but became more severe. She was forced to leave school when she was twelve. The seizures increased. Six months before operation (by then she was sixteen), in addition to epilepsy, she

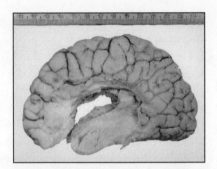

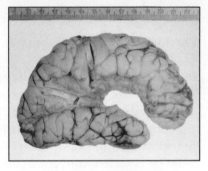

Specimen of excised right cerebral hemisphere (N.P. 178-36) a) lateral surface; b) medial surface. The specimen was photographed under the direction of Professor Eric A. Linell, and published in the article by Williams and Scott which appeared in *J. Neurology, Neurosurgery and Psychiatry* vol. 2 (New Series), 1939: 313-321.

THE ORIGINAL PHOTOGRAPHS SHOWN HERE WERE PROVIDED BY PROFESSOR WILLIAM HALLIDAY.

suffered fits of rage and terrifying visual and auditory hallucinations, but it was the severity of the epilepsy that convinced McKenzie to operate.

At operation on June 22, 1936, on finding extensive brain destruction and scarring, McKenzie decided to remove what was left of the whole hemisphere rather than merely the extensive scar. He knew from his examination before operation the only function the damaged hemisphere still possessed was to induce epilepsy. If any movement or sensation was regained, and if the emotional and behavioural storms were calmed, so much the better.

The removal of the cerebral hemisphere is not a particularly difficult operation. Betty's course afterwards was "uneventful and she returned home to take over a large share of the responsibilities of the family household for the next 23 years." She never had another fit or temper tantrum, nor had to take another anticonvulsant drug, and the only hallucinations she had were voices calling her name. "On May 6, 1959 at the age of 39 ... she died suddenly and unexpectedly 20 hours" after an operation in another centre for gall stones. An autopsy was granted and the brain was sent to Eric Linell, Professor of Neuropathology in the university (see illustration p.114).

McKenzie cured the epilepsy when it could not be controlled by medication. The prime indication for the operation ever since has been the same — intractable epilepsy. The operation was not generally adopted at the time; it seemed too radical, too "experimental." When R.A. Krynauw (1950)[54] in South Africa published his favourable experience with his first twelve patients, the procedure became acceptable. Krynauw was unaware of McKenzie's work of fourteen years earlier because it was not published. Replying to a request from Paul Bucy, secretary of the Section on Nervous and Mental Diseases of the AMA, for a copy of the paper for publication in the *Journal of the American Medical Association*, McKenzie wrote on February 6, 1939:

> *I am sorry but the paper which I presented in San Francisco has never been completed for publication. We have continued to study this patient and new things keep turning up. I must make an effort to get something out this year.*

McKenzie spoke from his manuscript, which he never surrendered, but his replies to questions in the discussion of the paper were recorded by a stenographer. The *Journal* sent him a copy of the discussion transcript to proof, but the editor's request remained unanswered in the TGH file with the original manuscript, where it lies to this day.

Through hearsay, the paper attracted attention from surgeons, neurologists, physiologists, pathologists, psychiatrists and psychologists. It was the first time a detailed neurological and psychological assessment had been made in a human adult before and after hemispherectomy for a benign condition incurred at birth. McKenzie lent the file to Denis Williams, a leading neurophysiologist in London, during his tenure of a Rockefeller Travelling Fellowship. Williams collaborated with John Scott,[55] who held a University of Toronto Fellowship in Physiology, in a

1939 article on "The functional responses of the sympathetic nervous system of man following hemidecortication."[56] The paper was not important from the strictly clinical standpoint as it dealt with certain reflex pathways involving changes in limb circulation in response to cutaneous sensory stimulation. But the authors astutely seized the opportunity the case provided to demonstrate, by comparing the sensory and cutaneous vascular reflexes of the two sides of the body with each other, that the human sympathetic system has no functional representation in the cerebral cortex in a manner analogous to voluntary motor and sensory representation. For the historian and clinician, the article remains the only publication to describe some of the neurological and pathological features of the case (including two photographs of the removed hemisphere), although detailed neurological examination, sensory, motor, visual and psychological, by Botterell and McKenzie, are preserved in the file.

The publication by Williams and Scott took the pressure to publish off McKenzie to some extent. At least his key role in Betty's management was on the record. Although the initiative to use the uniqueness of the case to study a certain physiological function was Williams's, McKenzie saw to it that the honour was shared by the contribution of Scott from his own medical school. In 1939, with war looming (Canada was at war before the year was out), he foresaw the burden he would have to carry as soon as the other active staff neurosurgeons in the medical school, Harry Botterell, Bill Keith and Palmer McCormick, enlisted and the resident staff shrank drastically. To write the article he needed uninterrupted peace, which would, as far as he could see, be denied him for the duration of the war. In any event, he did write four articles during the war but they were less demanding than a paper on this unique case would have been.

Clinical articles have been the backbone of surgical literature from the beginning of the twentieth century until soon after World War II. The authors have been mainly university appointees, but without any university salary. Universities, strapped as always for funds, left it to the appointed clinicians to fend for themselves out of the proceeds from their private practices. In return for teaching, carrying out research, writing and generally upholding and advancing the reputation of the medical school (and themselves), the academic staff was given priority access to "private" beds for their "private" patients. In Toronto, until medicare arrived, as elsewhere in the country, about seventy-five percent of beds in a teaching hospital were designated "public" where the occupants received free medical and surgical care from the appointed staff. This left a teacher to earn his living in his office from referred consultations and from the few "private" beds available. The burden was often heavy for the staffman, particularly in surgery, if he was to carry out his clinical duties conscientiously in the "public" wards and in teaching and original writing. When the load became insupportable it usually meant publication, teaching and private practice suffered — in that order.

R. Douglas Wright, Professor of Physiology in the University of Melbourne, noticed in the Williams and Scott article that E.H. Botterell, "in an article to be published later," carried out after the operation an exhaustive sensory examination of Betty. Because of the great neurophysiological interest of the case, Wright asked McKenzie for a reprint of their paper and to let him know "the subsequent happenings" to the patient. McKenzie, on August 10, 1943, had to reply,

I am sorry to say that the war has interfered with the publication of Betty, the girl on whom we removed the right cerebral hemisphere. This patient still remains reasonably well and I anticipate and expect that some day we shall get the case published.

Eighteen months after the operation the patient was readmitted to hospital for detailed assessment aimed at providing answers to questions on certain human brain functions the neurophysiological world was waiting for. Botterell carried out over several days a thorough sensory examination with the intention of writing the paper for presentation to McKenzie for approval and proofing. But then the war came and the task was relegated to "work in progress," the death knell to much creative clinical writing. After the war Botterell drafted the article under McKenzie's and his name, but Botterell did not pursue it with enthusiasm. He was gradually taking over the direction of the neurosurgical service from McKenzie; he had his practice, his teaching responsibilities, the organizing of spinal injury cases in the city and province and guiding the architectural and future plans of the neurosurgical unit in anticipation of the move into its new quarters.

After Betty's operation, McKenzie kept in touch with her by acknowledging the many chatty letters she wrote him in well-formed longhand, and through her periodic visits to the hospital. Not only was Betty his patient, but she lived near Tillsonburg, the town where Irene McKenzie had her roots, not far from Monkton, his own birthplace. Irene's father,

Fred Biette, a prominent bank manager in the district, reported to his son-in-law on her progress and sometimes drove her to Toronto for her appointments with McKenzie. The concern McKenzie and Biette had for Betty during her life assured there would be no resistance from the family to an autopsy, which was eventually carried out by Eric Linell.

Harry Botterell dusted off Betty's file and on January 22, 1960 wrote to McKenzie, the latter by then in his eighth year of retirement:

> *Here is the draft of a paper on "Hemispherectomy" which I though it would be nice for Tasker[57] to work on. This he has done and I have added a bit and edited it somewhat … I hope you will really give this manuscript the full treatment so we can get it published reasonably soon.*

By this time McKenzie also had little enthusiasm for it and the file stayed with Botterell until Ronald R. Tasker received it. Two more hemispherectomy cases by the neurosurgical staff were added to Tasker's draft, which was then passed back to Botterell for review. When Harry Botterell died in 1998 the file was put in Tasker's care again. It may find its way to the university archives or continue as "work in progress" or be accepted for publication as a historical document.

Eric Linell, with R.M. Clark, in 1954 wrote an article that modified the contemporary view of the cause of hemiplegia occurring at birth or in infancy.[58] It had been assumed that neonatal hemiplegia was due to trauma at birth due either to moulding of the foetal head during its passage down the birth canal, to the application of forceps during a difficult labour and delivery, or to cerebral haemorrhage or thrombosis from a primary blood disorder. Linell's case was of a female with erythroblastosis foetalis who died one and a half hours after birth. He was able to demonstrate a cerebral infarct in the territory of the middle cerebral artery that he attributed to a placental embolus which, therefore, must have occurred *in utero* and probably before labour.

McKenzie's 1936 operation, anticipating Krynauw's report on his results in South Africa by fourteen years, went unheeded. A place on the programme of an annual meeting of a section of the American Medical Association is no substitute for publication. It is not surprising his paper remained unnoticed. Neurosurgical wisdom at the time would have recalled Dandy's report in 1928 of four hemispherectomies that left no encouragement to practising neurosurgeons to do the same. Had McKenzie published the case, there is little doubt other young patients with intractable epilepsy would, in selected cases, have benefited.[59]

Lobotomy (nos. 33, 43)

The era of lobotomy for certain psychological disorders opened and closed during McKenzie's active career. Like most leading neurosurgeons in North America and Europe, McKenzie and the University of Toronto practised in the field.

It all started with J.F. Fulton and C.F. Jacobsen when Fulton gave an early paper of their work at the Second International Congress of Neurology in London in 1935. Here they reported experiments on the result of resection of the frontal lobes of chimpanzees.[60] Fulton and his colleagues did not publish their mature work until 1948,[61] by which time they had something more informative to write about than the preliminary report of 1935. Meanwhile, Egaz Moniz (1874–1955), Professor of Neurology at Lisbon, Portugal, who attended the 1935 meeting and saw the evidence for change of mood and personality in Fulton and Jacobsen's chimpanzees, decided the correlation between chimpanzees' and humans' behaviour was sufficiently close to warrant a trial of partial isolation of the frontal lobe connections in man to relieve certain chronic and severe mental illnesses.[62] Moniz was not a surgeon, so he enlisted his neurosurgical colleague Almeida Lima to do his bidding. Lima, like neurosurgeons elsewhere who participated in lobotomy programs, was the handmaiden of the psychiatrist partner. McKenzie was no exception. In 1936, Freeman and Watts wasted no time reporting a single lobotomy[63] case in a patient with agitated depression, but delayed a more considered monograph on the whole developing subject of surgery on the brain for different psychological disorders until 1950.[64]

At Toronto, McKenzie joined forces with the university psychiatrists led by the department head, Professor Aldwyn Stokes. Lobotomy, by then widely practised in the world, did not yet suffer the condemnation it later received, particularly in the United States. It was estimated by Fulton that at least 20,000 lobotomies were carried out before 1951. Organized clinical studies on the great majority of patients were lacking, so that, "in spite of this wide clinical experience with frontal lobe lesions, a comprehensive therapeutic assessment of lobotomy is still not possible. As a result, among neurosurgeons today [1973] there is only scattered interest in this field, and among those who are interested, there is little consensus as to the rationale and method of therapy" (Livingston).[65] In his article, Livingston deplored the damaging effect of outcries against any form of brain surgery, even for the most crippling mental disorders. Many would-be researchers in psychophysiology were not prepared to put up with the virulence of opposition and deserted the field to apply their talents elsewhere. A decade or two passed before important research in human psychophysiology regained momentum.

The main reason, however, that the interest in lobotomy faded in the late 1940s and 1950s was the arrival of effective psychotropic drugs. Lobotomy, in any of its several anatomical forms, could not be countenanced until a full trial of drug therapy was applied, and then only the most afflicted patients who did not respond to medication would be accepted for operation.

Stokes and McKenzie anticipated Fulton's and Livingston's challenges by carrying out their own clinical study of lobotomy over the years 1948 to 1952. Miller, the executive psychiatric member of the group, reported the team's experience in a monograph published in 1954.[66] (It was funded and published by the Province of Ontario in 1954 but bears no date or reference number nor publication data other than the coat-of-arms of the Province of Ontario and the name of the Minister of Health, MacKinnon Phillips. Small wonder the work of the research group led by Stokes and McKenzie is virtually unknown!)

Prediction of result and actual result were scored on a point scale assessment following pre-operative and post-operative examination. Weekly conferences were held to discuss patients' diagnosis, history, extent of incapacity, result of psychometric and metabolic tests and electroencephalography; in fact an exhaustive clinical survey from all interests involved — psychiatrist, neurosurgeon, internist, statistician, nurse, occupational therapist and social worker — was presented in conference both before and after each operation.

The operation of lobotomy (synonym: leucotomy) was the standardized closed, bilateral incision through the white matter anterior to the frontal horns of the lateral ventricles, a protocol abandoned after the closure of the study to a smaller, infero-medial lesion, in keeping with the changing opinion of the day. One hundred and fifty operations were carried out by McKenzie with a mortality of two percent, one patient from massive haemorrhage and one from brain abscess. The cause of death was not determined in the third patient who died at home six months after operation, but for statistical purposes it was recorded as an operative death.

This is not the place to comment on the many aspects of the monograph of 107 pages, nor to resurrect the physiological arguments over the best placement of the lesion, arguments which in the sixties and seventies had given way to passionate ethical and religious challenges to any brain procedures bearing the label "psychosurgery."[67, 68]

While the Toronto program was underway, a parallel pathological study was approaching publication.[69] It comprised autopsy information lacking in the Toronto series with only two deaths, but which was complementary to it. Meyer and Beck at the Maudsley Hospital in London had carried out post-mortem examinations on 102 brains from patients who had received standard bilateral pre-frontal lobotomy for a variety of psychological disorders of, generally speaking, the same nature as the Toronto patients. The purpose, of course, was to correlate site and size of the surgical lesions with the type of psychological disorder and the result of operation. The cause of death in three cases was the lobotomy procedure. The other ninety-nine patients who had had lobotomies died later from a great variety of conditions that might be encountered in any department of pathology, and were unrelated to the surgical lobotomy. It was a qualitative pathological report with no claim to statistical application in therapy.

McKenzie continued his interest in lobotomy after his retirement from the university. He joined with the staff of the (psychiatric) Ontario Hospital, Hamilton, in an assessment of lobotomy on the "disturbed wards" with B.A. Boyd and W.H. Weber, who published their findings in 1958. In those days, psychiatric hospitals in Ontario were (and still are) government institutions, unlike general hospitals that have their own boards of governors. They were identified by the name of the town where they were built — Ontario Hospital, Hamilton, or Toronto or Whitby, etc. — so as not to disturb the sensitivity of patients and the public with the dreaded title of "mental hospital." The authors' avowed aim was to concentrate "on the disturbed patients who present a difficult nursing problem, not so much to get patients out of hospital as to relieve the overall nursing problem." The apparently cynical concern over staffing rather than patients' welfare is misleading. It was simply a way of identifying the severity of mentally ill patients by their violence and other grave symptoms of psychological disturbance that incidentally threatened to deprive the institution of essential nursing staff, either from resignation or lack of applicants.

The Toronto program began in 1948. The "standard" bilateral lobotomy was carried out in 150 consecutive patients. To make the lesion in the frontal lobes, McKenzie's leucotome, an instrument devised by himself and manufactured by Eugen Scheerle of the J.F. Hartz

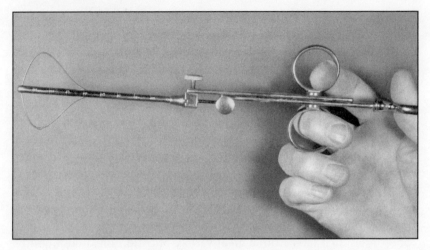

McKenzie's first leucotome. The shaft is marked in centimetres. The size of the "snare" in subsequent models was progressively reduced.

Co., was still preferred for patients who were so disturbed they were "destructive, noisy and assaultive ... required supervision in their eating, dressing and toilet habits ... [and were] unable to mix with other patients or do consistently useful work on the wards." The authors concluded the procedure was worthwhile in this category of illness. Assaultiveness, destructiveness and noisiness were greatly reduced. Many patients came to live out of hospital who otherwise would probably have required indefinite in-patient care.

From an analysis of the psychometric tests of sixty-one patients who were available for detailed post-operative study (having received pre-operative testing), Miller found greater improvement in those with an I.Q. above 100; they had "higher performance [scores] than verbal scores, a small degree of performance 'scatter' and relatively high scores on Picture Completion, Picture Arrangement and Similarities subtests of the Wechsler-Bellevue Scale. On the Rorschach test, absence of anatomy responses and presence of human movement were of good prognostic implication." These results would have been a guide to the selection of patients for lobotomy in the future had pharmacotherapy not arrived to supplant surgical lobotomy.

Miller, however, continued his study of the Toronto program by examining the same patients again in 1962, ten years after the Toronto study ended.[70] It was, nonetheless, a useful "academic" report: useful, should a lobotomy have to be considered for a patient in the future, and "academic" to bring closure to the project by an informative long-term follow-up.

There can be a few clinical procedures whose merits are more difficult to assess objectively than lobotomy. As Miller pointed out, even a comparison of results from other centres may be of little value. "There is considerable variation [in the published reports] in the clinical response to lobotomy as experienced by different investigators. To a large extent this reflects the [inconstancy of] clinical criteria used in the selection of cases for operation [by the different authors]."

By the time Miller conducted the 10-year follow-up of the Toronto study, 133 of the original 150 patients had been examined by him. Seventeen had died. There was evidence of improvement in certain categories, but a comparison with treatment by modern medication was not and cannot now be made. Sixty-one percent of patients who had a lobotomy before 1952 were working in the community in 1962. Thirty-nine percent did not benefit from the operation sufficiently to live out of hospital but they were "better adjusted to the hospital environment." Seventy-five percent were "able to work productively, and in 38% this work was of high calibre."

Neurosurgeons and psychiatrists of the lobotomy era need no defence or apology for their efforts. Anguish, pain and despair, depression and mania, groundless guilt and deluded paranoia, all were of a severity and chronicity in numbers not encountered in a mental hospital today. Insulin-induced coma, malaria-induced and body-warming hyperthermia, and electroconvulsive therapy were commonly administered in certain categories of mental disturbance. Physical restraint to protect the patient from himself or herself was a standard resort. Hospital staff became expert in quickly subduing a violent patient by wrapping the patient in a warm, wet sheet. The alternative or combined management for such severely disturbed patients was a prescription for depressants, hypnotics or narcotics to induce sleep until the next dose was due. At least one room in a mental hospital was lined with padded walls and floor and fitted with a door that could be locked from the outside. Even the Toronto General in McKenzie's time had a few small barred and locked rooms for the temporary containment of patients violent from alcohol or from some form of mental illness. McKenzie was familiar with the custodial scene for all types of mental illness; he had no misgivings about the need for and value of lobotomy. He accepted his responsibility for operation as he did in all patients who needed his surgical intervention, regardless of diagnosis and procedure.

In an attempt at a more rigorous statistically-controlled study (no. 43) McKenzie and G. Kaczanowski declared there was no benefit from the operation. The article was based on 183 patients on whom McKenzie performed the same procedure as in his earlier series, and all the psychiatric assessments, pre-operative, post-operative and longer term, were by Kaczanowski. The operations were carried out between 1955 and 1957 and the paper came out in the *Canadian Medical Association Journal* ten months after McKenzie's death in 1964. The authors discuss the reasons for their failure to detect any advantage in the procedure in spite of a modest success of the Toronto Study as reported earlier by Miller. Apart from possible incomparable preoperative diagnoses and criteria for operation, the study was launched *after* psychotropic drugs had taken hold in psychiatric practice. Lobotomy (leucotomy is the synonym the authors use) was not undertaken until the newer and more effective medications were tried; the hard core of patients resistant to treatment by the new drugs also remained unrelieved by lobotomy. Consequently, comparison between the two studies is invalid on account of the arrival of psychotropic drugs administered to the later group.

By the time he established himself through his publications and his clinical skills, McKenzie was well known in the surgical world of Canada, the United States and Britain. His publications on trigeminal neuralgia, Ménière's syndrome, a "minor" modification of Cushing's silver clips, the treatment of spasmodic torticollis, and his honest reviews of the results of his surgical treatment of tumours, abscess, head injury and pain were topics new and important. Yet the question is often asked, "Why have we only heard of Penfield?"

Edward Archibald, as the Professor of Surgery at McGill and knowledgeable about the possibilities of surgery of the nervous system, steered the decision leading to the creation of the Montreal Neurological Institute and the application of the Rockefeller grant to its building. When he met Penfield he knew he had discovered the man to head the Institute. Amiable but strong in resolve, a Rhodes Scholar, Princeton graduate, student of Sir Charles Sherrington at Oxford, the famous experimental neurophysiologist, and regarded with favour by Sir William Osler, the Regius Professor of Medicine at Oxford, Penfield was altogether an outstanding candidate to fulfill Archibald's hope for the future of McGill's medical school.

McKenzie's story could not be more different. Although he was the Silver Medallist in his final year in medicine at Toronto, he did not hang around when war was declared in 1914, the same summer as his graduation. With several of his medical colleagues at Toronto, he volunteered for overseas service in the Canadian Army Medical Corps (CAMC). Many graduated medical men applied for junior intern jobs for six or twelve months before enlisting for war service. They were promised positions at TGH to continue their medical training when they returned. Those who enlisted immediately without entering the intern programme were automatically denied a guaranteed appointment. McKenzie was such a one. When he came back he had no sponsor to satisfy his craving to train as a surgeon. He started a general practice close the to TGH to support his young family. After a few years of applying unsuccessfully to Professor Starr's office for a surgical internship, he obtained by chance a residency with Harvey Cushing. Thus his neurosurgical career began. He had no more education in basic science than he had absorbed as a medical student. He began his climb at the very bottom, inadequately prepared, without money or encouragement other than a somewhat unenthusiastic assurance that if the Boston appointment with Cushing worked out he would be given a probationary year as an intern back at TGH.

The contrast between the early careers of the two young men, McKenzie and Penfield, could not be more striking: the one educated to the hilt, the other merely educated. Penfield, with his career carefully mapped before it started, debonair, sponsored by world renowned men, a brilliant academic career already behind him; and McKenzie, reticent, without sponsorship, patient but equally determined to gain his desire to be a surgeon. He eventually joined Penfield on the top of the neurosurgical mountain.

McKenzie had no stomach for the diplomacy of administration at which Penfield and Botterell excelled. At first he received only lukewarm encouragement, but he persevered. Penfield was set up at McGill with complete research, surgical, neurological, laboratory and nursing teams of his own choosing, a massive centre of research and service to the public. Penfield, at the head of a supporting galaxy of stars he advised McGill to appoint, was the right man to shine in public and to justify McGill's large expenditure on the Institute. In Toronto, no special funding was allotted to neurosurgery because the specialty didn't exist until McKenzie was well under way. Of course everyone had heard of Penfield. He was the leader of an institute that was McGill's glory, a gift to the country and beyond.

McKenzie was a gift to no one when he started at TGH, but even before he had arrived there he had written a good, thoughtful article on spasmodic torticollis on his own initiative that passed Cushing's scrutiny but also won his printed comment. Thereafter McKenzie published an average of almost two papers every year. None of them was trivial; some introduced important new procedures, others were designed to inform practitioners how surgical treatment can be valuable in certain conditions. He reported his original concepts of certain diseases and how he treated them. These were directed at the neurosurgical readership. Most articles were written by him alone: long-term results following surgery for tumours, spasmodic torticollis, a variety of painful conditions, brain abscess, Ménière's syndrome.

His interests were also those of leading neurosurgeons at the time. He was well judged by his peers who voted him president of the two leading societies in the United States, the Harvey Cushing Society and The Society of Neurological Surgeons. McKenzie chose to shun publicity because it was against his nature; but he was happy and at ease in the company of his peers, delivering his papers at annual meeting of his societies. On the other hand, Penfield had to keep in the public eye for the sake of the Institute, McGill and the parent Victoria Hospital. They served the public largely from the proceeds of public funding. Fortunately Penfield was at ease in public speaking and in mingling with the leaders of society. When the flow of public money threatened to slacken, he spoke and wrote on the importance of corporate support to anticipate retrenchment of government funding. McKenzie's duty was to excel at neurosurgery for the sake of the university's and hospital's reputations. There was no call for publicity of the type Penfield had to deliver.

ENDNOTES — CHAPTER 4

1. Bodman, R. and D. Gillies. *Harold Griffith: The Evolution of Modern Anaesthesia*. Toronto: Dundurn Press Ltd., 1992.
2. Griffith, H.R. and G. Enid. Johnson. "The use of curare in general anaesthesia." *Anaesthesiology* 3 (1942): 418–420.
3. The original handwritten MS with Cushing's editing has been deposited in the archives department of the Toronto General Hospital.
4. Charles Edward Dowman, Jr. (1892–1931). Founder member of the Society of Neurological Surgeons; President 1930–1931.
5. McKenzie, K.G. "The surgical treatment of spasmodic torticollis." *Clinical Neurosurgery* 2 (1955): 37–43.

6. Rossitch, E., S. Khoshbin, P.McL. Black, M.R. Moore and H.R. Tyler. "Kenneth McKenzie, Harvey Cushing, and the early neurosurgical treatment of spasmodic torticollis." *Neurosurgery* 28 (1991): 278–282.

7. This and other charts from the 1920s and 1930s were rescued from the shredder in the 1980s. The hospital had run out of storage space. The notes (no. 58804, first admission 23 January 1924; 58815, second admission on 1 June 1924) in this as in all other charts of the period were written on poor quality acid paper. Any surviving charts of neurological or neurosurgical interest during this period have been deposited with the Toronto General Hospital archives department.

8. Mixter, W.J. and J.S. Barr. "Rupture of the intervertebral disc with involvement of the spinal canal." *New England J. Med* 211 (1934): 210–214.

9. The cordotomy knife was McKenzie's design.

10. Fothergill, J. "Of a painful affection of the face." In *Medical Observations and Inquiries by a Society of Physicians in London*. Vol. 5. London: T. Cadell (1776): 129–142.

11. Jannetta, P.J. "Treatment of trigeminal neuralgia by micro-operative decompression." In *Neurological Surgery* 3rd edn. Youmans, J. (ed.) Philadelphia: W.B. Saunders Company (1990): ch. 144.

12. Adson, Alfred Washington (1887–1951), Founder Member of the Society of Neurological Surgeons in 1920; President 1932–1933.

13. Transcript of conversations (taped) between T.P.M. and C.G.D. dated March 1987 (16 pp), and "summer" 1987 (6 pp). (Archives and Records Management Services, University of Toronto library, 120 St. George Street, Toronto, ON, M5S 1A5.) Quotations in this section are from this source.

14. Horsley, V., J. Taylor and W.S. Colman. *Brit. Med. J.* 2 (1891): 1139–1143.

15. Frazier, C.H. and W.G. Spiller. *The Philadelphia Medical Journal* 10 (1902): 594–597.

16. Sjöqvist, O. "Studies on pain conduction in the trigeminal nerve. A contribution to surgical treatment of facial pain." *Acta Psychiat. Neurol.*, supplement 17 (1938): 1–139.

17. Walker, A.E. "Mesencephalic tractotomy. A method for the relief of unilateral intractable pain." *Arch. Surg.* 44 (1942): 953–962.

18. Charles George Drake (1920–1998) was McKenzie's resident during the time the work on mesencephalic tractotomy was undertaken.

19. Walters, J. Allan. Senior physician (neuropsychiatry) University of Toronto, Toronto General Hospital and Wellesley Hospital.

20. Frederick P. Dewar (1911–1990). Professor of Orthopaedics at the University of Toronto and Toronto General Hospital.

21. Cushing, H. "The control of bleeding in operation for brain tumors. With the description of silver 'clips' for the occlusion of vessels inaccessible to the ligature." *Annals of Surgery* 54 (1911): 1–19.

22. Macewen, W. *Pyogenic Infective Diseases of the Brain and Spinal Cord.*

Meningitis, Abscess of the Brain, Infective Sinus Thrombosis. Glasgow: J. MacLehose and Sons, 1893.

23. Cope, Z. "Seventy years of abdominal surgery." In *Science Medicine and History.* Underwood, E.A., ed. London: Oxford University Press. Vol. 2 (1953): 343.

24. Stephanov, S. "Surgical treatment of brain abscess." *Neurosurgery* 22 (1988): 724–730. The author reviews the literature under tube drainage, marsupialization, migration method of Kahn, tapping only, aspiration, excision.

25. Jefferson, G. *Sir William Macewen's Contribution to Neurosurgery and its Sequels. The Centenary Macewen Memorial Lecture, Glasgow, 1948.* Glasgow: Jackson, Son, and Co., 1950 (36 pp.). Briefly quoted in *Neurosurgical Classics,* compiled by R.H. Wilkins. American Association of Neurological Surgeons (1992): ch. 27 (391). Jefferson's essay from which Wilkins quotes is fully reprinted in G. Jefferson. *Selected Papers.* London: Pitman Medical Publishing Co. Ltd., 1960. The original printing is in *Glasgow University Publications* LXXXI (1950).

26. Tutton, G.K. Personal verbal communication (1951).

27. Tutton, G.K. Hunterian Lecture: "Cerebral abscess — the present position." *Ann. Roy. Coll. Surg. Engl.* 13 (1953): 281–311.

28. Le Beau, J.J. *Neurosurgery* 3 (1946): 359. In 1946 the "penicillin era" had only just arrived. Before 1946, sulphonamides had been available for about ten years but they were much less effective than penicillin and other subsequent antibiotics in the treatment of intracranial sepsis.

29. Kahn, E.A. "The treatment of encapsulated brain abscess." *JAMA* 108 (1937): 87–90.

30. Written in 1943 at the height of the war when, as the article also states, "it is so easy for a patient to get a job."

31. Turnbull, F. *Operating on the Frontier: Memoirs of a Pioneering Canadian Neurosurgeon.* Madeira Park, B.C.: Capilano Publishing (1995): 107. ISBN 1-55017-135-6. Partly because of popular alarm, the label "manic-depressive" has been replaced in medical jargon by the more comfortable but less descriptive term, "bipolar."

32. F. McKenzie to T.P.M. Interview (24 April 1987).

33. Turnbull. *Operating on the Frontier* (p.107).

34. E.H.B. letter to T.P.M. (28 June 1989). Queen's University Archives: Botterell box.

35. Cushing, H. *Tumors of the Nervus Acusticus and the Syndrome of the Cerebellopontile Angle.* Philadelphia and London: W.B. Saunders Company, 1917.

36. Hullay, F. and G.H. Tomits. "Experiences with total removal of tumors of the acoustic nerve." *J. Neurosurg.* 22 (1965): 127–135.

37. McKenzie, K.G. and E. Alexander, Jr. "Acoustic neuroma." *Clinical Neurosurgery,* 2 (1955): 21–36.

38. Guttmann, Sir Ludwig. *Spinal Cord Injuries: Comprehensive Management and Research.* 1st edition (731 pp.). Oxford: Blackwell Scientific Publications, 1973.

39. Frank Turnbull (1904–2000) was appointed resident to McKenzie at the Toronto General Hospital in 1931. His autobiography, *Operating on the Frontier: Memoirs of a Pioneer Canadian Neurosurgeon,* is published by Capilano Publishing (1995), Madiera Park, B.C., V0N 2H0.

40. Turnbull letter to TPM (23 March 1988). The quoted passage is taken from a draft of F.T.'s MS which appeared in a slightly different form in *Operating on the Frontier* (107) (see ref. 39 above).

41. Crutchfield, W.G. "Further observations on the treatment of fracture-dislocations of the cervical spine with skeletal traction." *Surg. Gynec. Obstet.* 63 [1936]: 513).

42. H.H. Hyland was McKenzie's opposite number in neurology at the TGH. He brought clinical neurology up to date following his appointment as full-time junior neurologist by Prof. Duncan Graham. He had spent eight months at the National Hospital, Queen Square, London, under Gordon Holmes, George Riddoch and Sir Charles Symonds (Cosbie, W.G. *The Toronto General Hospital 1819–1965: A Chronicle.* Toronto: Macmillan of Canada [1975]: 197).

43. William S. Keith (1902–1987) was McKenzie's first full-year resident in 1930. He became the first neurosurgeon appointed to the Hospital for Sick Children in Toronto and later, with the neurologist John Silversides, built up a combined neurology-neurosurgery unit at the Toronto Western Hospital, University of Toronto. It was later expanded into the present neurosciences unit by amalgamation with neurology and neurosurgery from the Toronto General Hospital. (Fleming. J.F.R. "In Memorian. William Strathearn Keith." *Canad. J. Neurol. Sci.* 15 [1988]: 165–166).

44. Keith, W.S. "Spinal epidural granuloma." *Proc. Roy. Soc. Med.* 37 (1944): 376–378.

45. For a full discussion of the early debate on the causal mechanism of trigeminal neuralgia and hemifacial spasm, each of relevance to Ménière's syndrome, see W.J. Gardner, "Trigeminal neuralgia." *Clinical Neurosurgery* 15 (1968): 1–56.

46. For a later article by Jannetta (he was strongly influenced by Gardner) on the whole subject of conditions due to cranial nerve distortion by intracranial arteries and veins, including Ménière's syndrome, see P.J. Jannetta, "Cranial Rhizotomies." In *Neurological Surgery.* 3rd edition. J.R. Youmans, ed. Philadelphia: W.B. Saunders Company (1990): Ch.161 (4169–4182).

47. Jannetta, P.J. "Neurovascular cross-compression in patients with hyperactive dysfunction symptoms of the eighth cranial nerve." *Surg. Forum* 26 (1975): 467–468.

48. Dandy, W.E. "Treatment of Ménière's disease by section of only the

vestibular portion of the acoustic nerve." *Bull. Johns Hopkins Hospital* 53 (1933): 52–55.

49. TGH archives. File T6 22.2.3.

50. Maria Wishart (1893–1982) trained in medical art under Max Brodel at Johns Hopkins 1922–1925. In 1926 she was appointed the first Director and Staff Artist at the medical school in Toronto. In 1945 she founded the university's School of Medical Art and offered a three-year diploma course. She retired in 1962.

51. Barber, H.O. and P.E. Ireland. "Surgical treatment of hydrops of the labyrinth. The clinical results following differential section of the eighth nerve." *Laryngoscope* 62 (1952): 566–576.

52. Dandy, W.E. "Removal of right cerebral hemisphere for certain tumours with hemiplegia." *JAMA* 90 (1928): 823–825.

53. McKenzie's paper was never published but is cited as if it had been in some texts by the date (1938) he gave it at the annual AMA meeting. Example: L.D. Cahan and P.H. Crandall, in Youmans 3rd edition, Vol. 6: Ch. 165, cites: McKenzie, G.: "The present status of a patient who had the right cerebral hemisphere removed." *JAMA* 3 (1938): 168–183. The title and author's name are correct, but there is no such article in the journal referred to in the pages quoted, nor elsewhere.

54. Krynauw, R.A. "Infantile hemiplegia treated by removal of one cerebral hemisphere." *J. Neurol. Neurosurg. Psychiat.* 13 (1950): 243–267.

55. John W. Scott (1916–1998). The first clinician in the Toronto medical school who, having the necessary credentials, was appointed simultaneously to the departments of medicine, surgery and physiology.

56. Williams, D.J. and J.W. Scott. "The functional responses of the sympathetic nervous system of man following hemidocortication." *J. Neurol., Neurosurg. and Psychiat.* 2 (New Series) (1939): 313–321.

57. Ronald R. Tasker. Neurosurgeon and neurophysiologist. Professor of Surgery (Neurosurgery), University of Toronto. He was among the first to introduce computer-assisted cerebral and spinal stereotaxy to neurosurgery, in collaboration with Leslie W. Organ, physicist.

58. Clark, R.M. and E.A. Linell. "Case report: prenatal occlusion of the internal carotid artery." *J.Neurol., Neurosurg. and Psychiat.* 17 (1954): 295–297.

59. Carson, B.S., S.P. Javedan, J.M. Freeman, E.P.G. Vining, A.L. Zuckerberg, J.A. Lauer and M. Guarnieri. "Hemispherectomy: a hemidecortication approach and review of 52 cases." *J. Neurosurg.* 84 (1996): 903–911.

60. Fulton, J.F. and C.F. Jacobsen. "Functions des lobes frontaux; étude comparée chez l'homme, les singes et les chimpanzés." *Rev. neurol.* 64 (1935): 552.

61. Crawford, M.P., J.F. Fulton, C.F. Jacobsen and J.B. Wolfe "Frontal lobe ablation in chimpanzee." *Assoc. Res. Nerv. Dis. Proc.* 27 (1948): 3–58.

62. Moniz, E. "Essai d'un traitement chirurgical de certaines psychoses." *Bull.*

Acad. Méd., Paris. 115 (1936): 385–392. For an English translation see R.H. Wilkins (ed), *Neurosurgical Classics*. Copyright and publisher, American Association of Neurological Surgeons, 1992. ISBN:1-879284-09-X.

63. Freeman, W. and J.W. Watts. "Prefrontal lobotomy in agitated depression. Report of a case." *Med. Ann.* D.C. 5 (1936): 326–328.

64. Freeman, W. and J.W. Watts *Psychosurgery in the treatment of mental disorders and intractable pain*. Springfield, Ill: Charles C. Thomas, 1950.

65. Livingston, K. "Neurosurgical Aspects of Primary Affective Disorders." In *Neurological Surgery*. J.R. Youmans (ed). Philadelphia: W.B. Saunders Co. (1973): ch. 106.

66. Miller, A. "Lobotomy. A Clinical Study." Toronto Ontario Department of Health (1954). This exhaustive study, organized and written by Dr. A. Miller, Clinical Teacher, Department of Psychiatry, University of Toronto and Medical Specialist, Toronto Psychiatric Hospital, covers the years of McKenzie's participation.

67. Morley, T.P. (ed.) *Current Controversies in Neurosurgery*. Philadelphia: W.B. Saunders Co. (1976): Ch. 30.

68. *Current Controversy in Psychiatry*. (J.P. Brady and H.K.H. Brodie, eds. Philadephia: W.B. Saunders Company, 1978). Chapter 3, "The Ethics and Effectiveness of Psychosurgery," should also be consulted for an appreciation of both sides of the argument while it raged.

69. Meyer, A. and E. Beck. *Prefrontal Leucotomy and Related Operations: Anatomical Aspects of Success and Failure*. Springfield, Ill: Charles C. Thomas, 1954.

70. Miller, A. "The lobotomy patient — a decade later. A follow-up study of a research project on lobotomy started in 1948." *Canad. Med. Assoc. J.* 96 (1967): 1095–1103.

TGH from College St., Architectural Rendering, 1938.
Courtesy of University Health Network Archives, Toronto.

FIVE

TORONTO GENERAL HOSPITAL

The first Medical Board of the York General Hospital on King Street was struck in 1819 under the authority of the Parliament of Upper Canada. There was delay in its construction, but once completed it was first used in 1824 as a makeshift legislative building after the original building burned down. In 1829 it opened its doors to 52 patients, and to 136 patients the next year. Cholera, insanity and malnutrition were among the serious illnesses tended in the hospital. By 1856 a new Toronto General Hospital was built on Gerrard Street to replace the squalid, dirty and small building of the York General. The first patients were admitted in 1856. The present TGH on College Street opened on June 18, 1913 with 550 beds, increased to 600 the following year. Under a new Toronto General Hospital Act of the Provincial Legislature (1906) the governance and financing of the hospital would be shared between the City of Toronto, the University of Toronto and those elected by the hospital subscribers. The Chairman of the first Board was Joseph Flavelle.[1]

Kenneth McKenzie might have walked the wards of the new TGH before he graduated in 1914, but he spent his working life in them after he returned from overseas to his junior position as surgical resident to

C.L. Starr, the Professor of Surgery. From the time of his appointment to his retirement, the hospital did not change much structurally. The largest public wards, each with thirty beds, were housed in south-reaching wings from the east-west main building with its handsome façade on College Street. At the south end of each ward, a large open balcony gave a place for the ambulant patients to sit out in summer months and chat. There are two of these wings, each with wards on three storeys, and another two smaller wings with their own wards, also on three floors.

Outside, to the south, lay the hospital's garden and extensive greenhouse and potting shed where the full-time gardener and assistant grew flowers for the wards and the senior administration and nursing offices. The balconies, greenhouse and gardens have vanished since the Second World War, surrendered to the never-ending need for more hospital construction. The central part of the top floor of the main building was given up to the intern and resident quarters, with their private dining room, single bedrooms and sitting room where billiards and beer could be enjoyed (the beer was provided by a well-known brewer in time for the evening meal served by a maid assigned to the quarters, chosen for her tolerance). The greatly increased number of interns and residents after the war, many of them married, the need for space for other purposes, the periodic playful indiscretions by the residents on the dormitory floor, all contributed to the final closing of the doctors' quarters. They had been treated well in return for working for virtually no pay: free beer and perhaps ten dollars a month for pocket money.

The house staff, interns and residents, were content with a pittance in place of a salary because they knew that once the resident period was over (one to three or four years) they were financially secure for as long as they practised. And real doctoring, under graded supervision by their more senior colleagues, interspersed with regular, formal contact with the attending staff, was what they had been looking forward to during years of medical studentship. The pressure of work, day and night, was particularly onerous on the neurosurgical intern and resident who gladly accepted the experience. Discipline was strict under the chief resident and professional etiquette, while not expressly taught, was absorbed by example. The residence was a tight ship in the twenties and thirties.

McKenzie's twenty-nine years as neurosurgical chief in Toronto passed before the technological era gathered speed. His thoughts were with Cushing, preoccupied with symptoms and signs, forever searching for

Janet Kirby (née MacMillan), McKenzie's first operating room nurse, 1931–1942. "She was K.G.'s first O.R. nurse, really first assistant with a second nurse scrubbed. She taught me to do a subdural in real time when I had never even done one."
— E.H.B. TO T.P.M., JULY 1978

improvement in his own diagnostic and operation skills and in prognosis. The era drew to a close as technological techniques began to supersede reliance on symptoms and physical examinations for accurate diagnosis. But McKenzie never lost his dexterous supremacy in the operating room nor his wise clinical judgment.

Charles Drake[2] (1920–1998) was sent to Toronto by his alma mater, the medical school at the University of Western Ontario, to advance his training in anticipation of his return to London, Ontario. It was planned that he should start as junior intern in medicine and progressively climb the intern-resident ladder to equip him to sit the fellowship examinations of the Royal College of Physicians and Surgeons of Canada. He spent the first year as junior intern rotating month by month through different specialties, the last being in neurosurgery under McKenzie, which changed Drake's plans; he had come under K.G.'s spell. "I couldn't believe what I saw Ken McKenzie doing. It was always with a sense of wonder that I helped him in the operating room. I was utterly fascinated."

John Wilson Scott (1915–1997),[3] who spent a three-month rotation as McKenzie's assistant between graduating and signing on with the Royal Canadian Navy during World War II, was astonished at McKenzie's dexterity. "Two brain tumours in the morning and sometimes a short-case as well" was not unusual. McKenzie's concentration and composure while operating impressed him. On one occasion during an operation, the high stand with all the instruments was knocked over with a shattering crash. There was a long pause. McKenzie looked up at his scrub nurse, Janet Wallace. "Please warn me before you do that again." You couldn't catch him off balance.

Janet Wallace[4] was with McKenzie a little over three years. She recalls

when, just out of training school, she
worked with McKenzie for the first
time:

> Before the operation started, Dr.
> McKenzie came over to me and said,
> "I understand you're going to be
> scrubbing for me." And he said, "I
> will tell you once what I want, I will
> tell you a second time what I want,
> and the third time I'll expect you to
> know." Well of course that just made
> my stomach flip. I can't remember
> what operation it was, probably a
> brain tumour, and at the end of it he
> hadn't asked Rosie to scrub. I'd fin-
> ished it! He came back into the room
> afterwards and said, "I think we're
> going to get along all right." And
> that made my day ... Even though I

Janet Wallace, in Royal Canadian
Army Medical Corps uniform
during World War II, was
McKenzie's second operating
room nurse, 1936–1939

only worked [with him] for a little over three years I think in retrospect they were the happiest years of my career. You always knew
when you'd done well; you knew when you hadn't done so well. Not
just what he said particularly, although if you had been a little bit off
some day he'd say, "Bad night last night?" That's all. You didn't
expect praise from him. You didn't need it.

Wallace said of his operating technique, "I never saw anyone that
matched him. He never made a mis-move, was economical, and very
easy in that you knew exactly what he wanted. If he changed his mind
and wanted something else he gave you time to get it. He was really a
very easy person to work for. Demanding yes, but easy."

During the war, between 1941 and 1944, Wallace was in charge of the
O.R. at Basingstoke under senior surgeon W.V. Cone[5] from Montreal.

> I found him difficult. I received a letter from Dr. McKenzie because
> there were problems between Montreal and Toronto. There always
> had been. He said that [the difficulty] was understandable. We could
> always learn from somebody, as well as contribute. Do not forget
> that. Then he went on telling me about Toronto, what was hap-

pening there, and he ended up by saying, "But never forget that you have been well trained." By him, of course. I wish I'd kept the letter. It was really a masterpiece because he was sort of saying, "Now, behave yourself, but don't give in. Keep Toronto's end up."

McKenzie's contemporary, Professor Edgar A. Kahn of the University of Michigan medical school, said of him: "Kenneth McKenzie was closer to wisdom than any other neurosurgeon I have ever known."[6]

Administration, however, was not McKenzie's strong suit. He naïvely assumed that it should only be necessary to present a sound, carefully drafted proposal to the superintendent of the hospital or the chairman of the board to assure its adoption. If they couldn't see the merit of his request there was nothing more he could do about it; he chose not to waste further time and effort in fruitless attempts at persuasion. Harry Botterell, on the other hand, who joined McKenzie's attending staff in 1945, responded to stonewalling very differently. He would not give up the struggle to convert unbelievers; he bypassed old hacks in government whose energy had been long spent, and broke through the

C.W. Jefferys, the artist of a popular illustrated series of Canadian history, bartered this picture for McKenzie's professional service. The caption reads: "The First Prescription in Canada.1536. Cartier learns from the Indians the use of Anneda, Hemlock, as a remedy for Scurvy."
— *JEFFERYS, C.W.*
THE PICTURE GALLERY
OF CANADIAN HISTORY.
TORONTO: RYERSON PRESS
(1942) VOL. 1: 77.

gatekeepers to reach the seats of real power. It was an exhausting exercise but no one played it more skillfully or with more determination. It was hardly surprising the two protagonists at times made an uncomfortable team.

Early planning for the future of neurosurgery at the TGH began in 1942.[7] Harry was overseas during the early years of the war so it had to be done by correspondence with McKenzie. Harry's friendship with Geoffrey Jefferson allowed him to pick Jeff's brain, and Jefferson to give freely of his advice. Harry kept Ken abreast of the conversations. At first, the question of the appropriateness of a Toronto Institute on the lines of Montreal's had to be settled between them. There was early unanimity in opposition to that model. The university, surely, would never favour such a radical departure from its time-honoured departmental and administrative structure whereby the major Departments (medicine, surgery, obstetrics, etc.) controlled the annual allocation of funds, while the constituent Divisions (e.g., neurosurgery, urology, othopaedics) did not.* And although the medical school after the war would be greatly expanded, the constituent university teaching hospitals in the city each jealously upheld what they considered their prerogative to provide full service to the community, including neurosurgical. Neither K.G. nor Harry was likely to get the necessary votes "in their pockets" before approaching the university with such a plan, even if they had wanted it.

The Toronto General Hospital was still the flagship of the fleet of several teaching hospitals — some doctors who unsuccessfully aspired to membership of its staff sourly called it the House of Lords, a sobriquet many TGH staff privately enjoyed. McKenzie was reluctant to support neurosurgical units in other teaching hospitals. He believed the premature extension of neurosurgery in the city and university would be harmful to the Toronto General, which was the main teaching hospital for undergraduates and residents. Dilution of examples of specific neurological diseases residents should experience at first hand would seriously damage their training. It was good for residents who aspired to a career in neurosurgery to shoulder a heavy clinical load, while residents in general surgery and other specialties required training in the fundamentals of head injury management. K.G.'s popularity sagged

---

*For details of the structure and history of the medical faculty at the hospital and university see: W.G. Cosby, *The Toronto General Hospital 1819–1965: A Chronicle.* Toronto: Macmillan Canada, 1975 (ISBN 0-7705-1184-8).

amongst other large teaching hospitals in the city, which saw their plans thwarted by his failure to lend his approval to their aspirations for neurosurgical residents.

The Toronto Western Hospital already had a neurosurgical service headed by **William Keith (1902–1987)**, McKenzie's first resident

(1930–1931). Keith's first staff appointment in neurosurgery was at The Hospital for Sick Children (1933). In 1936 he started another service concurrently at the Toronto Western Hospital. McKenzie covered Keith for emergencies at HSC when he was away, but he transferred patients from the Western Hospital to the General when delays for Keith's return would have put them in danger. The Western Hospital appointed Keith to its staff without the blessing of McKenzie, who was the true neurosurgical representative of the university. In those years some affiliated teaching hospitals arranged their own appointments to staff with only token reference to the university and, occasion-

William S. Keith at his cottage on the Oxtongue River, 1960

ally, not until after the hospital had irrevocably completed its contract with the newcomer.

During Keith's resident appointment to McKenzie's service their relationship was uneasy. Half a century later Keith recollected:

4 Oct '83

Dr. [W.E.] Gallie made it known that he was interested in having a neurosurgeon at HSC [Hospital for Sick Children] but never told me directly that there was or would be a job available ...

Dr. Gallie did arrange for me to be a Douglas Smith fellow at the University of Chicago under his friend D.B. Phemister but he also told me that Percival Bailey was starting up there as a neurosurgeon at that time. I spent much of my time in research on bone regeneration and also got X-ray pictures of the spleen (Reticulo Endothelial System) by injecting emulsions of Iodized and Bromidized oil Etc. I did examine on week ends all the sections of Brain Tumours Bailey[8] had brought from Boston and which he used to write his book. I went to all the neurological-neurosurgical rounds and I learned a lot that year 1929–1930. It was a big change from the narrower sphere of Toronto.

I was Ken McKenzie's House Doctor from 1 Oct. 1930 to 1 October 1931 — the first he had for a whole year. I recall in that year when he was doing a [tumour] case — I said this might be an oligo-dendroglioma. He said not a word then or later but went regularly after that to the Banting [Institute pathology department] to look at the sections of tumors. There was another time when I said the tumor must be a unipolar spongioblastoma (I think the term is now obsolete). He said not a word about that also.

The timing of Linell's transfer from anatomy to pathology is significant in this connection I think now. I was too innocent to think I might be a threat to K.G. but it became abundantly clear later on that that was the case ....[9]

Keith's antagonism towards McKenzie, still burning from the days of his residency, was later refuelled when McKenzie refused to expand the neurosurgical program by denying him resident support at the Western Hospital. Keith's reconciliation towards McKenzie did not come until after K.G.'s retirement, but he still believed McKenzie's decision to curb neurosurgery in the university had been wrong.

Norman Delarue (1915–1992),[10] who spent six months with McKenzie during the war, says of Bill Keith:

Norman Delarue c. 1950

Bill was a superb technician and had damn good clinical judgment in an off-hand sort of way ... His example in the operating room was without reproach. He was a doggone good surgeon, and I think he put people off by his rather dogmatic statements and his own personal aggression and his apparently[11] light-hearted approach to neurosurgical problems, something that Dr. McKenzie never had. He was very serious about neurosurgery and its position in the disciplinary hierarchy ... He [Bill] had one of the strangest antipathies I have encountered in our profession. It almost amounted to [his] feeling that K.G. was blocking development at the Western and Sick Kids. K.G. wanted his own unit to be the chief repository of neurosurgical advances in Toronto. I think the differences between the two men are the differences you encounter in any profession when great men are in competition ... Great men have to be aggressive ... and willing to ride roughshod over their opposition if they are going to make advances ... I guess K.G. had asserted that temperament on Bill and Bill, being recalcitrant, rebelled. Bill would like to argue the case, which K.G. would refuse to do.

Delarue had hit the nail on the head. Keith's animosity indeed centred on McKenzie's refusal to support enlargement of the neurosurgical unit at the Western Hospital, and over his determination to protect the TGH from competition from the other hospitals in the university.

Since Eric Linell's transfer from the Department of Anatomy to the Department of Pathology as neuropathologist was during the year (1931) Keith was with McKenzie, Keith's perceptive recollection has credence. Meanwhile, McKenzie's request to McMurrich to sanction Linell's changeover was immediately approved — a priceless irony in a painful little comedy. But McKenzie's reasons, which Keith and others believed were purely selfish to protect his reputation, were in fact altruistic and aimed at protecting standards, not himself.

Aware of the narrowness of his own neurological knowledge, McKenzie believed that neurosurgery as he practised it had almost run its course. Further neurosurgical advance — by which he meant operative skills and techniques — would not give generous academic returns in the future. It was not a symptom of moodiness, the sapping of mental energy and prescience; his confession was simply a recognition that, for surgery to play its part in the future, it had to identify with other neurologically inclined skills and technological inventions. It was an honest admission to himself of his own shortcomings, of the challenge of newer skills than his own. He had already seen the coming of radioactive compounds in cerebral diagnoses, the possibilities of neurosurgical stereotaxy, new techniques in imaging, in therapeutic radiation and diagnostic ultrasound, and these were only the beginning.

Eric Ambrose Linell (1891–1983)

Eric Linell was not one of the founders of Canadian neurosurgery, but he was a keystone in the structure of neurosurgery in the University. Until his arrival, Toronto neurosurgery, lacking a specialty division in neuropathology, was unfulfilled.

Linell was brought to Toronto by Professor Playfair McMurrich to teach medical students anatomy of the nervous system. Having graduated Bachelor of Medicine at Manchester University in 1914, Linell promptly volunteered for service in the Royal Navy at the outbreak of war. He was commissioned Temporary Surgeon Lieutenant and was assigned to the minesweeper HMS *Skip Jack*, operating in the North Sea. When the war was over he returned to Manchester to prepare for the higher degree of Doctor of Medicine, which he obtained in 1920. Linell's interest in human anatomy, particularly of the nervous system, led McMurrich to appoint him to the teaching staff of his department in Toronto where he worked until 1931. That year, at the urging of McKenzie and with the blessing of McMurrich, Linell transferred to Professor Oskar Klotz's Department of Pathology where he set up the Division of Neuropathology. Linell believed he had the university President, Sir Robert Falconer, to thank for his promotion to full professor when he moved over to the Banting Institute to take up his new job. It was also Linell's understanding his was the first full-time professorial appointment in neuropathology in North America and, probably, beyond.[12]

The University had already shown interest in the study of the nervous system by the appointment of Professor E.H. Craigie as comparative neurologist in the Department of Biology. He had contributed importantly to the anatomy of the blood supply to various parts of the brain in rats. In 1921 Clarence Starr granted partial independence of a surgical subspecialty within his department by the creation of the division of genitourinary surgery. It was the first sign of softening of the attitude he had clung to and a portent that recognition of a neurosurgical division could not be long delayed. Although McKenzie was appointed assistant surgeon in 1924, the year after completion of the probationary period as surgical resident, and although he became *de facto* the neurosurgeon for the hospital, the promulgation of the Division of Neurosurgery with McKenzie at its head was delayed until 1928. Not long afterwards, in 1931, Linell moved to the Banting Institute in his new role.

The newly built Banting Institute was the centre for pathology in the university. Situated opposite the Toronto General on College Street and connected to it by a tunnel, it was ideal for Linell and McKenzie. They got on famously with each other — "fitted beautifully" in Linell's words; the trio, McKenzie, Linell and his colleague in pathology, Mary Tom,[13, 14] was a harmonious and productive partnership. Tom was specializing in embryology when Linell arrived from Manchester in 1923. She and Linell moved from Anatomy to the Banting Institute at the same time and shared the reporting of microscopical sections brought over from McKenzie's service and from the general autopsy service. Gradually she took over the majority of the reports and, in so doing, became an unrivalled expert in the microscopic diagnosis of neuropathological material.

Linell's great contribution was the application of neuropathology to the support of the clinical faculty. At the same time, he and Mary Tom were bringing up their neuropathology trainees who, like students of all good teachers, eventually surpassed their mentors in new knowledge and techniques.

Linell's records, from the beginning, were complete and accessible. It pleased him that researchers in clinical studies depended on his files for information. Cay Bell, Linell's secretary at the Banting Institute, guarded with a proprietary interest the thousands of pages she typed and catalogued over the twenty-five years of Linell's appointment. She continued in the position for another fourteen years adding to the department's archival treasures.

Linell himself worked in clinicopathological rather than fundamental research. His contribution was akin to a lexicographer in the describing and interpreting of the gross and microscopic appearances of the specimens he studied. He worked in the mainstream of neuropathology of the period when the light microscope was the tool, when stains distinguished one type of cell from another. Histochemistry, the colour-labelling of chemical components of cells rather than simply their morphology, had not reached a stage of sophistication. And the routine study of tissues by electron microscopy was not available until Linell's active career was at its end. Linell and Tom together remained the leaders of the division until Linell retired. Tom stayed on during Jerzy Olszewski's (1914–1964) regrettably short five-year reign as Linell's successor.[15]

Once Bill Keith was appointed neurosurgeon to the Toronto Western Hospital, the McKenzie-Keith relationship became more tattered for the time being. By blocking the appointment of a career neurosurgical resident at the Western, McKenzie was only sticking to his beliefs. He deprived Keith of assistance as he had for so long deprived himself, and for the same reason — to ensure that residents in their last year of training received an abundance of experience at TGH so that the transition from tutelage to full patient responsibility would be imperceptible when they were set free. K.G. also held his stand against the enlistment of new neurosurgical staff at TGH right up to the time of his retirement in 1952, when an extra man was taken on by Botterell. But this still kept the total at only two, where it remained until two or three years later with the appointment of W.M. Lougheed and, shortly afterwards, R.R. Tasker.

It was clear to Botterell that changes were necessary in university and public medical care to correct the problems that surrounded him; the craftsmanship was in getting them done. His greatest disappointment was his inability to obtain a budget from the university from which he could pay for frills towards the education of the resident staff. The request for funded projects had to go through the Chief of Surgery. He was no longer in the army where power of rank made change comparatively easy. On the civilian stage, those adversely affected by change were, understandably, bitter in their recrimination. Botterell did not enjoy wounding the opposition; it was the price he and they paid to satisfy his conviction that reform was necessary. His extraordinary organizational skill was the secret to his greatest medical contribution: a lifetime devoted to the care of patients with spinal cord injury.[16]

Botterell proved that early death was not inevitable following severe injury to the spinal cord. Up to the period shortly before World War II, the complications of cord paralysis were overwhelming. The medical profession knew what ought to be done to prevent the debilitation which assuredly led to death, but no one with the necessary will, skill and experience would take it on. Medical and nursing attendants were almost as demoralized as patients. A paralyzed urinary bladder quickly led to infection and kidney damage; immobilization in bed from paralyzed muscles brought pneumonia in its wake; and deep, suppurating bedsores the size of dinner plates exposed naked bone, which in turn became infected. Too often it all led to the despair of patient, doctor and caregivers, relieved only by death's merciful release. A strong medical leader was imperative.

In the early stage of his association with K.G. before the war, seeing at first hand the deadly consequence of paraplegia, Harry began to interest himself in its management before the war drew him into the army. When he became officer in charge of neurosurgical patients at Basingstoke, his interest in spinal injuries was rekindled. He was instated following the departure of the Montreal neurosurgical team under W.V. Cone, recalled at Penfield's request to help with his clinical load at home.

During the "phoney" war of inactivity after the 1940 debacle at Dunkirk, Harry was sick with boredom. He arranged to leave the hospital to visit Geoffrey Jefferson and his busy neurosurgical unit at the Manchester Royal Infirmary (MRI). Jefferson was intermittently absent from Manchester on inspection tours for the Emergency Medical Service of which he was the chief neurosurgical adviser. Harry's arrival was of mutual benefit to the two men and the beginning of a close and lasting friendship. Jefferson put Harry in charge of the (civilian) neurosurgical service in the assurance it would be well looked after. For his part, Harry enjoyed the stimulus of a busy clinical load after prolonged inactivity at Basingstoke. It was during this time that Harry was able to discuss with Jefferson the future of neurosurgery at Toronto; characteristically, he was already planning for the long term when he would take over from McKenzie, a transition he was assured would come about.

Geoffrey Jefferson (1886–1961)[17] was in age a contemporary of McKenzie, but the two men had other things in common. Each had been pioneers and, like true pioneers, experienced if not overt opposition to their early advancement, at least an absence of enthusiasm or, equally oppressive, lukewarm recognition. Jefferson was appointed in 1923 to the staff of the Royal Salford Hospital in a minor category until 1925 when he was given the full status of Honorary Surgeon. He failed in his first application in 1922 for membership of the staff of the university's teaching hospital, the Manchester Royal Infirmary, in spite of rave testimonials from leading national scientific figures and senior professors from his own university at Manchester. When his second application in 1926 was successful, he was granted four beds in the MRI for his "public" (non-paying) neurosurgical practice. By 1932 his bed allocation increased to twelve male and twelve female in wards shared with his orthopaedic colleague, Harry Platt. They also shared the operating room. Jefferson had to wait until one year before his retirement in 1951 for his own department to be built, complete with beds, operating room, laboratories, secretarial space, and up-to-date radiological facilities. He was, in fact, slightly better off than McKenzie, whose new neurosurgical unit in the Toronto General opened six years after his retirement.[18]

At long last, in the late 1930s, Jefferson was promised his due at the MRI. A modern neurosurgical unit was approved but the war delayed construction. Approval coincided with the coming of neurosurgery's recognition by teaching hospitals and universities, at first in Edinburgh, London and Oxford. Many American medical schools were experiencing the same neurosurgical stirrings but these British institutions were still closer in spirit to Canada through their common constitutional roots, which were bound tighter by the camaraderie of a total of nine years in two World Wars. And over the previous hundred years or more, Canadian medical establishments had been generously impregnated by British, mainly Scottish, graduates of Edinburgh. The bonds began to loosen after World War II as the United States became dominant in medical technology while the United Kingdom, bombed and bankrupt, licked its wounds. The influence on Canadian practice of British neurological traditions and skills declined as the new generation of Canadian and American neurologists came into its own.

A formidable obstacle to the conquest of the complications of spinal injury was its cost. Highly skilled management and a lifetime of supervision of paralyzed patients were the only prescriptions for success. Once the fiscal burden was accepted by government the situation began to change. Before the war Canada, like other countries, particularly Great Britain and Australia, began to address the solution to rising health costs and the expectations of impatient electorates by exploring the feasibility of a state-run health service. The army in wartime, where costs were not counted, was in a position to tackle the care of the spinal-injured patient.

Botterell had the opportunity, energy and vision to rise to the challenge. He was ideally situated in his command of neurosurgery at the Canadian Neurological and Plastic Surgical Military Hospital at Basingstoke, England. As important as his rank of Lieutenant Colonel, however, was his ability, through judicious use of coercion, example and conviction to meld all ranks, patients and staff alike, into an effective team. Within the structure of the army he was able to get rid of staff who, for whatever reason, didn't pull their weight. Patients who threatened to give up or refused to obey treatment orders would be "Botterellized," as the technique came to be known. A quiet tongue-lashing by the Colonel in front of all the other paraplegic patients in the ward usually changed the sufferer's attitude. Only occasionally was it necessary to coerce the truculent or the downhearted with the admittedly empty threat of a charge of self-inflicted injury for failure to co-operate in the management of his disability. It was Botterell's proud boast that, once he had things running smoothly, there were no more bedsores at Basingstoke.

The leadership he offered quickly attracted followers among the staff. Patient despair yielded to confidence in the future. Certain paraplegic patients, led by John Counsell, began to plan the Canadian Paraplegic Society, which, with the support of the Department of Veterans' Affairs (Dr. W.P. Warner[19]) and the Director General of Medical Services for the Canadian Army (Dr. Brock Chisholm), assured the continuation of enlightened care in peace that Botterell showed to be achievable in war.

John Counsell was a patient with paraplegia from a gunshot wound looked after by Botterell during the war at the Basingstoke Canadian Military Hospital. To Harry he was "the leading patient who pioneered the rehabilitation of paraplegics."[20] His effectiveness in the cause was due to his drive and experience as a paraplegic patient and to his connections in high places. His mother was a friend of Prime Minister Mackenzie King and his sister married Walter Gordon, who became Minister of Finance in Lester Pearson's Liberal administration (1963–1968).

Brock Chisholm (1896–1971), a Toronto graduate in medicine, specialized in psychiatry achieving notoriety for outspoken opinions on the need for the application of Freudian theories to the upbringing of children. He developed a simple grading code for assessment of recruits during the Second World War to match mental, emotional and physical ability with the recruit's assigned branch or trade in the army:

PULHEMS: Physique. Upper limbs. Lower limbs. Hearing. Eyesight. Mentality. Stability.

His crowning distinction was as the first Director General of the World Health Organization of the United Nations. (For his biography see *Brock Chisholm: Doctor to the World* by Allan Irving. Markham, Ontario: Fitzhenry & Whiteside, 1998.)

Harry was sent home by the army in 1943 "for no very good reason, except … to meet with the executive of the Canadian Medical Association and tell them … that the medical people who were overseas took a very dim view of the fact that the Canadian Medical Association was discussing health insurance with the Government of Canada, without consulting people who were overseas."[21] It was Brock Chisholm, as Director General of Medical Services, who had alerted the serving overseas doctors to what was going on.

On his return, Harry went back to the base hospital at Basingstoke where he was in charge of the evacuated neurological casualties, while mobile neurosurgical units were sent to the battlefield. The organization for treatment of neurological battle casualties was a hot topic:

> The Montreal group wanted everything brought back to the base, to be operated on at the No. 1 Canadian Neurological Hospital … Cairns,[22] who was the British Senior Surgeon in the army, and was a friend of Ken McKenzie — Cairns and McKenzie felt very strongly there had to be a more flexible approach so that you should have a mobile neurosurgical unit that could be attached to a General Hospital or a Casualty Clearing Station — a Field Hospital as the US calls it. With two or three nurses, two or three orderlies, an anaesthetist and neurosurgeon and second surgeon … they could operate on the appropriate neurosurgical cases right there, early, because sometimes there wouldn't be air transport available [to evacuate patients to the base hospital] … There was a great terrible argument about this and Cone and Penfield were for the base operation and McKenzie and Cairns were for the mobile unit and … I thought you needed both, so I was easy.

Harry was ordered home by the army for the second time. His arrival in Toronto allowed him to relieve K.G. of some of the neurosurgical burden. At the outbreak of World War II, University of Toronto faculty members volunteered for overseas service in droves. The university promised their appointments would be held for their return. The resulting depletion of the younger permanent staff members and residents in training was so severe that senior staff and the few who were medically unfit for overseas duties were severely overworked. The medical school, with governmental approval, recalled some medical officers for a six-month crash course in field surgery and to give some relief to the overburdened staff left behind to look after the public at home.

Harry's instructions were to attend to the neurosurgical service at the Christie Street Veterans' Hospital, which, he found, was "really a disaster." McKenzie couldn't take care of it adequately because he was overwhelmed at the General. There were a hundred paraplegics rotting at Christie Street, their deaths expected in six months. Harry exploded.

In his spinal injury unit at Basingstoke no one developed a bedsore. Here everyone was victim to them and to all the other complications of paraplegia. He didn't mince his words in his report to the Director General of the Army, Navy, Air Force and to the Department of Veterans' Affairs (DVA). At first, but not for long, he was not believed. As a result of the report his chosen neurosurgeon, Captain Joseph Cluff, was immediately put in charge together with Nursing Sister (Lieutenant) Isobel Wilson. They made an incomparable duo. Key appointments were also made in radiology, urology and rehabilitation medicine on Botterell's recommendation. The situation was soon brought under control.

Harry picked **Dr. Albin Jousse**[23] to look after neurological and physiotherapeutic management of the injured. Al Jousse had been working with McKenzie as his medical neurologist for two years, an arrangement McKenzie considered indispensable to his own health and sanity. "Harry has stolen Al from me," he revealed ruefully to his family, but his expressed dismay went no further. He soon persuaded himself without much heart-searching that Jousse's place should be with the spinal unit.

McKenzie was well aware of his deficiency in medical neurology. It was difficult for him to stand up to the neurologists in the department of medicine whose diagnoses he sometimes felt compelled to question. Or he might see a neurological patient who, he believed, was wrongly denied surgical treatment. He had looked after many cases in Boston as Cushing's resident and learned the symptoms and signs of tumours and other masses of the brain and spinal cord. He had the diagnostic edge over his neurological colleagues in Toronto in some ways, but he recognized his weakness in non-surgical disease of the nervous system. He had enlisted the help of Albin Jousse, a young man with more knowledge of neurological disease than he had, to assist him in diagnosis and, importantly, to back him up *vis-à-vis* his neurological colleagues when surgery seemed to him appropriate. Even more important, Jousse took the time to talk to patients and their families, which McKenzie was unable to do adequately himself because of the many demands made on him. Jousse was wise beyond the ordinary, and a great support to McKenzie.

Jousse had enrolled in a general arts course at McMaster University, Hamilton, in 1934. His father encouraged him to graduate in optometry to pay for his medical course at U of T. He became disabled by an obscure life-long paralytic affliction of the cauda equina, which, in the beginning, ended his enjoyment of hockey. "We are eagerly awaiting the autopsy," he said sardonically during his oral history interview many years later. The disability also disqualified him from joining the armed forces. It very slowly progressed, but to the end of his life he remained mobile with the help of crutches and leg braces. He graduated in medicine in 1942 at U of T and became McKenzie's junior intern for seven months. For the next eighteen months he remained half time on McKenzie's service, teaching medical students neurological diagnosis and patient evaluation. The other half-time occupation was at the government mental hospital, 999 Queen Street West, where he carried out electroconvulsive therapy under the direction of senior staff psychiatrists. He was responsible for patients' neurological examinations, which gave him the opportunity to talk to and befriend those in his charge.

Because of Jousse's qualities of industry, dedication, humanity and calmness under stress, Botterell spotted him as the ideal physician to run his spinal injuries programme. At first Botterell had preferred a surgeon because so many of the later complications of spinal cord injury required surgical treatment. He sought the advice of his chief, but McKenzie was adamant that a surgeon would probably not be attuned to the unending care paraplegic and quadriplegic patients needed. McKenzie suppressed his dismay at the prospect of his own discomfort at losing Jousse and agreed to his appointment as Director of Lyndhurst Lodge, the centre for the care of spinal injuries in Toronto. It was right that Jousse should move; in his new position he was the key to the eventual success of the whole spinal care program.

McKenzie's early fear there wouldn't be enough work to go round if the neurosurgical service were enlarged, could not be sustained. It became essential to enlist other surgeons when the load was too heavy for him to bear. In the early 1930s, Bill Keith and Frank Turnbull were each with McKenzie for a full twelve months as residents with careers in neurosurgery ahead of them. When they completed their residencies McKenzie had to rely for help on surgical trainees who, as part of their education towards a life in other branches of surgery, were appointed for six or twelve months to his service. Harry Botterell himself came to the TGH as resident to the chief of surgery, W.E. Gallie. It was Gallie who directed him to McKenzie's service where someone with his capacity for work was needed to come to the rescue.

Harry's eagerness to appoint at least one extra permanent staffman at Toronto General was at odds with Kenneth's wish. While K.G. was head of the unit (until 1952) things did not change. Perhaps Harry pushed too hard for change and Ken simply dug his heels in. It wasn't until his retirement was imminent that Ken lifted the ukase to allow Harry, as his successor, to begin negotiations for a junior. By this time Ken had shifted the administrative load of running the service onto Harry's shoulders. But he never yielded to Harry's pleas for extra permanent surgical staff. K.G.'s refusal was a source of deep disagreement between him and Harry; it seriously threatened their friendship right up to the approach of K.G.'s retirement. But with Ken now on side, the negotiations with the university in the person of the Professor of Surgery, Dr. Robert M. Janes, began.

Harry was not prepared to wait another two or three years or more for a Toronto man to complete his training, so eyes were turned to the United States. Ken would go along with Harry's choice, whoever it might be, but Janes's approval could not be taken for granted. The short list (the long list drawn up so soon after the war did not contain many names of adequately trained men) was narrowed down to two. One had the stronger scientific background but was short on general surgical experience, while the other's background was the opposite. Harry, well aware of the rapid expansion of the scientific revolution in medicine and in neurosurgery particularly, favoured the one more likely to bring "scientific" distinction to the service, while Janes resisted the narrowness he feared would at this stage be a detriment to the practice and teaching of surgery. Additional appointments to the staff to satisfy the obligation to develop fundamental research and its application to neurological problems could be left until later. Harry yielded to Janes, his departmental chief, without too much soul-searching; whatever vision he had of the future of the service, he knew his personal priority at this time was to be relieved of the same intolerable clinical load McKenzie had endured; he would strengthen the scientific side soon enough.

The difficulties between K.G. and Harry were unavoidable. Their widely different personalities inevitably led to friction but, paradoxically, their very differences allowed for reconciliation. Harry did not fail to acknowledge and bow to K.G.'s seniority. He knew K.G.'s clinical skills and experience were superior to his own and his operating dexterity unrivalled. K.G. recognized in Harry the master of energetic negotiation. Each had the generosity to see in the other qualities he did not possess but which were necessary to the partnership. K.G.'s reaction to views or proposals contrary to his own was not infrequently a retreat into stony stubbornness. Once he made his mind up, he did not readily change it. When a surgical problem needed a decision, he would mull over it, usually without seeking the opinion of others. He had been on his own for a long time and he expected to work things out himself. He had a quiet self-assurance; once he made what he thought was a right clinical decision he stood by it. In the operating room and ward he was his own master, but outside the surgical arena he was at a disadvantage. He had little negotiating skill, mainly because he believed the reasonableness of his requests or opinions were self-evident, rendering negotiation superfluous. He dismissed rebuffs with a shrug of the shoulders. There was no point in attempting to convert philistines. He could wait.

There are three items in the TGH archives that cast some light on conflicting plans and their resolution between McKenzie and Botterell for the future of neurosurgery in the hospital and university.[24]

The first is *Memorandum of Interviews with Dr. K.G. McKenzie: Re: Combined Neurological Division. 15 April 1946.* Unsigned. It probably comes from the hospital Superintendent's office and was drafted by Mr. C.J. Decker, the Superintendent (the equivalent position today is hospital President), or by Dr. Charles Parker, the medical Assistant Superintendent. The carbon copy has no letterhead. It was not printed by McKenzie's typewriter.

Toronto, April 15, 1946

MEMORANDUM OF INTERVIEWS WITH DR. K.G. McKENZIE:

Re: Combined Neurological Division

Dr. McKenzie and I had a conference in regard to a Combined Neurological Division on March 9th, 1946, at which he outlined his ideas in regard to this matter.

Since then we have met and revised the outline slightly, and now date it April 15th, 1946.

Dr. McKenzie described his conception of a Combined Neurological Division. To his mind it would be unwise for such a division to supersede ordinary Neurology, whether Medical or Surgical, and he has no thought but that the present departments of Medical Neurology and Neurosurgery shall carry on as part of the Medical and Surgical Departments of the Hospital. He proposes that the combined Division be an extra.

It was agreed that the Heads of certain Departments should be the ones who would bring the matter up before the constituted authorities governing the University and the Hospital. The particular Heads of Departments who are interested at the present time are: the Professor of Anatomy, the Professor of Physiology, the Professor of Surgery, the Professor of Pathology. Professor Linell also is entirely sympathetic. The plan also has the approval of the Dean-elect.[25]

THE PURPOSE:
1. The purpose of the Division is to provide improved investigation and treatment of patients suffering from neurological disease.
2. Clinical research into Neurology.
3. Medical education in regard to Neurology, undergraduate Interne and post-graduate.

THE SPONSORS:
The sponsors of the Division would be —
    a. The Toronto General Hospital.
    b. The University of Toronto, with particular reference to Anatomy, Physiology, and Pathology.

THE BUDGET:
The budget to operate the combined Division should be independent of any clinical department in the Hospital or in the University.

ADMINISTRATION AND MANAGEMENT OF THE
COMBINED DIVISION:
The management of the Division should be under the direction of a Committee appointed by the University and the Hospital. This Committee should have an Honourary [sic] Chairman, and should have regular meetings, with one definite annual Meeting, at which the Officers for the ensuing year would be elected.

It should be recognized that the Chairman of the Division should be a practising physician or surgeon. The Secretary might be a member of the Pre-Medical Groups, such as Physiology or Anatomy. The Honourary Chairman should be the President of the University, or his nominee. Members of the Committee should be members of the teaching and active staffs on Neurosurgery, Medical Neurology, Physiology, Anatomy, and Pathology.

The memorandum is the only known document giving McKenzie's early views on a combined neurological division before he changed his mind on the course neurosurgery should take in Toronto. The Montreal Neurological Institute under Penfield had proved a triumph. For a number of reasons McKenzie and Botterell advised against a similar development in Toronto (see p.138). McKenzie made known his recommendation for a coalescence within the clinical and preclinical neuroscience faculty. If his suggestion were acted on, all neurologically related disciplines would come under one umbrella — neurosurgery, neurology, neuroanatomy, neuropathology, neurophysiology, neurochemistry — but without disruption of the existing departmental and divisional structure. The organisation would be more of a think-tank than a separate department.

The Botterell archives at Queen's University do not have any document that refers specifically to the memorandum. A year later, as will be shown, McKenzie abandoned his imaginative and expansive recommendations which could have brought into the fold all disciplines related to the nervous system, as Archibald and Penfield had so successfully coaxed McGill to do almost two decades earlier.

On March 5, 1947, McKenzie wrote to the Chairman of the Board of Trustees of the hospital, Norman Urquhart. The contents of the letter, judged by its total neglect of the substance of the earlier memorandum, strongly suggests McKenzie had given up hope of his dream coming true or that, in any case, he had changed his mind. Instead, his requests and recommendations have contracted in their scope to the interests of the neurosurgical service alone. This time McKenzie's office typewriter was used.

March Fifth, 1947
Mr. N.C. Urquhart,
Chairman, Board of Governors,
Toronto General Hospital.

Dear Mr. Urquhart:

I am going off to attend a surgical meeting and also to have
a vacation and will not be back until the end of the month.
    I believe that we have made some progress in furthering a
better set-up for the Neuro-surgical Service. Doctor Botterell and
I have talked a good deal about the problem and had quite a long
conversation with Doctor Parker and Mr. Longmore. I have also

talked about it at some length to Doctor MacFarlane [Dean of the Faculty of Medicine].

The problem as Doctor Botterell and I see it is somewhat as follows:

A. Ward "D" seems to be the only satisfactory place in the hospital where we can conceive of a concentration of our neuro-surgical cases. There are 42 beds in "D"; if 20 of these beds were made public and 22 semi-private I believe that there would be no financial loss to the hospital. At the moment the beds are all semi-public, the combination of semi-private and public which we suggest would I think mean some slight increase of income from Ward "D".

B. We have considered the problem of how to replace the semi-public beds on "D" which the whole staff now use and would suggest for your consideration the possibility of closing in say three more balconies in the private pavilion, this would provide eighteen beds. If in addition the accommodation in about ten private rooms could be doubled up the number of semi-public beds available would remain pretty much as it is now.

C. Another problem which must be taken into consideration is this: Both Medical and Surgical Neurological Services have badly needed an expert on electro-encephalography for some years. We are so far behind in the development of this work here that a certain group of patients have to be sent to Montreal to be adequately cared for. This fact has crystallized the problem in the Dean's mind and he is now taking steps to see if we can attract a suitable individual to fulfill this need. At the moment Doctor Ciprioni is being considered. He is now at Chalk River working on the Atomic Bomb problem. If such a man is obtained we had hoped that he might be housed in the corridor adjacent to "D" operating room. This would involve moving the large sterilizer, it was thought that some new temporary construction could be carried out so that this large sterilizer could be moved directly east. At the same time in the same manner some additional space could be obtained so that x-rays of our head cases could be made adjacent to our operating room. At the moment the arrangement in this regard is quite unsatisfactory as it is necessary to take patients under an anaesthetic from our operating room to the x-ray department.

These are some of the problems that we have been thinking about. When I come back the end of this month I will be in to see you. In

the meantime Doctor Botterell is thoroughly conversant with
everything we have been thinking out and you may wish to see him.
In general it seems to us that Doctor Botterell, you and I should try
and work out a plan which you felt was feasible and which you could
implement. If this is possible we could then carry the conversation
more or less officially to the President of the University and the Dean
and with their support get it through the Medical Advisory Board of
the hospital so that you could then bring it up before your Hospital
Board. Doctor Botterell and I are very anxious and hopeful that
something can be worked out that might be implemented this
coming summer.

You will be interested to know that we have attracted a highly
qualified young man from Boston [Eben Alexander, Jr.] who will
be with us during the first six months of 1948 for further training
in Neuro-surgery. This is the sort of thing that spreads the reputation
of our Hospital far afield.

Yours very sincerely,
K. G. McKenzie

The third preserved document is a letter signed by McKenzie to the
head of the Department of Surgery in the University and the TGH,
Professor Robert M. Janes. It is an elaboration of some points raised in
the earlier letter and an introduction of others. The difference in format,
style and address is striking. It is a letter that must surely have been
drafted by Botterell but which had to be signed by McKenzie, the divisional head. It was not printed by his typewriter.

Toronto, September 30th, 1947.
Professor Robert Janes,
Department of Surgery,
The Banting Institute,
University of Toronto,
TORONTO, Ontario.

Dear Professor Janes:

At your request Dr. Botterell and I are submitting a plan for the
expansion and improvement of the Division of Neurosurgery. These
recommendations, together with the existing set-up, will outline the
minimum requirement of an academic neurosurgical unit in a
teaching hospital.

ADDITIONAL SPACE ADJACENT TO "D" OPERATING ROOM IS REQUIRED FOR THE FOLLOWING:

1. To house an X-ray subdepartment and to allow the establishment of an adequate E.E.G. (electro-encephalographic) unit. It is contemplated that X-ray and E.E.G. units will serve the needs of both surgical and medical neurological services.

The X-ray establishment has been discussed with Dr. Gordon Richards and, in this instance, he approves of the principle of decentralizing neuroradiology. Dr. Richards has pointed out that the financial details of such a plan will have to be worked out between the Department of Radiology and the Toronto General Hospital.

The best administrative arrangements for establishing an electro-encephalographic unit in the Toronto General Hospital are still under discussion with the Dean and the Departments of Medicine and Physiology. It is anticipated that these discussions will be concluded in a few weeks. It must be pointed out that facilities for E.E.G. work of the exposed brain are an essential part in the investigation and surgical treatment of epilepsy. This necessitates the establishment of an E.E.G. unit, adjoining "D" Operating Room.

In addition facilities for photography of the exposed brain are necessary,

    a. To record the various positions of the electrodes used for recording electrical activity.
    b. The appearance of the brain before extirpation of an epileptogenic focus.
    c. After extirpation of a focus.

2. A minor operating room.

The establishment of a second operating room has become necessary to handle the volume of work at present being carried out. For the most part this room will be used for ventriculography, arteriograms and myelograms, difficult brain abscess dressings, etc.

3. Adequate secretarial, teaching museum and library space.

4. Adequate dressing room for nursing and surgical staff.

The preliminary survey of the space required has been discussed with the hospital architects. It has been demonstrated that it is possible to create the necessary additional space by extending the room on the east side of "D" Operating Room corridor, as well as "D" Operating Room proper, for a distance of about twenty feet.

It also will be necessary to house elsewhere the steriliser and linen room now off "D" Operating Room corridor.

Mr. Wilson, the architect, feels that $35,000.00 will cover the projected expansion. This figure is only tentative, for detailed plans have not been drawn up.

CENTRALIZATION OF NEUROSURGICAL PATIENTS

On an average some sixty neurosurgical patients are now widely dispersed over the hospital. As the service has grown the care of these patients has become increasingly difficult and unsatisfactory because of this dispersal. This unsatisfactory situation can be largely rectified by concentrating most of the neurosurgical patients on Ward D. This involves taking over forty-four beds now used for semi-public patients. Therefore, for such an arrangement to be equitable to the staff at large, it would be necessary to establish alternative arrangements for semi-public beds elsewhere in the hospital. It is understood that arrangements for new semi-public beds are now under consideration by the Chairman of the Board and the Professor of Surgery. It will be necessary to carry out certain structural changes if the proposal regarding concentration of neurosurgical patients in Ward D is accepted. Three types of patients must be accommodated — public, semi-public and private. Only a small number of private patients, probably four at most, are contemplated, though additional single rooms will be necessary for critically ill patients.

The ratio of public to semi-public patients, if Ward D is utilized for the Neurosurgical Service, will vary with the general economic situation in the community and any physical layout should be flexible in this regard. The achievement of the above plan should not call for any great major structural change or financial expenditure.

It is strongly urged, if these plans are accepted, that final detailed plans be worked out with the collaboration of an individual, who is an established authority on internal hospital arrangements and design. Dr. Jack MacKenzie of Montreal is one example of such an authority, who would probably be willing to collaborate with the firm of architects employed by the Toronto General Hospital.

Should you wish any further information regarding the proposals broadly outlined here, either Dr. Botterell or myself will be glad to obtain and provide for you the necessary data.

Yours very sincerely,
K. G. McKenzie

The picture seems clear. A new neuroscience arrangement had been fermenting in McKenzie's mind. He put his proposal before the Hospital chairman, Norman Urquhart, after talking it over with the chief executive officer, the Superintendent. During the succeeding year he must have had many discussions with Harry Botterell, who did not share McKenzie's vision. Instead of the envelopment of all interested parties in a grand scheme, Botterell insisted on concentrating on the limited but attainable goal of building the "best damn neurosurgical service on the continent," as he once promised. For Harry, the objective was paramount and the steps to its attainment were workable. Since he was to be involved in the planning and the inheritance of the service after McKenzie's approaching retirement, this was how it would have to be.

These memoranda contributed to the growing swell for greater enlargement of the hospital than had been considered a few years earlier. Dr. F.P. Dewar, the chief of the orthopaedic division and secretary of the newly formed Committee on Hospital Improvement, asked the division of neurosurgery for its views on physical and organizational expansion. A *Memorandum Regarding Neurosurgical Unit*, dated October 25, 1948, prepared by McKenzie and Botterell, was delivered to the committee. It was in two parts: the first from Botterell, the second from McKenzie. In tone and content each part is an echo of the earlier memoranda with some elaborations added. An attempt to meld the points of view into a single document both could sign is abandoned. Part I, by Botterell, bears his imprint of detailed planning for the neurosurgical service. It became the basis of negotiations for neurosurgery over the next ten years until the new building (the Urquhart Wing), with neurosurgery occupying the whole of the 12th floor, was completed in 1958.

In his contribution to the Memorandum, Part II, McKenzie first supports without reservation the recommendations of Part I:

> The Memorandum prepared by Dr. Botterell puts in writing most of the points and principles that rest in our minds. We have discussed and agreed upon them through the years. Naturally we have thought of the desirability of a separate Neurological Institute comparable to those established in Montreal, New York and Chicago … It is our considered opinion that there are many serious objections to a Neurological Institute. The problem is better met by the establishment of two first-class units (a) Medical and (b) Surgical collaborating within the framework of the Medical and Surgical sides of a University Hospital. It is of interest to note that the Neurosurgeons in England

have arrived at the same conclusion (see recent publication by
the Society of British Neurological Surgeons, Planning Committee,
1945–1947).

McKenzie then returns to his original theme of a blending with neurosurgery and (medical) neurology of related interests more or less on a
par with each other: neuropathology, neuroanatomy, applied neurophysiology, neuroradiology and psychiatry. But his listing of the allied
specialties is no more than to report "we have progressed a long way in
the establishment of a first-class Neurosurgical Unit ... One can enu-
merate the following assets when thinking of Neurosurgery in this
University" — here he lists the allied specialties. "In reality," he writes,
"[we] only lack certain physical space and added equipment" for the
development of the neurosurgical division.

The Memorandum marked the final resolution of their difference
over the form neurosurgery should adopt in hospital and university. It
was a template for the future pattern of the neurosurgical service. Part I,
with K.G.'s blessing, was a detailed, comprehensive and attainable recommendation, which, thereafter, was essentially unchanged during the
years of construction of the Urquhart Building. In Part II, McKenzie
accepted that his vision for co-operation amongst the allied disciplines
had already spontaneously evolved and therefore only needed to be
recorded. But he stresses his conviction that TGH must continue as the
most favoured teaching hospital in the university:

It seems to us important that all concerned with the future of our
Medical School accept the following conclusions with regard to the
Toronto General Hospital:

1. For the next ten or twenty years expenditures of considerable
magnitude will be necessary on the present Hospital.

2. Ultimately a completely new Hospital on a new site will be
necessary, comparable to the move the Hospital for Sick Children
is now making.

In other words, to prevent deterioration in our leading teaching hospital,
we must concern ourselves for the moment with 1 and not 2 ...

Shortly after this memorandum was received, plans were set afoot — if
they hadn't already been drafted — for the erection of the Urquhart

Wing. The original suggestions for architectural changes in the College Street building for upgrading the neurosurgical division were scrapped but the functional principles of layout were carried over to the new building. Neither McKenzie nor Botterell could reconcile their views in a single memorandum. McKenzie refused to surrender the recording of his collegial instincts, which remained in his dream of an amalgam of all related neurological interests (Combined Neurological Division), but he couldn't organize them into a detailed, practical plan. Botterell, more pragmatic, sketched in detail a plan that would work for the neurosurgical division alone, ignoring the related sciences. The only mention, for example, of neurology was a reference to the desirability of rotating neurologists-in-training through neurosurgery for their own good; the need for a similar enrichment in reverse for neurosurgeons-in-training is not mentioned! He wasn't disparaging a reciprocal exchange (he once arranged a period of medical neurological instruction for himself at Queen Square), but to introduce it into the memorandum would blunt the sharpness of his main thrust, the promotion of neurosurgery.

Kenneth George McKenzie, about 1940

Harry's vision had little in common with Ken's original memorandum, but he won the battle with superior organizational experience and well-honed administrative tactics. It cannot have been a happy time for either of them, but their loyalty to each other and to the institution they served endured. No one knew how deep was the rift between them, deepened by their disagreement over staffing. Their secret was well kept. But by the time K.G. retired some six years later, however deep or shallow the wounds had been, they were now healed and the old friendship was restored.

McKenzie, probably also in the mid-1940s, was approached by the President, Dr. Edward Hall of the University of Western Ontario (UWO), to move to London, Ontario, to set up or at least advise on a new neuroscience division or department along the lines of his Memorandum of 1946. There is no record of such an invitation in the archives of the UWO. Neither the late Professor Murray Barr, who wrote a history of the medical faculty, nor the one-time Dean of the Faculty, Dr. Harold Warwick, knew anything of it. Dr. Warwick was not surprised that no record of a meeting between the two men was found. Dr. Hall, he suggests, would not normally have recorded it unless the topic had advanced beyond the preliminary conversation. There is no mention of an approach to McKenzie in J.R.W. Gwynne–Timothy's history, *Western's First Century*. Nor has any documentation on the matter at Western come to light. But there is little doubt that conversations between KG and President Hall at UWO did take place.

Dorothy McKenzie and Margo Angus (K.G.'s daughters) are emphatic that the lively family discussions about UWO only came to an end when Irene put her foot down and refused even to consider a move to London. The timing of a move, in 1946 or 1947, would have come during the period of disagreement between K.G. and Harry over the need for extra staff and the future of neurosurgery at Toronto. Discussing his own article on K.G. ("Kenneth George McKenzie, M.D., FRCS: His Contribution to Neurosurgery 1923 to 1963," *Annals of the Royal College of Physicians and Surgeons of Canada* 15 (1982): 521–529) before publication, Harry said, "It clearly is not a genuine biographical sketch for the truly controversial issues *such as K.G.'s threatened move to UWO* ... are not touched."[26]

It is uncertain how seriously McKenzie's threat to transfer to UWO should be taken. As a mere subterfuge to strengthen his position on the amalgamation of the neurosciences at Toronto or to procure better physical resources for the TGH division, it was not at all in character. It was soon after this time that Harry strenuously and successfully opposed K.G.'s sending in his resignation to Professor Janes. K.G.'s admitted motive in doing so was weariness from overwork, but he might also have sought a move to UWO where he would have a voice in the building of a department along the lines he had suggested. The total rejection of the proposal by Botterell must have aroused in him anger and wounded pride that he kept to himself. But his silence on the matter was a diplomatic decision to preserve peace. That always had been his way at times of disappointment and it was the way he would handle it now. It was unthinkable, not only to K.G. but also to Harry, to disrupt a partnership on which the future of the service hinged.

Harry's plan for the future of the neurosurgical division won the day. His advantage was the knowledge that in a few years he would inherit the division as chief, but meanwhile he had to put up with K.G.'s obdurate refusal to add to the division's surgical staff until he was in charge.

It is a tribute to both men that they kept their serious disagreements to themselves. Harry was careful to follow protocol when the topic of the future of neurosurgery surfaced, always acknowledging K.G. as the chief. In letters or memoranda to administration, each was at pains to include the other in any opinion or decision expressed. There was to be no schism for the public eye. McKenzie's hope for a working conglomerate of faculty members interested in the nervous system did not get past the visionary stage. He had neither the special organizing skills nor the political and enduring commitment to give it the priority it needed if there was to be any hope of success. The idea was a good one. It would be adopted eventually in another guise throughout the university. Meanwhile he contented himself with his declining interest in practice and in the solving of neurosurgical problems that had brought him such distinction.

Harry's priorities were of a different nature entirely. He was par excellence an organization man, from the dawning of an idea to its final fulfillment. He was as restless as any politician and more successful than most in the realizing of his dreams. For almost ten years, from the mid-forties to the early fifties, he was the force behind McKenzie. He swayed him from the dreaming of castles in the air to a focus on the future of the division of neurosurgery. Once McKenzie accepted Harry's plan over his own, K.G.'s resentment faded. He saw the pragmatic advantages of it over the more idealistic proposal he had put forward. Harry would play to win if the game was his own; if it was not, he would have nothing to do with it. And K.G. must have known well enough that without an executive director to see it through, his plan could not get off the ground. He could appreciate the force of Harry's argument that a strong, rejuvenated neurosurgical service would have a greater influence over events than an assembly of departmental heads trying to work together for the benefit of the whole. This would surely be a prescription for rivalries ending in stagnation or dissolution.

McKenzie admitted he never had the stomach for sustained committee work. It bored him. It wasn't for the challenge of administration he had won a staff appointment in neurosurgery. To Harry, it was an art form at which he excelled. Once K.G. pondered and presented a proposal to the right people, he considered his work was done. He had better things to occupy his original mind: above all, innovations in neurosurgery, then fly-fishing and golf. Ken always checked out of the hospital with little or no notice when the pressure of work became insupportable, leaving his resident in sole charge. Harry, however, while still officially in tutelage as the resident, once turned the tables on K.G. Against his strongly held principles of duty and responsibility, Harry poked his head around the operating room door one day and announced he and his wife, Margaret, were going away for a few days. Keeping his eyes on the wound, Kenneth, betraying no emotion, said, "Have a good holiday, Harry."[27]

But Harry had no time for much in the way of recreation. He once sailed with George Boyer, the skipper and a senior colleague, up the east coast of Georgian Bay. The stress of his confinement and inactivity was relieved only by disembarkation and a return to the real world of organizational diplomacy. For Harry, every committee he sat on (almost always as chairman) was a challenge from beginning to end, particularly when confronted by opinions opposed to his own. Harry stifled K.G.'s original proposal to Urquhart by deflecting it to much needed improved neurosurgical facilities which had to take precedence over long-term planning for the whole neurological field.

K.G.'s memorandum, however, remained dormant but not dead. Its ghost came to life again for a short while in 1961. Having brought the neurosurgical service in TGH and the university up to date and set it soundly on course, Harry was asked by Dean MacFarlane to chair a committee to advise how best the proceeds from a large new donation received by the university should be managed and allocated among all the neuroscience interests. The Helen Scott Playfair Memorial Fund committee held its first meeting on March 31, 1961 in the EEG Department of the Toronto General Hospital. The committee consisted of:

Chairman	E.H. BOTTERELL	
	J. OLSZEWSKI	*Neuropathology*
	J.C. RICHARDSON	*Neurology*
	J.W. SCOTT	*Neurophysiology*

The reclining male figure symbolizes humanity, while the surgeon, his left arm raised, lends compassion and support

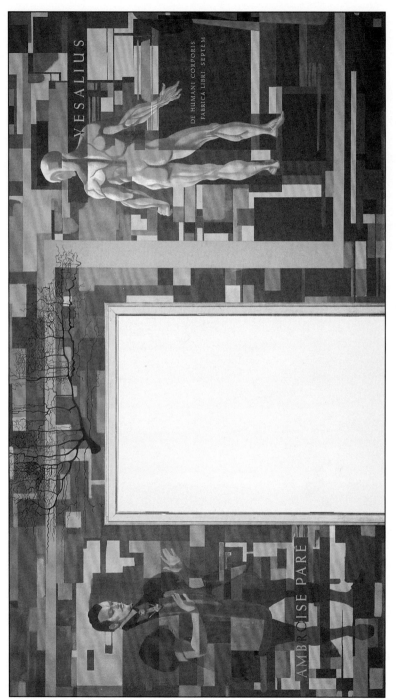

Ambroise Paré (1510–1590) is depicted to the left of the door; to the right, Vesalius (c.1514–1564) is honoured for his anatomy drawings

This section of the mural painted by Charles Fraser Comfort pays tribute to medical scholars Vesalius (c. 1514–1564), Galen (c.130–201) and Hippocrates (406–377 B.C.)

Commemorative panel of the mural painted by Charles Fraser Comfort
acknowledging the contribution of neurosurgeons

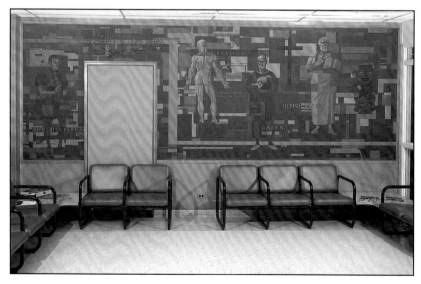

Part of the Charles Fraser Comfort mural that pays tribute to
medical scholars of the classical and renaissance period

The committee's report, abiding by its terms of reference, concerned the disposition of funds arising out of the bequest, rather than any departmental reorganization or academic priorities. The report did not go so far as McKenzie's 1946 Memorandum since its terms of reference only included the administration of the fund. The composition of the committee, in its departmental representation, partly reflected the 1946 memorandum's proposal.

The Playfair family's bequest was in the form of one million dollars in Tampax stock that appreciated greatly in the years after their donation to the University. Ten years later the University sold the shares, after a market collapse, at a great loss, provoking a fresh look at how the residue in the chest should be spent. Charles Hollenberg, Chairman and Professor of the Department of Medicine in the University, was asked to form the Playfair Fund advisory committee, which eventually recommended that the remaining moneys should be vested in neurophysiologic research related to Parkinson's disease, from which Mrs. Playfair had suffered, and that the Toronto Western Hospital should be the chosen site.

On October 19, 1972 an unsolicited report was sent to the Hollenberg committee which, had McKenzie been alive, would have been his dream come true. It was signed by representatives of the Neuroscience Institute Executive Advisory Committee, a new self-created body, not a recognized institute as officially defined by the University. Membership on this steering committee was drawn from Zoology (H.L. Atwood), Neuroanatomy (E.G. Bertram), Psychiatry and Neuroendocrinology (G.M. Brown), Neuropathology (J.H.N. Deck, Chairman), Neurology (W.J. McIlroy), Neurochemistry (M. Moscarello), Neuropharmacology (P. Seeman) and Neurosurgery (R.R. Tasker).

The recommendations were naturally more comprehensive than McKenzie could have proposed, but the committee's vision was no less bright than his of twenty-five years earlier. The essence of the report was to recommend the official acceptance by the university of an Institute of Neurosciences. This would, for the first time, bring together in one academic group medical and surgical clinicians and basic research workers in the burgeoning science of neurological function in health and disease. Although the committee members were senior and had distinguished scholastic reputations, nothing was heard again of their report.

If, as seems probable, McKenzie had indeed made suggestions to the University of Western Ontario along the lines of his original 1946 memorandum, then the idea enjoyed yet another, if stunted, resurrection elsewhere, this time to a more lasting life. The late Charles Drake

(1920–1998), the renowned neurosurgeon at UWO, and his eminent neurological colleague Henry Barnett,[28] had been contemporary residents at TGH in neurosurgery and neurology. Together at Western they built a productive *clinical* neuroscience department from which their publications put them and their university squarely on the world medical map, for which each was adorned with the Order of Canada. The "institute" concept as a convenient and effective way of tapping the best scholarly resources in a university, without spreading alarm and despondency amongst the top academic ranks, was partially adopted at UWO, but only in the clinical neurological sciences, without the participation of the basic neurological sciences divisions.

The idea came to McKenzie during the war at a time when expansion and reform throughout the university were in the air. No doubt he had been pondering the lead set by the MNI. His proposal was silenced, not so much because it was ill-regarded, but because it was untimely for the Toronto setting. His plan could not succeed until postwar reforms and staffing were brought up to date. The underlying plan in McKenzie's Memorandum of April 15, 1946 was buried and forgotten almost before the ink was dry. Later, it wasn't resurrected so much as reinvented. Its suppression prevented the publicity it would have had through discussion in Faculty Council. It does not appear in the minutes of the Toronto General's Board of Trustees that met every month. McKenzie saw the ideal but was unable to attain it. He was not born with the tireless energy of a persistent persuader of people in power. His talents and drive lay in clinical surgery, a compulsion that first snared him as a young man.

In the 1960s the University of Toronto began to adopt for general application the forgotten principles McKenzie outlined in 1946. The university created paper institutes to bring together academic staff members from different departments with a common interest. An important proviso in such conventions was to leave existing divisions, departments and faculties organizationally and administratively undisturbed. Far from creating bad blood between departmental heads, the movement added lustre to their separate crowns through their own staffs' participation in the work of an institute. The principle was so appropriate in the large, unwieldy University of Toronto that, before long, dozens of Institutes were created.

McKenzie's time at TGH exactly spanned the period between the two wars. Before Word War I, special investigations, whose purpose was to remove the uncertainty of the anatomical position and sometimes the nature of a lesion, had not progressed much beyond air studies and angiograms and analysis of the cerebrospinal fluid. The responsibility of the neurosurgeon lay heavily upon him. His two most welcome associates by the end of the Second World War were the radiologist and the anaesthetist, the one to guide him to the lesion and the other to ensure the patients' safe passage through the operation. New techno-logical discoveries such as stereotactic neurosurgery were in their infancy as McKenzie's retirement approached, but he could not muster the energy to master them.*

His published articles are a fair indication of where neurosurgery lay between the wars — dependence on his experience of neurological dis-eases and their course, the patient's history, the physical examination and the achievements and limitations of surgery. It may seem that clinical skills are at a lesser premium today with so many instruments and devices to make the performance of the surgeon more accurate and reliable. The old clinical skills are the yardstick by which the primary doctor makes the most important decisions. The secondary doctor, in this case the neurosurgeon, in receipt of many special tests and opinions as to diagnosis and even treatment, has to make his own diagnostic opinion, and to judge the merit of others who have been consulted. There is nothing to be taken for granted. He has to view the whole picture, just as McKenzie did. But the picture is larger and more detailed today.

ENDNOTES — CHAPTER 5

1. Cosby, W.G. *The Toronto General Hospital 1819–1965*. Toronto: Macmillan Canada, 1975. ISBN 07705-1184-8.
2. Transcript of conversations (taped) between TPM and CGD, March 1987 (16 pp), and "summer" 1987 (6 pp). (Archives and Records Management Services, University of Toronto Library, 120 St. George Street, Toronto, ON, M5S 1A5.) All direct quotations in this section are from this source.
3. John Wilson Scott (1915–1997). *Oral History Interviews*. Faculty of Medicine, University of Toronto. Vol. 39 (1982–1992). Hannah Institute for the History of Medicine/Associated Medical Services Inc.

*The ultimate sophistication to date in the field of depth recording in the brain for physiological data can be found in Tasker, R.R., Leslie W. Organ and P.A. Hawrylyshyn. *The Thalamus and Midbrain of Man. A Physiological Atlas Using Electrical Stimulation.* Springfield, Illinois: Charles C. Thomas, 1982. ISBN 0-398.04475-9.

4. Janet Wallace to TPM. Taped interview (November 1987). Extracts from the transcript of the tape.
5. Pruel, M.C., J. Stratford, G. Bertrand and W. Feindel. "Neurosurgeon as innovator: William V. Cone." *J. Neurosurg.* 79 (1993): 619–631. A full account of Cone's surgical achievements and a sympathetic study of his personality.
6. Kahn, E.A. "Random remarks on neurosurgery." *Clinical Neurosurgery* 12 (1977): 1–8.
7. Botterell, E.H. "Kenneth George McKenzie, M.D., FRCSC. His contribution to neurosurgery: 1923 to 1963." *Annals Roy. Coll. Phys. Surg. Canad.* 15 (1982): 521–529. 1982. Also published in *Surgical Neurology* 17 (1982): 81–89.
8. Percival Bailey (1892–1973). Trained in neurosurgery by Harvey Cushing. He studied the pathology of all the glial tumours Cushing had accumulated. He was appointed Professor of Neurology and Neurosurgery at the University of Chicago from 1928 to 1941, where he continued his interest in nervous system tumours and contributed generously to the neurosurgical literature on the subject.
9. WSK letter to TPM (4 October 1983).
10. Norman C. Delarue (1915–1992). Taped interview (January 1988). Graduate of University of Toronto Medical School. Professor, Division of Thoracic Surgery, Toronto General Hospital. Consultant, Princess Margaret Hospital.
11. In the transcript of the interview, "presumably" is the word Delarue used in place of my editorial "apparently," which I believe is closer to his intended meaning.
12. EAL letter to TPM (24 March 1963).
13. Mary Isobel Tom (d.1971). 1919 BA (U of T) with 1st class honours in physiology and biochemistry. Graduated in medicine (MB) in 1922.
14. "Obituary. Mary Isobel Tom." *Bull. Acad. Med. Tor.* 45 (1971): 29–30.
15. Jerzy Olszewski (1914–1964) had worked with Wilder Penfield at the MNI for eight years. On arrival in Toronto he devoted his exceptional talents to basic neuropathological research while Mary Tom headed the clinical section of the department.
16. Botterell, E.H. "The First Norman Dott Lecture." *J. Roy. Coll. Edinburgh.* 23 (1978): 57–64 and 23 (1978): 107–116. In this paper (published in two parts) Botterell sets down his life's experience in the treatment of spinal cord injury.
17. Schurr, P.H. *So That Was Life: a biography of Sir Geoffrey Jefferson.* London and New York: Royal Society of Medicine Press Limited, 1997. ISBN: 1-85315-305-2. This is a full account of Jefferson's life notable for its drawing on the life-time correspondence with Lady Jefferson from their meeting until the end of their lives.

18. Morley, T.P., ed. *The Opening of the Neurosurgical Unit. Toronto General Hospital. November 1958.* Toronto: University of Toronto Press, 1960.

19. Dr. W.P. Warner, Director General of Treatment Services for the Department of Veterans' Affairs, who was responsible for major reforms in DVA hospitals towards the end of the war and immediately afterwards.

20. E.H. Botterell. *Oral History Interviews.* Faculty of Medicine, University of Toronto. Vol. 3 (1979): 30–31. Copyright held by Associated Medical Services (Toronto). Index to the interviews, compiled by Martina Hardwick, was published in 1992, ISBN: 0-9691429-6-X.

21. Botterell. *Oral History Interviews.* Vol.3 (1979): 26.

22. Hugh Cairns (1896–1952). Born in Port Pirie, South Australia. Rhodes Scholar (1919). Awarded a Rockefeller Travelling Scholarship to Peter Bent Brigham Hospital as Resident to Harvey Cushing for one year (1926). Appointed the first Nuffield Professor of Surgery at Oxford (1937). For obituary notice and list of Cairns's publications see: Sir Geoffrey Jefferson, "Memories of Hugh Cairns." *J. Neurol., Neurosurg., Psychiat.* 22 (1959): 155–166.

23. Albin T. Jousse (1910–1993). *Oral History Interviews.* Faculty of Medicine, University of Toronto. Vol. 23 (1982–1992). Hannah Institute for the History of Medicine/Associated Medical Services Inc.

24. The first of three items appears to be the only existing or available record of McKenzie's original views on the future of Toronto neurosurgery and allied disciplines. All three documents were discovered, long misfiled, by Margaret Van Every, TGH Archivist.

25. Dr. Joseph MacFarlane.

26. EHB letter to TPM (25 June 1981).

27. Janet Wallace, R.N. to TPM. Transcript of taped interview (November 1987). Wallace was McKenzie's operating room nurse when this exchange took place.

28. Henry J.M. Barnett, OC. Professor Emeritus, Department of Clinical Neurological Sciences, University of Western Ontario; honoured by leading societies, universities and colleges in Canada, UK, USA, Russia and Japan for his extensive contributions to the neurological literature and international conferences.

Portrait of McKenzie by
Frederick Varley, RCA, painted 1952–53.
A pathological specimen of the brain base with
acoustic neuroma is depicted in the lower left corner.

SIX

RETIREMENT
AND EPILOGUE

Behind cedar rail fences and shrubberies in the shade of lofty trees, houses stand back from the winding road. The heavy scent of lilac hangs in the still air and puddles from the night's storm have received the first fallen blooms. The narrow road which follows the meanderings of the upper Don was deserted except for a schoolboy[1] on a bicycle pedalling dreamily from side to side of the deserted lane. As he came to a large, white house, he heard what seemed to be shots from an air rifle coming from the garden. He laid his bike on the edge of the road and, peering between the bushes, saw a man of middle age in shirtsleeves driving golf balls into a huge net at the end of the lawn. After each swing he stooped to pick another ball from a bucket beside the tee. The boy watched until the bucket was empty, and he marvelled at the display of concentration. He turned to pick up his bicycle as the player gathered the spent balls and started again.

For Kenneth George McKenzie, retirement was a happy time. Relieved of professional burdens and hospital and university responsibilities he could attend to his other interests with the same commitment he gave to the advancement of neurosurgery. Golf continued as his chief recreation. Periodically Charlie Drake would fly Ken to the annual pheasant shoot at Pelee Island; when they fished together Charlie picked up some tips of the art, for Ken could drop a fly gently as thistledown over the nose of a risen trout.

On McKenzie's retirement his old residents and associates commissioned his portrait by Frederick Varley, RCA (1881–1969), one of the last living members of the original Group of Seven.[2]

The donors "had the portrait painted primarily to serve two objectives: 1) the recognition of Ken McKenzie's great contribution to neurosurgery to the Toronto General and the University of Toronto as the first Canadian neurosurgeon, and 2) to the neurosurgical division adding to its tradition, strength and atmosphere."[3]

When McKenzie and Varley first met, each was uncertain he wanted to go through with the proposal. It was essential they should take to each other. They were similar in age, at the end of their active careers, straightforward and not afraid to speak their minds; a couple of old dogs circling, waiting for the other to make his move. After a trial sitting, Varley declared his willingness to go ahead and McKenzie agreed but with some reservation; he said he didn't like Varley's insistence on his sitting still for so long in an awkward position on the edge of a table.[4]

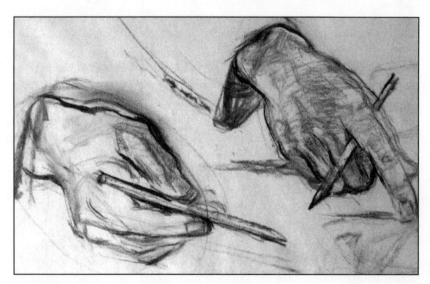

Pencil sketches of McKenzie's right hand drawn by
Varley in preparation for McKenzie's portrait.

— PHOTO COURTESY OF MARY WILDRIDGE

But it turned out to be a productive and cordial liaison. McKenzie, a smouldering cigarette in the left hand, is pointing with his right index finger to a piece of paper lying on the table as though drawing the student's attention to a lecture note. Nearby, almost out of the picture, is a specimen from Boyd's pathology museum of an acoustic neuroma embedded in the cerebello-pontine angle of the brain, the lesion McKenzie considered the ultimate challenge to the neurosurgeon.[5] The picture has all the power of Varley's earlier paintings, honest and uncompromising, and is as fine as any portrait he produced. Each man soon came to enjoy the other's company, but the association ended with the picture's completion.

It was the donors' hope that after the death of the survivor of the McKenzies' partnership the portrait would be given to the Toronto General Hospital to hang in the neurosurgical department for as long as the department existed. Some family members felt it deserved greater public display, as in the McMichael Collection at Kleinburg, or in the National Gallery in Ottawa. Negotiations after Kenneth's death between Mrs. McKenzie and the TGH, with the family's acquiescence, secured the picture for permanent display in the Division of Neurosurgery. The responsibility for the portrait while it hung in her home was a burden Mrs. McKenzie did not want to bear, particularly as she now lived alone. She hoped the hospital would assume ownership and with it the insurance she was not able to provide. (The portrait now hangs beside Alfsen's portrait of Harry Botterell in the Toronto Western Hospital where the neuroscience divisions of TGH and TWH have been unified.)

The hospital was therefore asked to accept the portrait as sole owner. In a letter written on July 31, 1972 to Mrs. McKenzie, J.A. McNab, the Executive Director, said, "I wish to give you every assurance that we will hang the portrait so that it will always be given the prominence it deserves, both as a tribute to Dr. McKenzie's leadership in the field of neurosurgery as Canada's first neurosurgeon and as a highly treasured art form...." Mrs. McKenzie was "delighted" at the turn of events: "All that I desired is in writing. I have the original letter in my Will, and one of the copies I am going to have taped on the back of the portrait...."[6] Once the transfer of the picture was promised by the hospital, Mrs. McKenzie entrusted it to the care of William Lougheed of the neurosurgical division who hid it in his home until it was insured (for $50,000) and the hospital constructed a Plexiglas case to fix it to the wall to secure it against vandalism and theft. Finally, the hospital promised that "in the event that the Toronto General Hospital ever ceases to have

Group in TGH garden to celebrate McKenzie on his retirement in 1952.
Standing, back row from left: J.C. Richardson, Carlton Smith, John W. Scott,
Allan Walters, R.I. Harris, Delbert Wollin, Aldwyn Stokes, Henry J.M. Barnett,
William J. Horsey, Norman Shenstone. *Middle row*: Eric Linell, William Edward
Gallie, Herbert H. Hyland, R. Glenwood Spurling, Loyal Davis, Eustace Semmes,
Edgar Kahn, Winchell Craig, Albin T. Jousse. *Sitting*: William D. Stevenson,
Frank Turnbull, Joseph Cluff, Eben Alexander, E. Harry Botterell, Kenneth
G. McKenzie, Palmer McCormick, Charles G. Drake, William S. Keith

a neurosurgical unit, the Hospital undertakes to present this portrait
to the National Gallery in Ottawa."

The portrait was unveiled on May 3, 1952 at a ceremony in the division's nerve centre, "D" operating room (DOR). To quieten his emotion
and to complete his speech without stumbling, K.G. drew up a prompt
card on which he wrote:

Notes for portrait unveiling in D.O.R. at noon May 3/1952.
1. Party and portrait arranged by past residents and students.
2. Reactions when Harry told me about it.
3. Wife's reaction — nicest part of it all, up until now somewhat
doubtful about her choice of husband — now quite sure he must be
some "punkin."
4. Story of having portrait done ending with gradually getting through
patient doctor relationship to real friendship and on my part at least
the full realization that Mr. Varley is a fine gentleman that you could
go fishing with — in addition he is a first class artist.

On the back of the card was a list of six names to remind him to give credit to the current operating room nurses who had helped him through many difficult cases: Mary MacIsaac, Ruth MacAulay, Elizabeth Hanna, Joyce Scrimgeour, Helen Binsell and Heilwig Horstman.

Not long after the portrait was completed and handed over to the McKenzies, K.G., ever determined, decided to try his hand at water-colours. While the experiment was not an artistic success, it satisfied his curiosity. K.G. had talked of his aspiration to John Scott, who persuaded his friend Charles Comfort,[7] an artist of great distinction, to hold evening classes for a few medical staff members. About ten would-be artists gathered in Rosedale one evening a week in The Studio Building (which was originally put up by the Group of Seven). Among the students were Kenneth and Irene McKenzie (Irene had true artistic talent), John and Grace Scott, Rick and Freda Richardson, Reg Haist and Tom and Helen Morley. Comfort was the epitome of patience and contributed generously to the repairing of the students' works. K.G. concentrated with eyes half-closed against the smoke curling up from a cigarette held loosely between wet lips. Irene would occasionally break the silence with a hissed, "Kenneth, stop sniffing." They were memorable evenings.

Kenneth and Irene at home c. 1945

So Kenneth settled down to a happy life with Irene free from the anxieties of neurosurgery and the hassles of administration. Irene was the constant, intelligent companion, soothing, boosting, adjusting to Ken's moods, sensitive to his preferences, and frank about her own. With Rosedale Golf Club only minutes away from home, Ken and Irene spent much of their time on the course. She was an enthusiastic golfer but not quite so good as her husband. Golf had been important to him all his life. Like wrestling, it was a solo sport where you depended on yourself alone to achieve excellence. Bill Lougheed, who returned from Boston to work with K.G. just before his retirement, recalls Kenneth's devotion to the game:[8]

> When I came back [from my year in Boston with Bill Sweet] as resident, he used to have me turn all his bone flaps and close them and I never knew if I was going to do the case or not ... because if it was his golf day ... you knew you were going to be closing the dura at 11:30 for sure, no matter what ...

In his retirement he began preparing a manual on golf. "I will try to write something that will assist other golfers," he records. He began writing on January 1, 1957, covering upwards of fifty pages in his notebook, but he never finished it. He roughed out in pencil diagrams of body positions at different stages of the swing, but he clearly realized his artistic limitations, for he suggests the ideal swing could best be demonstrated by a movie of a golf pro in bathing trunks.

Indeed, nothing could better illustrate his commitment to any undertaking than his passion for improving his golf, a passion that bore him

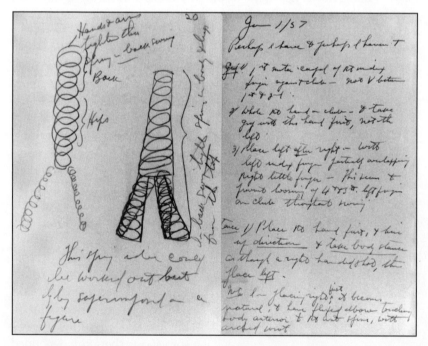

Pages from McKenzie's notebook for his proposed manual on golf

The McKenzies camping with K.G.'s trailer

aloft to membership in the Canadian Seniors team. One of his ideas was to fix a sort of whistle to the club head to analyze its speed at different stages of the swing. For another he tried attaching a small bell (of the type normally used on a cat's collar) to the tee to warn him when the driver struck the ball too low. He taught his children — those who would submit — to keep the head down and eye on the ball by connecting nose to ball with a length of fine thread. When Margo was thirteen or fourteen, she and her father won the Father and Daughter (Ontario) golf competition.

McKenzie admired invention and technical skill. As soon as he identified a problem he set about seeking its solution. In the early days of family camping, he assembled an ungainly, heavy trailer that carried supplies for three weeks and, with patience and strength, could be converted into a sleeping tent. When his son-in-law designed re-usable building construction forms to replace wooden planks for poured concrete, McKenzie was as excited as the inventor. In the coffee break between operations he could not hold back from sharing with his assistants his enthusiasm for the inventor and the invented. Perfection was his aim in all that his enthusiasm led him to.

McKenzie's home from the 1950s to 1972, 2 St. Margaret's Drive
in Hogg's Hollow, Toronto

Like many perfectionists he forced his obsessions on his children
but did not in the long run forfeit their affection. He had a proprietary
devotion to his children and grandchildren, no less intense for its being
rarely, if ever, uttered. Family discipline, Ken believed, was important,
even essential to good order and the shaping of character: breakfast at
7:45 a.m. sharp; the five-minute warning bell for dinner. Shades of St.
Andrew's! His O.R. nurse, Janet Wallace, however, remembers a slightly
different story, told to her by his children: "He would be supposed to
drive them to school in the morning and would simply drive out of
the garage and take off without them. Sort of typical ..." she added.

There was a constant coming and going of out-of-town visitors at
2 St. Margaret's Drive, and before that at the Roehampton home. The
children were expected to be present at dinner, the girls serving under
instruction from Irene and the watchful eye of Kenneth. Sometimes the
training he inflicted was excruciatingly embarrassing to the children.
The girls might be taken by their father to do the grocery shopping.
Since the estimation of the ripeness of a melon could not be left to the
shopkeeper, Ken would take a knife to it and judge for himself before
he bought it. Sometimes the girls would be sent with a certain amount
of money to do the family shopping unsupervised.

On one occasion when he had to attend a meeting in New York, Ken packed the children into the car and took them with him, "for the experience." He took Dorothy, who was twelve, to the Algonquin Hotel for dinner. The hotel in those days was famous for its cuisine and particularly for apple pie. Ken told Dorothy he doubted the art of making apple pies could survive the death of the chef. So he summoned the great man and asked him if he would teach his daughter how it was done. "Certainly," the chef replied. And to Dorothy he said: "Be here at eight o'clock tomorrow morning." Dorothy must have shown promise because the next morning the chef said, "I have to leave now. I would like you to make six pies to be ready for dinner tonight." Dorothy was furious to have her one day in New York ruined, but her talent for cooking, especially apple pies, dates from that day. She came away with *Feeding the Lions: An Algonquin Cookbook* by Frank Case (1942).

Irene was K.G.'s unfailing port in a storm. During the early years when Ken received a less than enthusiastic welcome from the hospital staff, when war separated the couple and, as if their constancy should be further tested, when they were apart during the Cushing year, and then again later when he was outmanoeuvred by Harry Botterell's superior tactics for the organization of neurosurgery in the university and hospital, Irene never wavered in her support of Ken. The Boston episode had been particularly difficult; money was tight and the family had grown and Irene was on her own in Toronto with three small daughters.

Irene McKenzie, 1948

Towards the end of Kenneth's life, the family's fear that Irene would collapse once Ken was no longer around was a misjudgment. She had, it appeared, never failed to do Ken's bidding, to give of herself to please him. But when the time came, she took a renewed lease on life, living in the cosy house at 5 Donino Drive Ken bought for her in 1961 in anticipation of his death (he had already discovered the enlarged lymph nodes which he correctly assumed were evidence of a malignancy.) When it became too much of a burden to keep up the Donino house, Irene moved to Belmont House, where some of her friends had already retired to.

The harmony she enjoyed with Ken was the product of her own resolve to support him. It was not, as some believed while Ken was alive, a sign of subservience to a demanding husband. On the contrary, Irene was the strength that underpinned the partnership. She died on the first of January, 1986, twenty-four years after Kenneth, at the age of ninety-four.

The last public recognition of K.G.'s place in the neurosurgical pantheon was six years after his retirement. In 1958, the American Academy of Neurosurgery came to the Toronto General Hospital for its annual meeting. It was Harry Botterell's show, prepared down to the last detail and consequently it went off without a hitch.

The recently built wing at the General (later named for Norman Urquhart, Chairman of the Board of Trustees) contained the new neurological and neurosurgical divisions with admirable facilities. Harry headed off a proposal by the hospital that the opening should be a part of the grand opening of the building itself, with the full complement of political, civic, university and professional representatives. He would have no part in a ceremony that, by its size and importance, would dilute the attention he intended to focus on the division of neurosurgery. He therefore arranged a date with the hospital well into the future so that preparations for the occupation of the twelfth floor would be completed, but before the whole building was ready. Charles Comfort was commissioned to produce a mural painting with a neuro-

Part of the mural painting by Charles Fraser Comfort on the Twelfth Floor of the Norman Urquhart Building, Toronto General Hospital.

— COURTESY THE TRUSTEES OF THE TORONTO GENERAL HOSPITAL

At the formal opening of the Toronto General's new neurosurgical division in 1958. In front of a part of Charles Comfort's mural painting (from left), Sir Geoffrey Jefferson, K.G. McKenzie, E.H. Botterell, T.P. Morley, W.M. Lougheed.

surgical theme to cover two walls of the visitors' waiting area on the neurosurgical floor. His work was completed in time for the opening.[9]

For the walkabout by the visiting neurosurgeons the twelfth floor was hurriedly filled overnight with beds and all basic equipment and furnishings. The next day the grand tour was followed by papers by distinguished members of the university and the profession:

Chairman, E. HARRY BOTTERELL, M.D., *Chief of Service,*
    Neurosurgical Division, Toronto General Hospital
CLAUDE T. BISSELL, *President, University of Toronto*
K.G. MCKENZIE, M.D., *Retired Chief of Service, Neurosurgical*
    Division, Toronto General Hospital
SIR GEOFFREY JEFFERSON, F.R.S., *Emeritus Professor of*
    Neurosurgery, University of Manchester
WILDER G. PENFIELD, O.M., *Director, Montreal Neurological*
    Institute

F.G. KERGIN, *Professor of Surgery, University of Toronto*
JESS D. HERRMANN, M.D., *President, American Academy*
  of Neurological Surgery
The Reverend Dr. CHARLES FEILDING, *Dean of Divinity,*
  Trinity College, University of Toronto.

In his speech McKenzie recalled operating on a patient with tic doul-oureux. Since Cushing had never helped him to learn the fine points of the procedure,

> ... before coming home [from Boston] a visit to Dr. Adson of the Mayo Clinic proved most helpful ... For the first time I could see what was being done ... With a kitchen chair and attached dental head rest I became reasonably adept with this procedure and can recall one such operation going rather well when Professor Archibald was looking on. I have the feeling that it was then that he decided that Montreal should have a neurosurgeon and so Canada acquired Dr. Wilder Penfield.

So sang McKenzie in his swan song (for the full text see Appendix G). No wonder a crash of delighted laughter filled the auditorium.[10] No one enjoyed the dig more than Penfield himself.

Ken had told Harry he wasn't sure he wanted Penfield at the party. "Why are you inviting him?" he asked. "Because of who he is. Of course he must be invited." It wasn't the first time Harry overruled Ken without breaking protocol. Ken had toiled on his own beside the dazzle of Penfield and the MNI. He had none of the benefits showered on Penfield, as it seemed. He was not dissatisfied with his efforts in developing the art of nervous system surgery as skilfully as anyone, but he knew where his shortcomings lay. He felt uncomfortable rated beside Penfield with his sophistication, urbanity and international acclaim. There was no other reason to protest, however mildly, his invi-tation. There was no hint that Penfield ever disparaged, even by faint praise, the neurosurgical structure McKenzie had been trying to build in Toronto. Whatever the reason for the coolness or indifference between the two founders, McKenzie's humour on this occasion was, if any were needed, a healing balm, a pleasantry for friendly laughter.

The evidence — from a letter written the next day in his own hand[11] — is that K.G. was pleased to have been honoured by the meeting and the speeches.[12] The distance between him and Penfield had closed. As for Harry's part in the commemoration, K.G. wrote:

Dear Harry,

A very wonderful week for you and for me too. Your Academy of Neurological Surgeons are a grand group. The scientific papers and discussions and the general good fellowship was outstanding. Took me back to the earlier days of the Senior [Society] group when we were still young enough to carry a meeting in a similar fashion.

You must be pleased and satisfied with the way everything went and I hope that now you can relax for a bit.

In particular I want to thank you for arranging the binding of my papers. In time along with the [Varley] portrait they will find their way into the TGH neurosurgical library ...

Also sending a note to Wilder and Jeff thanking them for the time they spent on their so very excellent speeches. They set the tone — impressive for an occasion not to be passed over lightly.

Again, Thanks for everything,

Yours sincerely
Ken McKenzie

Kenneth planned the management of his last months himself. His friend Clifford Ash advised and directed radiation treatment for the protracted illness Ken had discovered a few years earlier. Treatment delayed the inevitable progression of the disease and allowed him to live a normal life until the end was near. He received the approach of death much as he had accepted rebuffs in the past. There was nothing much to be gained by "kicking against the pricks." He had some bodily pain that he controlled with analgesics but, to outward appearance at least, he felt no dread, no anxiety. Wrapped in the comfort of the Donino home and the quiet assurance of Irene, with the children and grandchildren nearby, he cancelled the prescribed radiation treatments. Three days later, on February 11, 1964, asleep in his own bed, he died in peace.

ENDNOTES — CHAPTER 6

1. CHT
2. The original Group of Seven were Frank Carmichael, Lawren Harris, A.Y. Jackson, Frank H. Johnston, Arthur Lismer, J.E.H. MacDonald, and Frederick H. Varley. Of these, Varley was the only one who paid attention to portraiture, the others being taken up with the wild scenery of the

Canadian Shield (see: Thoreau Macdonald. *The Group of Seven*. Toronto: The Ryerson Press, 1944. And numerous subsequent editions in The Canadian Art Series.)

3. EHB letter to TPM (24 May 1972).
4. Reported by W.M. Lougheed.
5. William Boyd (1885–1979). Professor of Pathology, University of Toronto. His many lucid pathology textbooks for students and practitioners sold over one million copies, he revealed with unabashed joy as he broke open the champagne (see Ian Carr. *William Boyd: Silver Tongue and Golden Pen*. Toronto: Associated Medical Services Inc./Fitzhenry & Whiteside, 1993).
6. Letter to TPM from Mrs. McKenzie (13 August 1972).
7. Charles Fraser Comfort RCA. (1900–1994). Professor, Department of Art and Archaeology, University of Toronto; official Canadian War Artist in the Italian Campaign with the 1st Canadian Infantry Division 1943–1944. Produced numerous mural paintings for institutions including the neurosurgical division at the Toronto General Hospital, Norman Urquhart Wing, and the Toronto Academy of Medicine. Represented in most major galleries in Canada, including the National Gallery. Director of The National Gallery, Ottawa.
8. WML to TPM. Taped interview (15 March 1989).
9. For the artist's description of the significance of the figures, the names he chose and of the symbolism of the background, see Appendix F.
10. An audiotape of the papers given at the meeting is preserved in TGH archives.
11. Letter from K.G.McK to EHB (9 November 1958). Queen's University Archives: Botterell box.
12. The proceedings of the meeting's programme were collected in a presentation book, *The Opening of the Neurosurgical Unit, Toronto General Hospital, November 8, 1958*. T.P. Morley, ed. Toronto: University of Toronto Press, 1960.

Appendix A

Alexander Felstead McKenzie: A Chronology

1864   Born in Goderich, Ontario.
1884   Graduated in medicine, University of Toronto.
        Practised under Dr. Smellie on CPR, June–December.
1885   Attended the New York Polyclinic postgraduate course.
        Practised in Belgrave, Ontario for 4 years.
1889   Married Margaret Pake (1864–1951) of Wingham, Ontario.
1892   Kenneth George born.
        Family moved to Toronto where A.F. practised.
1895   Moved to Mitchell (April) and to Monkton (August).
1916   To Toronto. For a short time A.F. was Assistant Medical
        Superintendent of the Toronto General Hospital.
        Practices established at various times in Oakville, Toronto
        and Alliston.
1925   Returned to Monkton.
1954   Died. Buried in Maitland cemetery at Goderich.

APPENDIX B

A.F. McKenzie's
Publications

1. Fibro-cystic tumour of the uterus. Hysterectomy. Exhibition of specimen. *Dominion Medical Monthly* (Sept. 1898). (Read before the Huron Medical Association, Aug. 3, 1898.)
2. Some features of medical nomenclature. *Dominion Medical Monthly* (May 1899): 233–241.
3. The clinical significance of tracheal breathing. *Dominion Medical Monthly* (July 1906). (Read before the Huron Medical Association, May 30, 1906.)
4. Two respiratory symptoms of serious import. *Canadian Practitioner and Review* (July 1909). (Read at the annual meeting of the Ontario Medical Association, June 1909.)
5. Medical heresy. *Canadian Practitioner and Review* (March 1913): 127–138. (Read before the Huron Medical Association, September 11, 1912.)
6. Acrodynia: a report of three cases in rural practice. *Canadian Medical Association Journal* (Jan. 1923): 43–47. (Read at the annual meeting of the Ontario Medical Association, May 1922.)
   A probable case of aortic thrombosis. *Canadian Medical Association Journal* (Nov. 1931): 594.
8. Notes on one hundred obstetrical cases in rural practice. *Canadian Medical Association Journal* (August 1934): 175.

Appendix C

A.F. McKenzie's Unpublished Papers

These papers are preserved in original manuscripts or typescripts by the family of K.G. McKenzie.

1. The Local Medical Association. Paper read at a meeting of the Ontario Medical Association held in Peterborough, May 27, 1915. (Twelve typescript pages.)

2. A Suggested Nomenclature for Two Respiratory Symptoms. (Five typescript pages and one handwritten page. Undated. Six references, the latest dated 1916.)

3. On Longevity. Paper read at a family and friends' party in August 1949 to mark the 60th anniversary of the McKenzies' wedding. (Seven typescript pages.) A photocopy of this paper can be obtained from Stratford–Perth Archives, Listowel Division, Gowanstown, ON, N0G 1Y0.

APPENDIX D

K.G. McKENZIE'S PUBLICATIONS IN CHRONOLOGICAL ORDER

1. —— and M.C. Sosman. "The roentgenological diagnosis of cranio-pharyngeal pouch tumours." *Am. J. Roentgenol.* 11 (Feb. 1924): 171–76.
2. "Intrameningeal division of the spinal accessory and roots of the upper cervical nerves for the treatment of spasmodic torticollis." *Surg. Gynec. Obst.* 39 (July 1924): 5–10.
3. "The diagnosis and treatment of brain tumours." *Ontario Journal of Neuro-Psychiatry* (Dec. 1925).
4. "The surgical treatment of trigeminal neuralgia." *Canad. M.A.J.* 15 (Nov. 1925): 1119–24.
5. "Paraplegia associated with congenital scoliosis; report of case." *Arch. Surg.* 15 (Aug. 1927): 222–30.
6. "Some minor modifications of Harvey Cushing's silver clip outfit." *Surg. Gynec. Obst.* 45 (Oct. 1927): 549–50.
7. "Some remarks concerning neuro-surgical cases." *University of Toronto Medical Bulletin* (May 1928).
8. "The treatment of abscess of the brain." *Arch. Surg.* 18 (1929): 1594–1620.
9. "The management of cranio-cerebral injuries." *University of Toronto Medical Journal* (May 1929): 215–19.
10. "An outline of the diagnosis of spinal cord tumours." *Canad. M.A.J.* 21 (Dec. 1929): 696–701.

11. Linell, E.A., and ———. "Astrocytoma of cerebrum showing extensive involvement of opposite cerebral hemispheres." *J. Path. Bact.* 34 (March 1931): 195–9.
12. "Surgical and clinical study of 9 cases of chronic subdural haematoma." *Canad. M.A.J.* 26 (May 1932): 534–44.
13. "Intracranial division of the vestibular portion of the auditory nerve for intractible vertigo with two case reports." *Transactions of the Academy of Medicine, Toronto* 14 (Nov. 1932).
14. Turnbull, F.A., H.H. Hyland, and ———. "A staphylococcus infection producing an inflammatory mass simulating a spinal cord tumour." *Canad. M.A.J.* 28 (April 1933): 415–17.
15. "Observations on results of operative treatment of trigeminal neuralgia." *Canad. M.A.J.* 29 (Nov. 1933): 492–6.
16. MacDonald, A.E. and ———. "Sympathectomy for retinitis pigmentosa." *Transactions of the American Ophthalmological Society* 32 (1934): 172–90.
17. "Fracture, dislocation, and fracture-dislocation of spine." *Canad. M.A.J.* 32 (March 1935): 263–9.
18. "Mental disorders in relation to trauma." *Ontario Journal of Neuro-Psychiatry* (Dec. 1935): 27–34.
19. "Intracranial division of the vestibular portion of the auditory nerve for Ménière's disease." *Canad. M.A.J.* 34 (April 1936): 369–81.
20. "Glioblastoma; a point of view concerning treatment." *Arch. Neurol. Psychiat.* 36 (Sept. 1936): 542–6.
21. "Extradural haemorrhage." *Brit. J. Surg.* 26 (Feb. 1938): 102.
22. "Cranio-cerebral injuries, Part 1." *University of Toronto Medical Journal* 3 (Jan. 1938): 126–32.
23. "Cranio-cerebral injuries, Part 2." *University of Toronto Medical Journal* 6 (April, 1938): 281–92.
24. From *Handbook on Cancer* (Canadian Medical Association, Toronto, 1938), chapter 19: "Brain and Spinal Cord Tumours."
25. "In Memoriam: Harvey Cushing, 1869–1939." *Am. J. Psychiat.* 96 (Jan. 1940): 1001–7.
26. "Post-operative results in lesions involving spinal cord and cauda equina." *Canad. M.A.J.* 42 (March, 1940): 209–13.
27. ——— and E.H. Botterell. "Common neurological syndromes produced by pressure from extrusion of intervertebral disc." *Canad. M.A.J.* 46 (May, 1942): 424–35.
28. "One aspect of the posttraumatic syndrome in cranio-cerebral injuries." *Surg. Gynec. Obst.* 77 (Dec. 1943): 631–3.
29. "Perforator and ball burr." *J. Neurosurg.* 1 (Jan. 1944): 58–9.
30. Delarue, N.C., E.A. Linell and ———. "Experimental study on the use of tantalum in the subdural space." *J. Neurosurg.* 1 (July 1944): 239–42.

31. "Brain abscess." *British Surgical Practice* 2 (March 1946): 323–36.

32. MacDonald, I.B., ——— and E.H. Botterell. "Anterior rhizotomy; accurate identification of motor roots at lower end of spinal cord." *J. Neurosurg.* 3 (April 1946): 421–25.

33. ——— and L.D. Proctor. "Bilateral frontal lobe leucotomy in treatment of mental disease." *Canad. M.A.J.* 55 (Nov. 1946): 433–41.

34. ——— and F.P. Dewar. "Scoliosis with paraplegia." *J. Bone and Joint Surg.* 31B (May 1949): 162–74.

35. "Brain abscess: progress in treatment." in *Essays in Surgery*. University of Toronto Press (1950): 332–7. Presented to Dr. W.E. Gallie.

36. ——— and E. Alexander, Jr. "Restoration of facial function by nerve anastomosis." *Ann. Surg.* 132 (Sept. 1950): 411–15.

37. Lawson, F.L. and ———. "Scalenus minimus muscle." *Canad. M.A.J.* 65 (Oct. 1951): 358–61.

38. "Symposium: surgical treatment of hydrops of the labyrinth; the residual hearing following partial resection of the VIIIth nerve." *Laryngoscope* 62 (June 1952): 562–5.

39. "Pain; surgeon and patient." Royal College of Physicians and Surgeons of Canada, Report of Annual Meeting and Proceedings (October 3 and 4, 1952). *Lecture in Surgery*, 48–59.

40. Drake, C.G. and ———. "Mesencephalic tractotomy for pain; experience with 6 cases." *J. Neurosurg.* 10 (Sept. 1953): 457–62.

41. *Clinical Neurosurgery*. Baltimore: Williams and Wilkins. Vol. 2. (1955): Ch.1. "Intracranial Astrocytomas"; Ch.2 "Acoustic Neuroma"; Ch.3. "Surgical Treatment of Torticollis"; Ch.4. "Ménière's syndrome"; Ch.5. "Trigeminal Tractotomy."

42. ———, E.A. Linell and H.H. Tucker. "Astrocytoma in the cerebral hemisphere of adults." *Proceedings of the Second International Congress of Neuropathology* (1955) London. Excerpta Medica Foundation, Amsterdam.

43. ———, and G. Kaczanowski. "Prefrontal leucotomy: a five year controlled study." *Canad. Med. Assoc. J.* 91 (1964): 1193–1196.

Appendix E

Neurosurgical Residents who Completed their Training under
K.G. McKenzie

1930	W.S. Keith
1931	F.A. Turnbull
1936	E.H. Botterell
1942	C.P. McCormick
1946	W.D. Stevenson*
1948	E. Alexander, Jr.
1948	J.W. Cluff
1949	C.G. Drake

* Stevenson spent three years with McKenzie. On completion of his neurosurgical training he was sought and soon appointed as head of the division of neurosurgery at Dalhousie University in Halifax. As the first neurosurgeon in the maritime provinces he had to make his own way and develop sympathetic university and hospital allies, in which he was, in time, notably successful. The neurosurgical service at the Victoria General Hospital has grown, with other specialities, into an important academic teaching and treatment centre. (See Mukhida, K. and I. Mendez. "The contributions of W.D. Stevenson to the development of neurosurgery in Atlantic Canada." *Canad. J. Neuro. Sci.* 26 (1999): 217–223.

APPENDIX F

MURAL PAINTINGS, NEUROSURGICAL UNIT, TORONTO GENERAL HOSPITAL

These murals were painted by CHARLES FRASER COMFORT, *President of the Royal Canadian Academy of Arts and a professor in the Department of Art and Archaeology, University of Toronto. Text by the artist.*

In these mural paintings the artist has recalled and paid tribute to medical scholars of the classical and Renaissance periods and commemorated the contribution of modern neurosurgery in its treatment of injuries and disorders of the human brain and the peripheral nervous system.

On the east wall the mural painting is dedicated to the scholarly accomplishments of the past. Romantic in colour and tone, the involved background symbolizes the labyrinthine complexity of the human mind, its penetration and integration with the corporeal identity of the personalities represented.

At the extreme right is a representation of a prehistoric Peruvian ceramic figure, showing a native trephining with a tumi. This indicates the ageless antiquity of the practice of cranial trephining which extends back to Neolithic man.

The dawn of recorded systematic thought on the problems of cranial surgery is represented in the figure of Hippocrates (406–377 B.C.). It was he who first classified skull fractures and stated the indications for operation. He is represented here as a teacher.

The divine mystery of the spirit which inhabits the mind is symbolized in the Cross. It also implies pain and human suffering, afflictions which neurosurgeons have striven so diligently and earnestly throughout time to mitigate and relieve. The Cross is placed in the composition in such a way that it also serves as a time marker, separating those men and developments which preceded the life of Christ from those which followed.

The great landmark in the centuries following Hippocrates is Galen (c. 130–201A.D.). He enlarged upon the five types of skull fracture discussed by Hippocrates and described in detail two methods by which bone may be removed. He is shown in the mural, lecturing on these methods.

Vesalius (c. 1514–1564) is the great anatomist whose drawings and dissections were the first to add to Galen's concepts of the anatomy of the brain. He also gave us the first clear description of internal hydrocephalus. The tree-like image above the doorway is a magnification of a single brain cell. To the left of the doorway is Ambroise Paré (1510–1590), whose contributions are among the classics of medical literature.

It would be manifestly impossible, and even redundant, to attempt representations of all those surgeon-scholars who have contributed to the development of neurosurgery in the past. Those included in the composition are men of unquestioned rank.

The mural painting on the north wall is dedicated to the post-Listerian developments in neurosurgical practice. This is a commemorative panel, acknowledging the contribution of neurosurgeons since this branch of surgery became a separate specialty under the guidance of Sir Victor Horsley about 1890.

The reclining male figure symbolizes humanity in the broadest sense. Lending support to this figure is a neurosurgeon, his left arm raised in a strong but compassionate gesture. Above the head of the reclining figure is a crystalline form, symbolizing the restoration of mental perception and spiritual clarity. As opposed to the romantic colour and tone of the adjoining historical painting, this panel is free from emotional colour and given a regular form and tone of the adjoining historical painting, which the artist associates with asepsis, anaesthesia, and the modern approach to localization of cerebral function.

To the right of the figure of Humanity appear the names of some of the distinguished neurosurgeons whose knowledge and skill have made possible the extraordinary advances in this field within the period stated.

To the left of the figure appears the name of Dr. K.G. McKenzie who, as the first neurosurgeon in Canada, established neurosurgery at the Toronto General Hospital*.

In the upper areas of the painting appear the names of some scientists and scholars, other than neurosurgeons, whose theories and discoveries have contributed vitally to the great advances that have been made in neurosurgical practice since Lord Lister published his paper, "The Antiseptic Principle of the Practice of Surgery," in 1867.

---

*Dr. E.H. Botterell's name has been added beneath McKenzie's.

APPENDIX G

K.G. McKENZIE:
VALEDICTORY

Those of us who graduated from Toronto Medical School around 1924 had clinics and lectures in two Toronto General Hospitals. My memories of undergraduate days seem to centre more vividly about the old hospital on Gerrard Street. I am sure I became interested in surgery from the moment I sat in the large gallery of the main operating theatre and witnessed Dr. Herbert Bruce remove an appendix, with speed, drama, flourish, and great skill. My recollections of this new College Street Hospital, which opened its doors in 1913, seem to centre mostly around such outstanding teachers in medicine as Drs. Alex MacPhedran, J.A. Oille, and G.S. Strathy.

Before 1921 the surgeons on the Toronto General Hospital staff were individually amongst the finest. However, they did not have the organization or facilities for the training of young surgeons. Such young men had to go to England, the United States, or the continent for most of their post-graduate work. This situation rapidly changed when Dr. C.L. Starr was appointed Professor of Surgery in 1921. He became busily engaged in all the problems of the three teaching services in General Surgery on Wards A, B, and C. The surgical specialties within the framework of General Surgery were yet to be established. Urology had made a start, largely as a diagnostic service for the general surgeons who did most of the actual surgery. Gradually, urology became the first specialty with an entity of its own. The next to develop was neurological surgery, already established in a few centres in the United States under the leadership of such outstanding surgeons as Cushing and Frazier. Sir Victor Horsley, the pioneer in England, had died in Mesopotamia from heat stroke and overwork. I can recall seeing Sir Victor there once during the first World War. In 1921 the indications for neurosurgical procedures were few in this hospital as in most centres. The mortality rates and results were most discouraging. In fact, it was considered a decidedly unpromising field for a surgical career. However, the specialty did get a start in this hospital in 1923, somewhat earlier than in most centres. This came about in the following manner.

A Canadian, William Mickle, born on a farm near Guelph, Ontario, graduated from the Toronto Medical School with the Gold Medal in 1866. He went to London, England, for further studies and remained there throughout his active career as head of a large mental institution. He left $50,000 to the University of Toronto to establish two annual Fellowships. One named in honour of his father, Charles, has been awarded annually since 1921 to a member of the medical profession who has done most during the preceding ten years to advance sound knowledge of a practical kind in medical art or science. The second award, in 1922, was made to Dr. Harvey Cushing, then at the height of his career in neurosurgery. With Toronto in mind, Dr. Cushing asked Dr. C.L. Starr to send a young man to him for a year to fill an unexpected gap in his house-surgeon staff. Thus, one K.G. McKenzie, an unknown young man, thirty-one years of age, married, with three children, making a living in general practice in downtown Toronto, ready for any sort of change that involved further experience in surgery, asked Professor Starr for this appointment and was accepted. I suspect that the competition was not very keen as Professor Starr had already gathered in the really competent young surgeons for his General Surgical Services.

In 1923, I returned from an exciting and stimulating year in Boston with the great master surgeon, Harvey Cushing. He had not only given me an opportunity to learn some of the principles of neurosurgery but, in addition, had taken an interest in the financial welfare of the McKenzies and passed on the Mickle Fellowship money to my wife and our children. All these happenings had in them a big element of luck and timing and we were indeed fortunate. One can feel sure that it would have given William Mickle the greatest satisfaction if he could have foreseen the award of his Fellowship to Dr. Cushing, and through this award the start of neurosurgery in Toronto because William Mickle, the donor of the Charles Mickle Fellowship, spent his life studying and writing about diseases of the nervous system.

On returning to Toronto I became the second C.L. Starr resident in General Surgery, succeeding Dr. Robert Janes who was the first. Some of the early cases during this year are still vivid in my memory. Perhaps one of the most fortunate for me was a patient of Dr. C.L. Starr's, with progressive paralysis of the legs. I think I must have put myself in Dr. Starr's good books when a benign spinal cord tumour was localized and successfully removed. These were the days when a localization and diagnosis was made entirely by clinical examination without the aid of X-rays and contrast media.

The first section of the sensory root of the fifth nerve to cure the dreadful pain of tic douloureux was an achievement, as I was not at all sure I could successfully do the operation. Certainly it was a difficult procedure as I saw it with Dr. Cushing. On his Service, a resident never got very far with a case before it was taken out of his hands and the three- or four-hour operation was finished by the Chief. Yet I knew this operation would be one of my first responsibilities on returning to Toronto. Fortunately, before coming home, a visit to Dr. Adson of the Mayo Clinic proved most helpful. He had been through the fire and took me under his wing. For the first time I could see what was being done and felt that his particular technique could be duplicated. The underlying principle, of course, was the sitting-up position with the patient positioned so that blood ran out of the field and did not continuously obstruct the surgeon's vision. With a kitchen chair and attached dental head rest I became reasonably adept with this procedure and can recall one such operation going rather well when Professor Archibald was looking on. I have the feeling that it was then that he decided that Montreal should have a neurosurgeon and so Canada acquired Dr. Wilder Penfield.

An appointment to the General Surgical staff of this hospital followed the year as resident. Just enough cases had turned up to justify the notion that it might be good to have someone interested in neurosurgery as a sideline to general surgery. The future was a bit obscure, to say the least. One had to have the temperament to face a high mortality and the frequent indifferent results obtained in those days. Would there ever be enough patients to develop an adequate surgical team? Also, and of some importance, how could one make a living, particularly as the general surgeons proposed to continue with the care of head injuries! One's training seemed sketchy — not so much in history taking, examinations, and diagnosis as in one's ability to see some of the operations through from start to finish. These, and other questions and problems, were best answered by the old phrase, "sink or swim!"

What of the next ten years or so, years that were before the time of the "Academy of Neurosurgery"? Some fifty members of this Society are here today as part of their annual meeting. In particular, they wish to be with their contemporary member, Harry Botterell, to help him open the new wing in style. Perhaps some will return to their own centres in the United States prepared to needle their own hospital boards with a "Why can't we have something like they have in the Toronto General Hospital?" I look back to the time when an operation was scheduled in any one of the general surgical operating rooms that happened to be free in the afternoon. The nurses and house-surgeons were tired because they had already completed a full day's work. For the most part it was their first experience. These were the days before suction, endotherm, and the tracheal tube to assist the anaesthetist. Control of bleeding from the brain depended on the application of fresh muscle obtained, not always with good grace, from a surgeon who had done an abdominal operation in the morning. Because of the difficulties with anaesthesia and the control of haemorrhage, the operations were long and exhausting to all concerned. This has changed and the cardio-vascular surgeons have taken over and hold the all-time records for long operations!

Gradually, in neurosurgery, the basic operating room techniques and nursing care improved. Miss Gunn, an outstanding personality and superintendent of nurses, was a tower of strength. Special neurosurgical operating room nurses were appointed. Miss Janet MacMillan (now Mrs. Kirby), here with us today, was the backbone and pioneer of the surgical team from 1930 to 1942. Increased work and gentle persuasion brought about an operating room for neurosurgery alone; general surgery said good-bye to us with a sigh of relief and D.O.R. was born deep down in the basement. There, for the first time, we were able to handle both private and public patients in one operating room and thus organize our work efficiently without waste of time and effort.

Many tales could be told of D.O.R. Janet has refreshed my memory of an episode shortly after Dr. Botterell became my colleague. He complained bitterly about the heat in this basement room and undertook to cool it by having a large fan blow over a still larger cake of ice. This home-devised cooling system was really very inefficient and was a great trouble to Janet as she was small and in danger of drowning in the resulting puddle of water on the floor. She solved this problem by dipping the wall thermometer in ice-water, thus dropping the temperature to the chilling point and making everybody happy. Along this same theme, I can recall the time we were agitating for green drapes to cut down light glare — a change from white to green seemed to be an innovation that met with resistance. My young son, then aged about ten, felt that the problem could be solved if all wore green-tinted glasses to make the white drapes appear green! I have often wondered what was wrong with the suggestion. D.O.R. grew to two complete operating rooms and the necessary number of nurses and orderlies. The green drapes remain, but the good old operating table and instrument stand that I helped design and could always work, have been replaced by tables that are almost as complicated as the modern car. I sometimes wonder if the coffee is as good as it used to be. Could it be that one grows old?

Adjunct services gradually developed. Neuropathology was started within the framework of general pathology by Professor Eric Linell in 1931. Under his and Dr. Mary Tom's direction it has grown to be an important teaching unit. It has always co-operated to the full with those of us responsible for the care of the patient. In the same vein I refer to Dr. D.G. Wollin, responsible for X-ray neurological diagnosis, and to Dr. John Scott, with his academic future in the Department of Physiology but with appointments on both the medical and the neurological divisions of this hospital. This double appointment, clinical and pre-clinical, in our medical school, may prove to be a signpost for the future. It is one way that our great pre-clinical departments can attract young doctors. Otherwise, these important fields may be taken over by pure scientists who have not got a medical degree.

Throughout the years, neurosurgery has continued to carry its share in the over-all teaching of this surgical school. A big concentration of cases makes it possible for students in their final year to spend a stimulating week on the Service. They acquire some fundamentals in diagnosis and a knowledge of what may be done with neurosurgical problems. A graduate preparing for the fellowship in general surgery may spend a period of months on the Service and so round out his training. The knowledge acquired by four such men each year has stood them in good stead when they have gone out into practice within a university or non-university setting. Over and above all this, some men have spent a longer period on the Service as part or most of their training to become specialists. Such men head university neurosurgical posts in three Toronto hospitals and in Vancouver, London (Ont.), Halifax, Kingston (Ont.), and Winston-Salem in the United States. Others fill important positions in non-university communities.

One should think of the medical school and surgical departments as a whole when considering the various specialty divisions. During my active surgical career I have seen the specialties of urology, neurosurgery, plastic surgery, orthopaedic surgery, and, just recently, cardio-vascular surgery, develop as off-shoots from the parent, general surgery. What of the future? The wheel turns; will it turn completely? Might not the ear, nose and throat specialty broaden its field and become more attractive for well-trained young surgeons and again become a part of the Department of Surgery? If this should happen in this hospital there would be no general surgeons, as the remaining field of abdominal surgery would, of necessity, become a specialty division. Many would be gravely concerned by such a development. However, specialization and the restriction of any one surgeon's activities may be the price one has to pay in a school such as this, concerned with the care of patients, teaching, research, and thus the maintenance (always difficult) of an established international reputation.

This hospital will not willingly relinquish the reputation it has acquired as a teaching institution. Future hospitals boards may find themselves concerned with further expansion and facilities in this regard. Some day in Toronto there may be a situation comparable to that in London, England, and a graduate in medicine here will have received all of his clinical training in one hospital. The three big teaching hospitals in Toronto would then have to compete for medical students! Such competition should be interesting to the boards of our hospitals and stimulate an increasing interest on their part in the welfare and needs of the teaching staff. Organization should be such that the highly trained staff doctor is enabled to earn an adequate living without waste of effort and time. Only by doing this will there be sufficient energy and initiative left to teach and stimulate the constant stream of young men and women which passes through the doors of such a hospital as this. Of course, we are profoundly grateful for all that this and past boards of the Toronto General Hospital have accomplished. Let it be kept in mind, however, that a new era is always in the offing; nothing is ever quite finished. How dull life would become if changes and progress should cease!

Dr. Botterell, my closing few sentences are directed to you more than to the many interested friends gathered here for this occasion, the official opening of a new wing in the Toronto General Hospital, planned by you for the needs of the Neurosurgical Service.

To you, I say, "Dreams can come true!"

As your Chief of the Neurosurgilcal Service for some years, I too, had dreams but time ran out when I reached the University's retiring age in 1952.

University retirement usually carries with it some problems and regrets. They, such as they are, amount to little when I look back and realize how well I had chosen when I asked you to become my colleague in 1934. You have shouldered an increasing burden since then with good humour and co-operation and for some years I have known that the planning of the neurosurgical wing would go forward under your able direction. You are still at the height of your career, with plenty of time on your side for continued direction of the unit which now consists of three active surgeons.

I wish Harry Botterell, and Tom Morley, and Bill Lougheed, and all of you who are associated with the Toronto General Hospital Neurosurgical Service, years of health and satisfaction in your exacting field.

References

Gallie, W.E. "The University of Toronto Medical School: Fifty Years' Growth," *The Medical Graduate*, (Medical Association of the University of Toronto), vol. 3, no. 2, 1956–57.

Clarke, C.K. *A History of the Toronto General Hospital* (Toronto, 1913).

The University Monthly, University of Toronto Alumni Association (December 1917).

Paper read on November 28, 1958 at the Toronto General Hospital on the occasion of the opening of the new neurosurgical unit and the annual meeting of the American Academy of Neurological Surgery.

GLOSSARY

TERMS AND ABBREVIATIONS

AMA — American Medical Association

ansa lenticularis — a system of nerve fibres deep inside the brain

arachnoid mater — membrane covering brain and cord containing fluid

aspiration — withdrawal of fluid collection (e.g., blood, pus) with needle and syringe

cauda equina — nerve roots streaming out from the lower end of the spinal cord likened to a mare's tail

CMA — Canadian Medical Association

CMAJ — Canadian Medical Association Journal

craniopharyngioma — a developmental anomaly in the form of a tumour or cyst related to the pituitary body

dura mater — tough outer covering membrane of brain and cord

endothelioma — tumour arising from the lining layer of blood vessels

etiology — cause of illness

erythroblastosis foetalis — abnormality of foetal bone marrow cells that produce red blood cells

glioma — tumour of brain cells other than nerve cells

granuloma — collection of cells in the form of a tumour during normal process of tissue repair

haematoma — blood clot

infarct — area of dead tissue due to a failure of blood supply

laminectomy — surgical removal of bone (lamina) to expose the spinal cord

lesion — local area of disease

lobotomy (leucotomy) — surgically produced lesion in frontal white brain matter

marsupialization — abscess opened to the outside to allow drainage without excision of the abscess

medulla — junction of spinal cord with brain stem

medulloblastoma — a malignant tumour of brain

Ménière's syndrome — condition of sudden paroxysmal vertigo and vomiting due to disturbance of inner ear semicircular canals

mescencephalic tractotomy — incision of spinothalamic tract at midbrain level

OMA — Ontario Medical Association

osteotomy — operation that involves cutting into bone

myelogram — spinal X-ray image following injection into spinal canal of contrast material

papilloedema — swelling in the retina indicating raised intracranial pressure

pituitary fossa — depression in skull base containing pituitary body (gland)

spinothalamic tractotomy — incision in spinothalamic tract in cord or midbrain

subarachnoid space — space covering brain and cord containing fluid

tractotomy — incision of a neural tract in the spinal cord, medulla or midbrain

trigeminal neuralgia — face pain in the distribution area of the trigeminal nerve

ventricle — chamber in the brain containing fluid

version — obstetrical manoeuvre to change the position of the foetus *in utero*

INDEX

abscess *see* brain abscess

acoustic nerve, 107–13

acoustic neuroma, 57, 79, 100–101

Adson, Alfred W., 79

air, injection of, 63

alcohol, injection of, 75

American Medical Association, 113–14

anaesthesia, 64–65

anatomy, knowledge of, 69

Angus, Margo (McKenzie), 162, 177

Archibald, Edward, 35–36, 38, 47, 124–25

Ash, Clifford, 183

aspiration, 90

Banting Institute, 142–43

Barber, Hugh, 112

Barnett, Henry, 166

Bell, Cay, 143

Betty, 114–18

Botterell, Edmund Harry, 35, 39–40, 100, 112, 118, 182–83

as administrator, 137–38, 144, 146–47, 150–52, 164

and Division of Neurosurgery at TGH, 151–52, 159–61, 163

on spinal injuries, 102–03, 144–45

World War II service, 144–45, 146–49

Boyd, B.A., 121

brain abscess, 89–92

brain lesions, 101–02

British influence, 146

Cairns, Hugh, 109, 110, 148

calipers *see* skull calipers

Canadian Army Medical Corps (CAMC), 24, 25

Canadian Neurological and Plastic Surgical Military Hospital (Basingstoke), 103, 136, 146–47, 148